TABLE ⬦ OF ⬦ CONTENTS

DOWNLOAD YOUR FILES

Downloading your files is simple. To access your digital files, please go to the last page of this book and follow the instructions.

For technical assistance, please email: info@vaulteditions.com

Copyright

Bibliographical Note

This book is a new work created by Vault Editions Ltd.

ISBN: 978-1-922966-75-9

VAULT EDITIONS

ART SUPPLIES YOU'LL NEED

Pro Tip: These tools are all helpful to have, but not all of them are essential. You don't need a full kit to begin your manga journey: a simple pencil or pen and a piece of paper are enough. Fancy materials can make the process smoother, but they won't replace the value of practice. What matters most is that you start drawing, experiment freely and build confidence through repetition. Everything else can be added later as your skills grow.

Once you're comfortable, try a few different mark-making tools to see what they naturally encourage. A fineliner, brush pen, felt tip, mechanical pencil, or a cheap fountain pen will each produce a different kind of line and texture. Even small changes like paper type can shift the feel of your marks. Smooth paper gives crisp edges, while textured paper creates broken, grainy lines that can be perfect for shading.

You can also explore more experimental materials for texture and atmosphere. Ink washes, diluted marker, graphite sticks, charcoal, crayons, or even a basic sponge and a bit of ink can create interesting tones and backgrounds. You don't need specialist supplies. Test what you have, keep what you like, and leave the rest. The goal isn't a perfect toolkit, it's building control and range through steady practice.

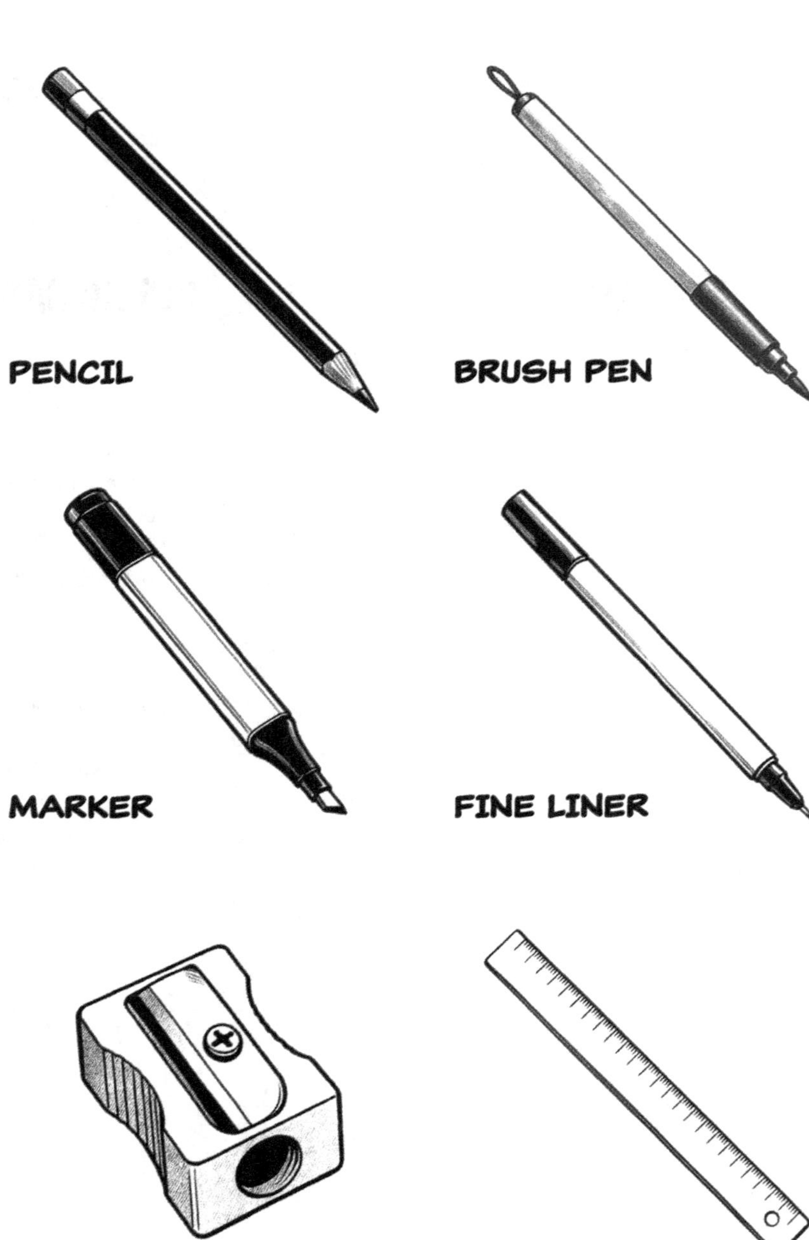

PENCIL

BRUSH PEN

MARKER

FINE LINER

SHARPENER

RULER

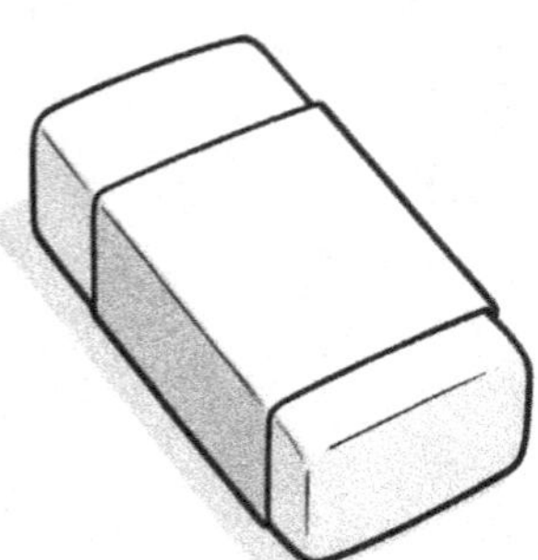

ERASER

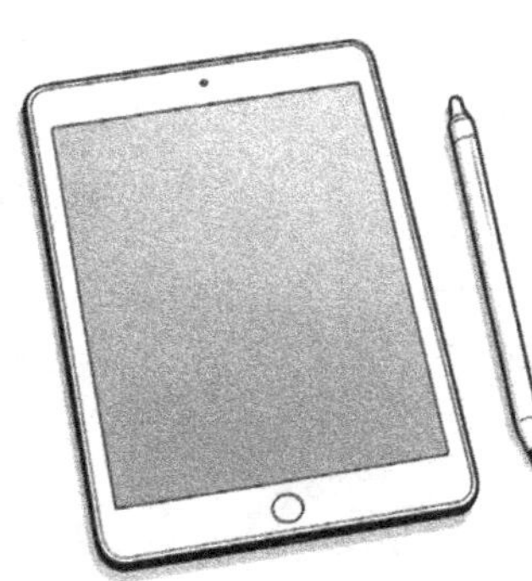

TABLET

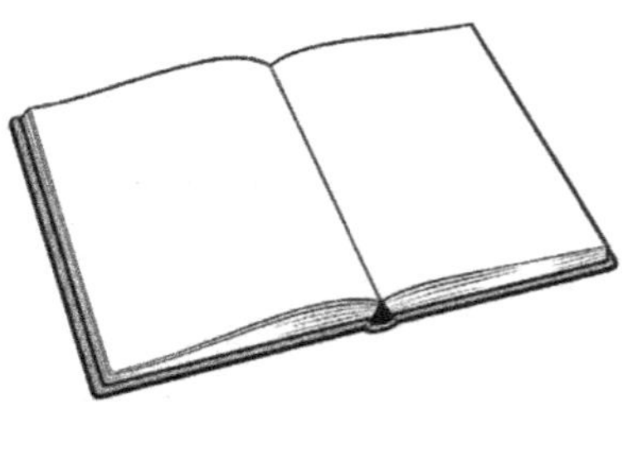

SKETCH BOOK

GRADIENT VALUE SCALES

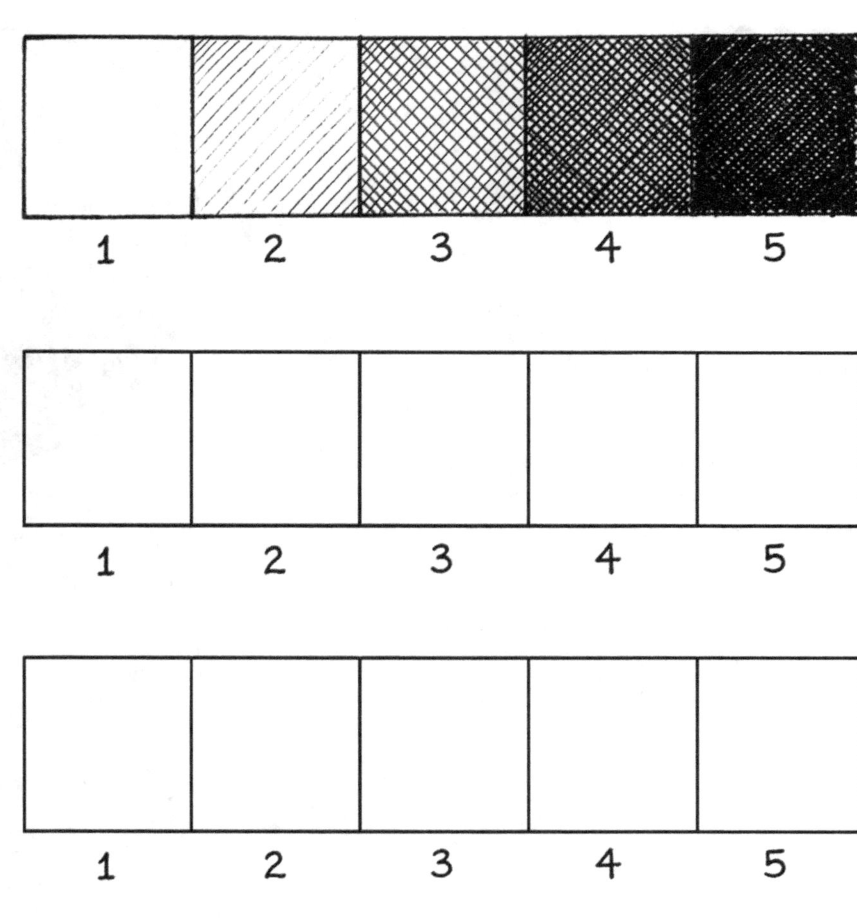

A value scale is a simple way to practise shading from light to dark. Each box represents a step in tone, helping you control how much ink you place on the page. If you can make clean, even value steps, you will find it much easier to shade faces, objects, clothing, and backgrounds with confidence.

Fill the boxes from 1 to 5. 1 is the lightest value, leave it almost white. 2 is a light grey, use sparse marks with plenty of paper showing. 3 is a midtone, increase the density so the white gaps shrink. 4 is a dark value, pack your marks close but keep them tidy. 5 is the darkest value, aim for near black with minimal white showing. Keep your hand pressure consistent and change the value by changing the density of your marks.

FUNDAMENTAL MARK-MAKING

Mark-making is the foundation of ink drawing. Instead of blending tones like you would with graphite, you build value using repeated, deliberate marks. Different mark types create different textures, so they do more than just darken an area. They can suggest form, material, atmosphere, and focus.

The four techniques shown here are some of the most common. Hatching uses single-direction lines for clean, graphic shading. Cross-hatching layers lines in multiple directions to create richer, darker values. Stippling uses dots to build soft gradients and grainy texture. Scumbling uses loose, looping marks for an energetic, sketchy feel. The best choice depends on the mood you want and the surface you are describing.

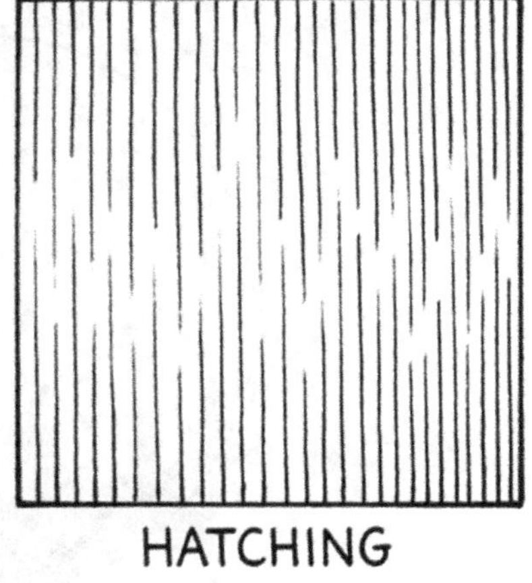

HATCHING

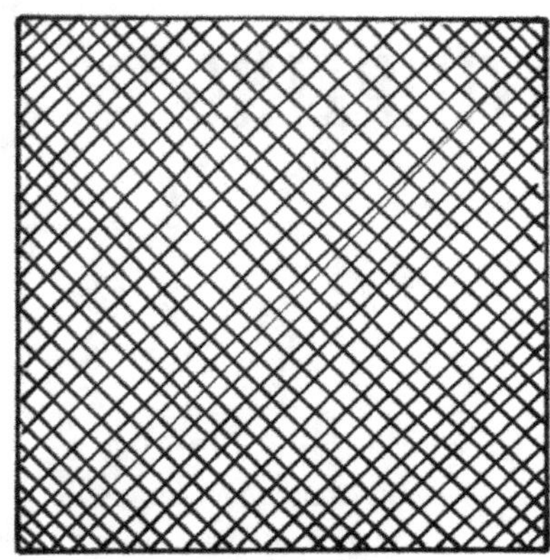

CROSS-HATCHING

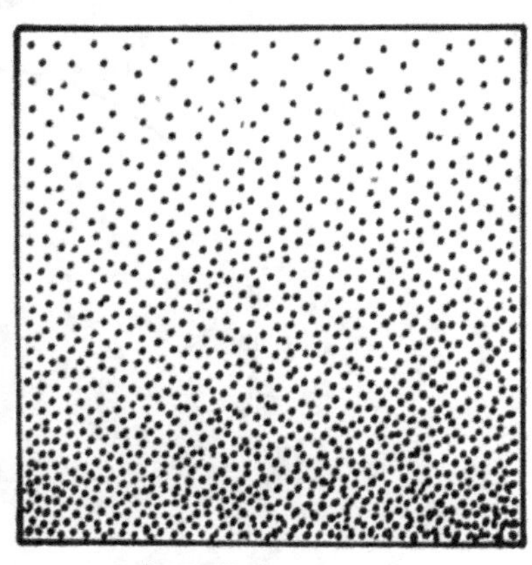

STIPPLING

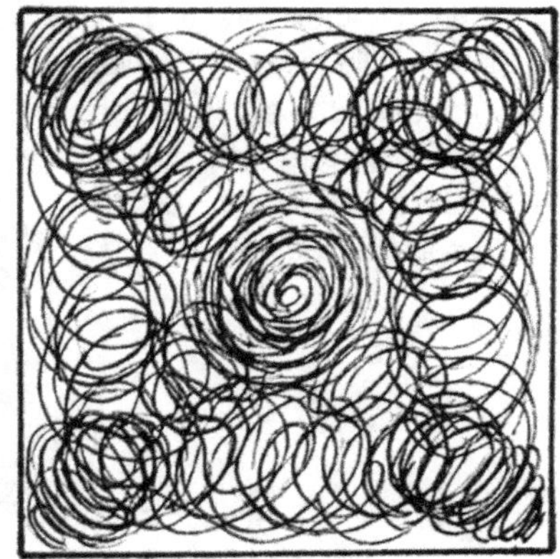

SCUMBLING

CROSS HATCHING

Cross hatching builds shading by layering sets of parallel lines at different angles. Choose a light direction first, then lay a first hatch layer with clean, evenly spaced strokes, keeping pressure consistent and controlling darkness by spacing. Add a second layer that crosses the first only where you need deeper value, and if needed add a third layer just in the darkest accents. On curved forms, slightly arc the lines so they wrap the surface, and let the spacing open up toward the light so the highlight stays mostly clean paper.

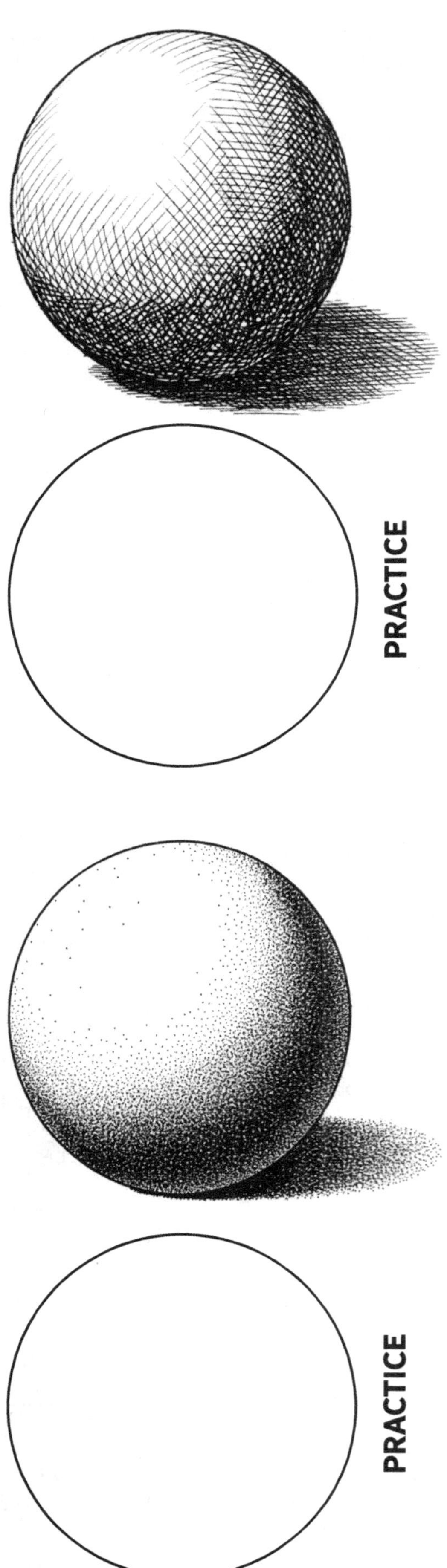

PRACTICE

STIPPLING

Stippling builds shading with dots. Choose a light direction first, then place dots in the shadow areas using consistent pressure and dot size. Control value by density: pack dots tightly for darks, spread them out for midtones, and let them thin to almost nothing as you approach the highlight. Keep the transition gradual, and reserve the densest clusters for the deepest shadows and contact areas.

PRACTICE

SCUMBLING

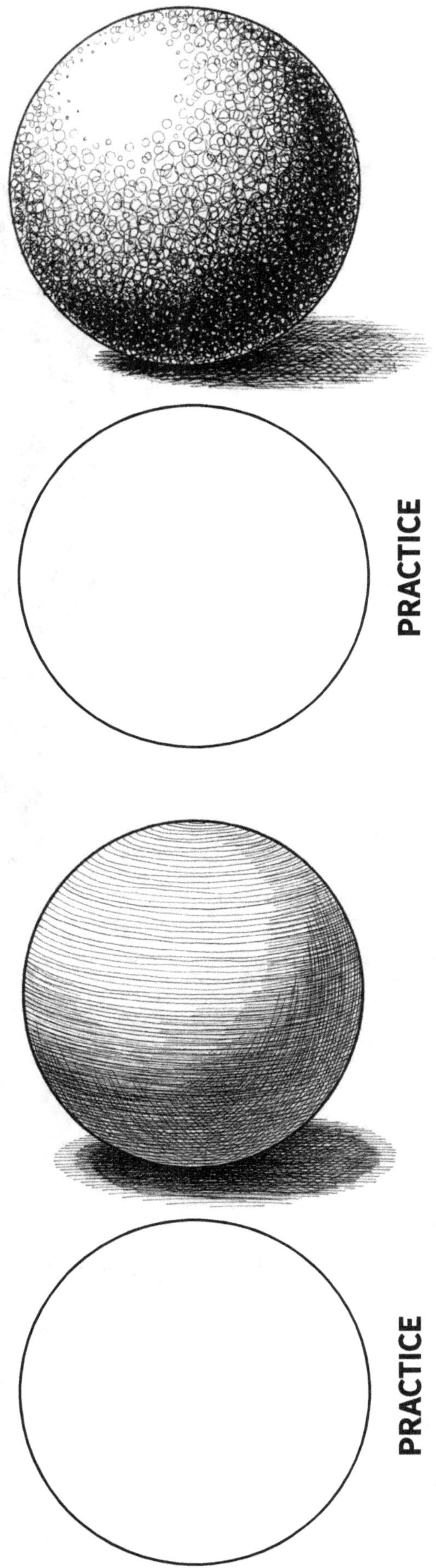

Scumbling, also know as scribbling, builds shading with small, controlled, looping marks instead of straight lines. Set your light direction first, then start in the shadow areas with tight, tidy loops, keeping your pressure consistent and controlling value by how densely you pack the marks. As you move toward the light, space the loops out and let them break up so the highlight stays mostly clean paper. On curved forms, follow the surface with the flow of your scribbles so they "wrap" the object, and keep the darkest accents confined to the deepest shadow areas rather than spreading heavy texture everywhere.

PRACTICE

HATCHING

Hatching builds shading with a single direction of parallel lines. Pick a light direction, then place your first hatch strokes in the shadow areas, keeping pressure consistent and controlling value by changing the spacing. To make a smooth fade, keep the line angle the same and gradually open the gaps as you move toward the light, letting the highlight stay mostly clean paper. For curved forms, arc the strokes slightly so they wrap the surface, and deepen the darkest areas by adding more lines (closer together) rather than switching

PRACTICE

SKULL RACER

Pro tip:

Start with the circle, then draw the
helmet shell about one sixth wider all
round, with the jaw dropping roughly half
a circle below the bottom edge.

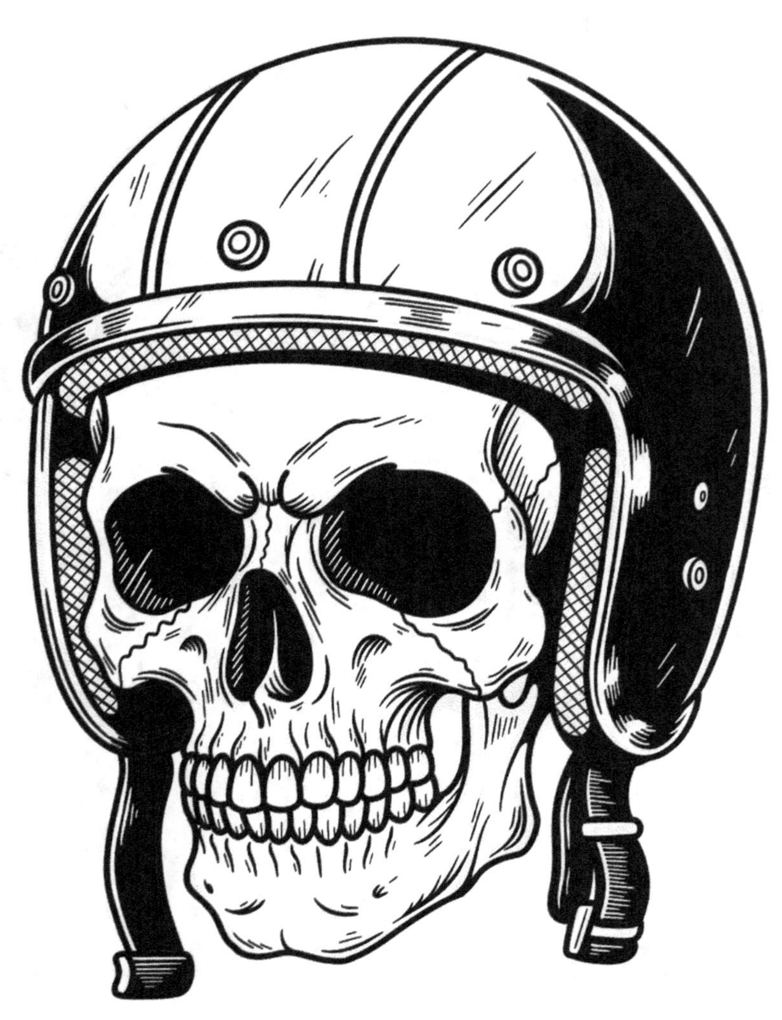

01

02

03

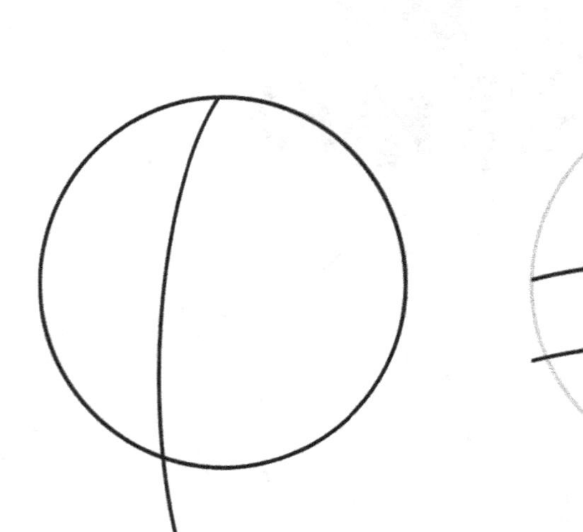
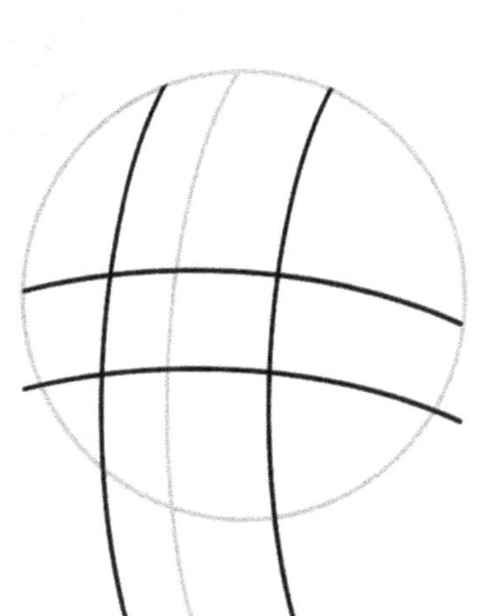
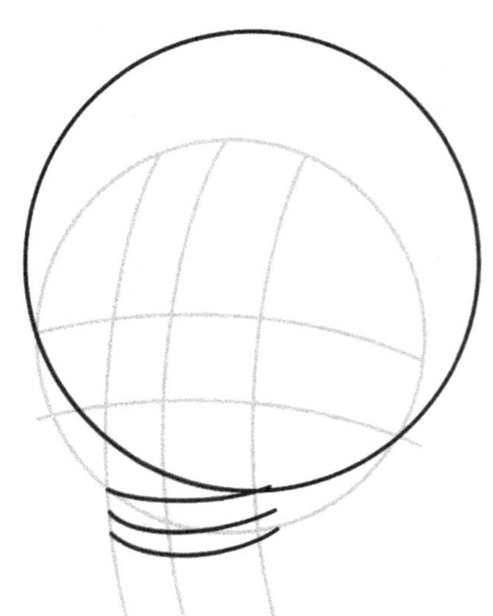

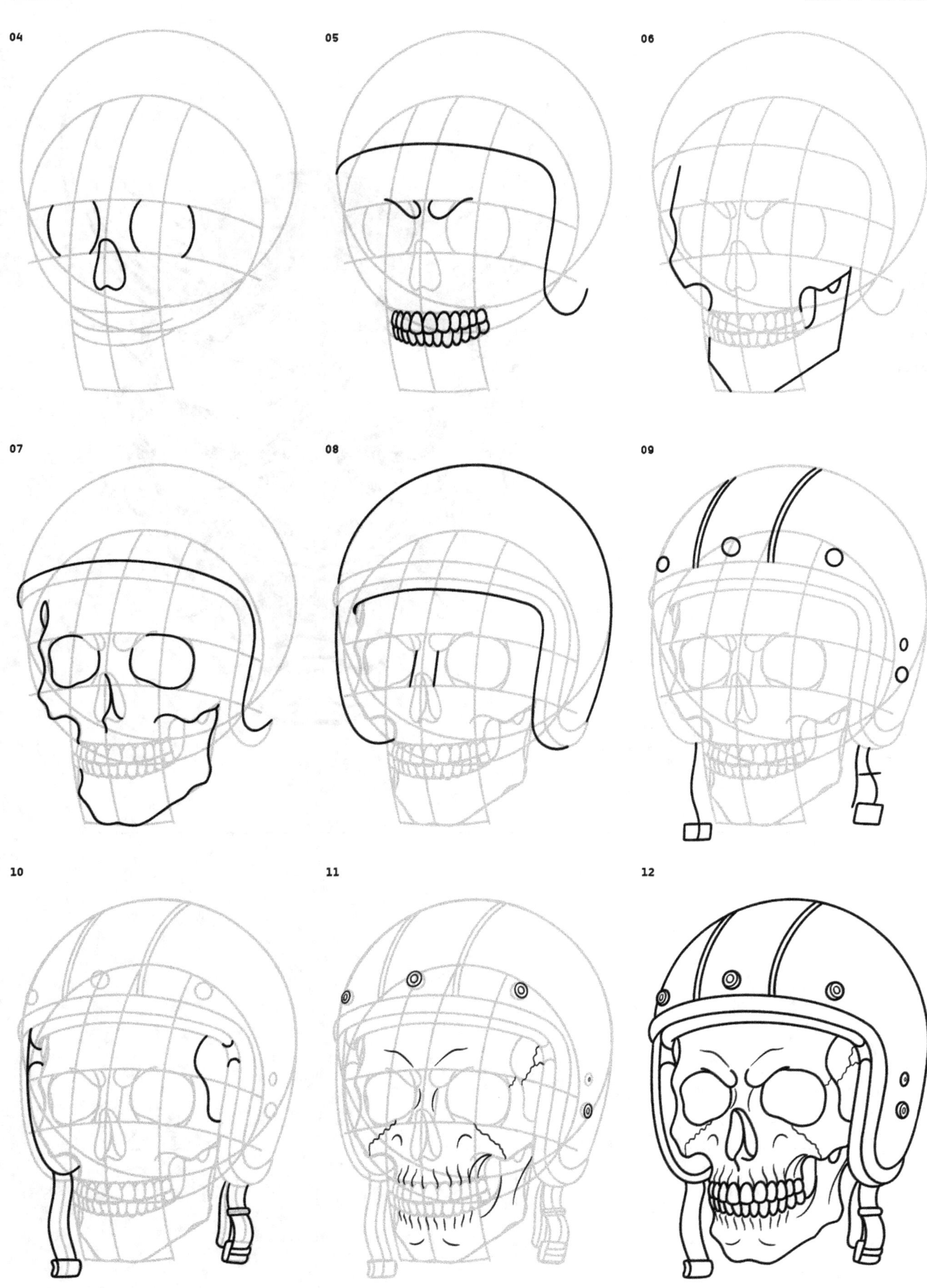

04
05
06
07
08
09
10
11
12

ONI MASK

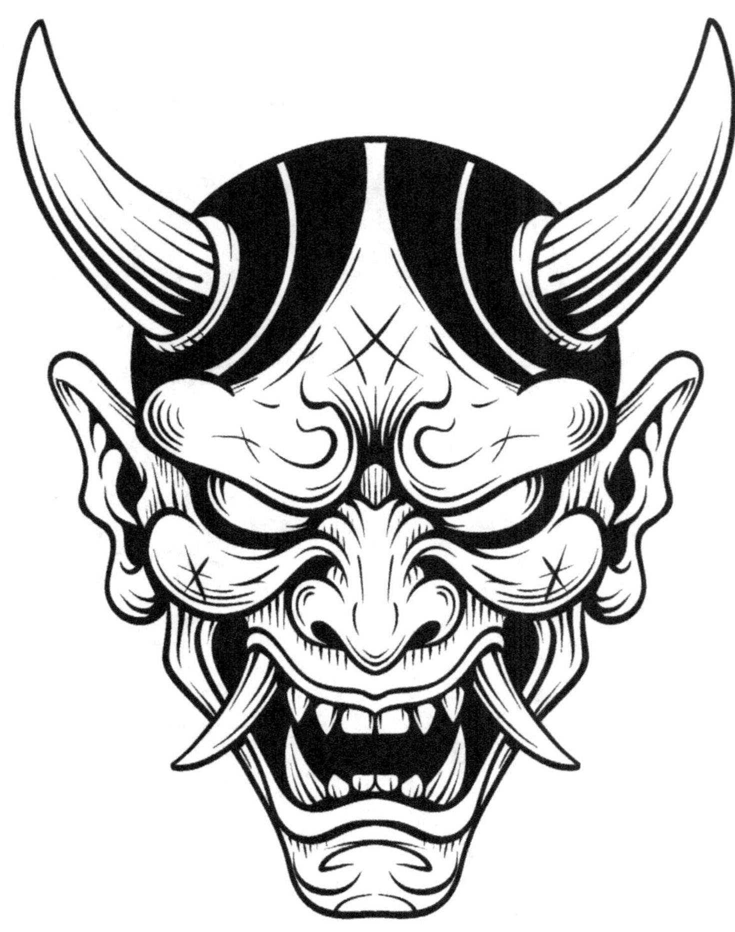

Pro tip:

Set the horn bases at the circle's upper thirds and let each horn sweep out about half a circle's width from the centre line.

---

01   02   03

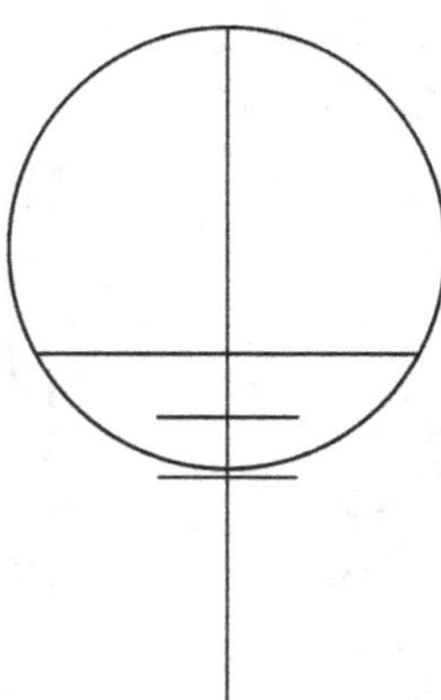

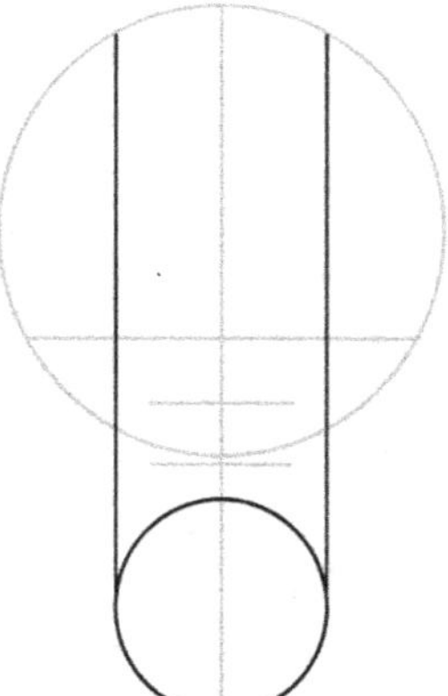

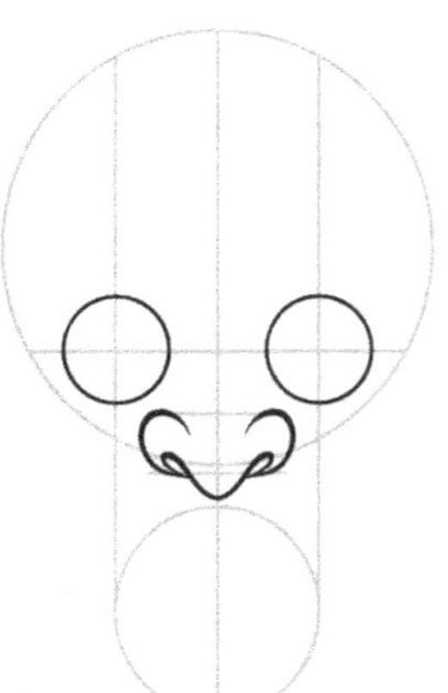

04

05

06

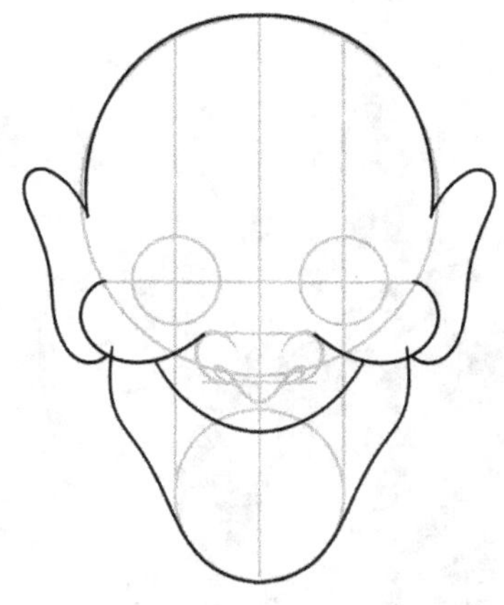

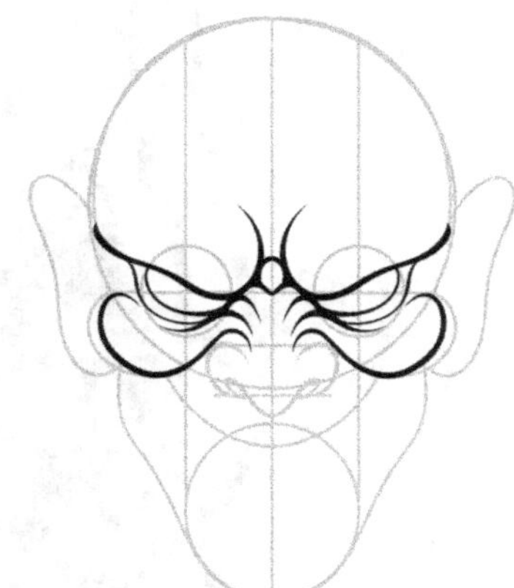

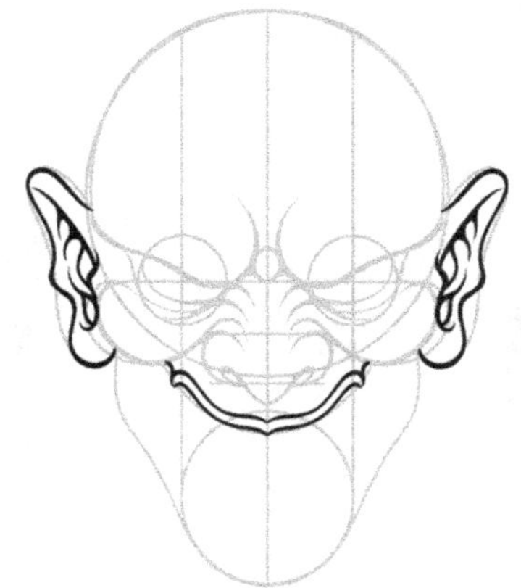

07

08

09

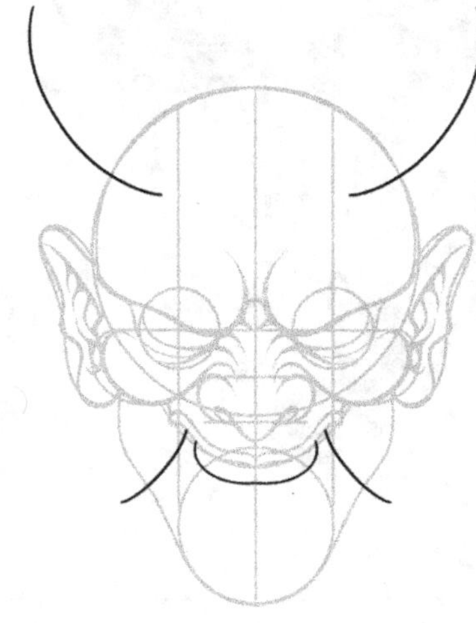

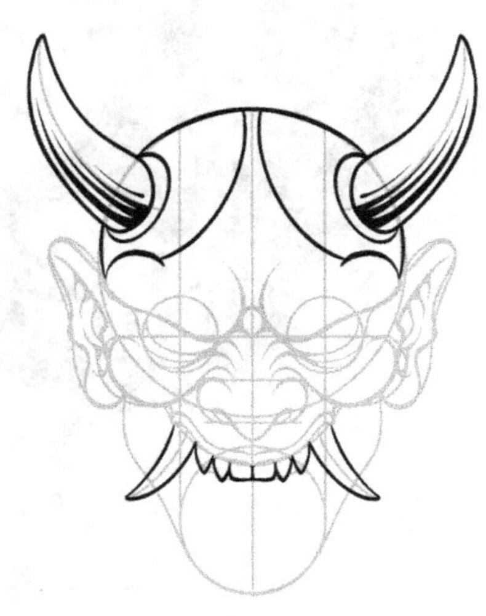

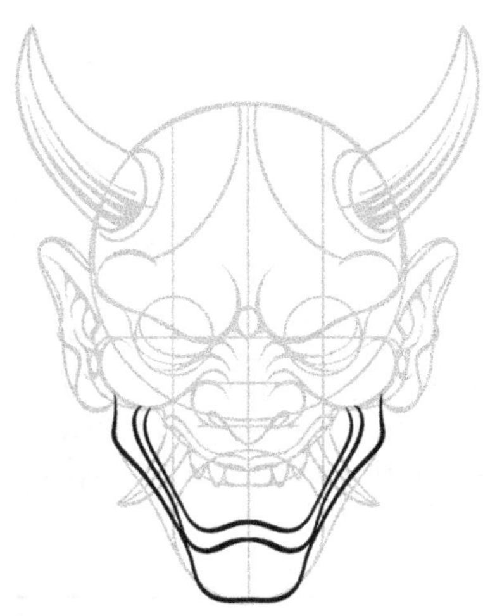

10

11

12

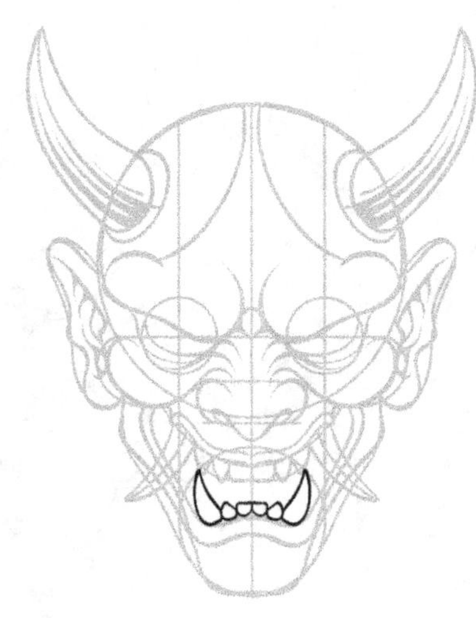

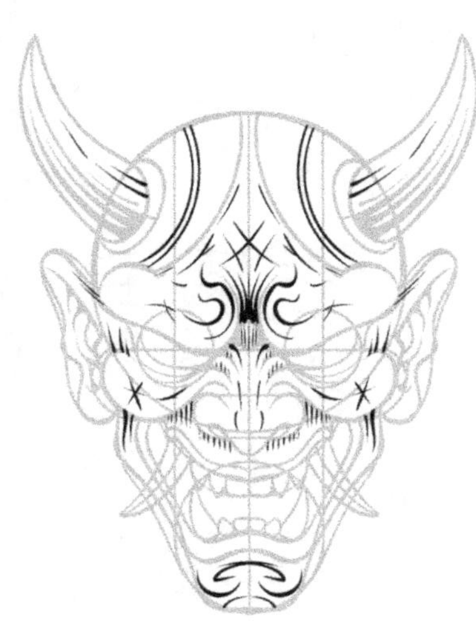

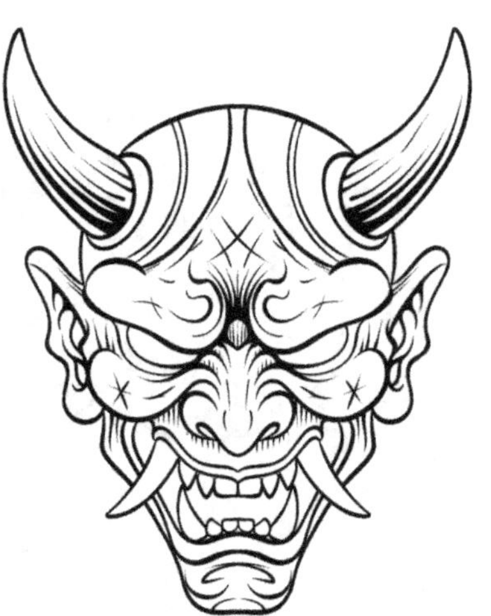

HOW TO DRAW COOL THINGS

DOBERMAN

Pro tip:

Use the centre line to aim the muzzle, then extend it about half a circle beyond the head so the Doberman's snout looks properly proportioned.

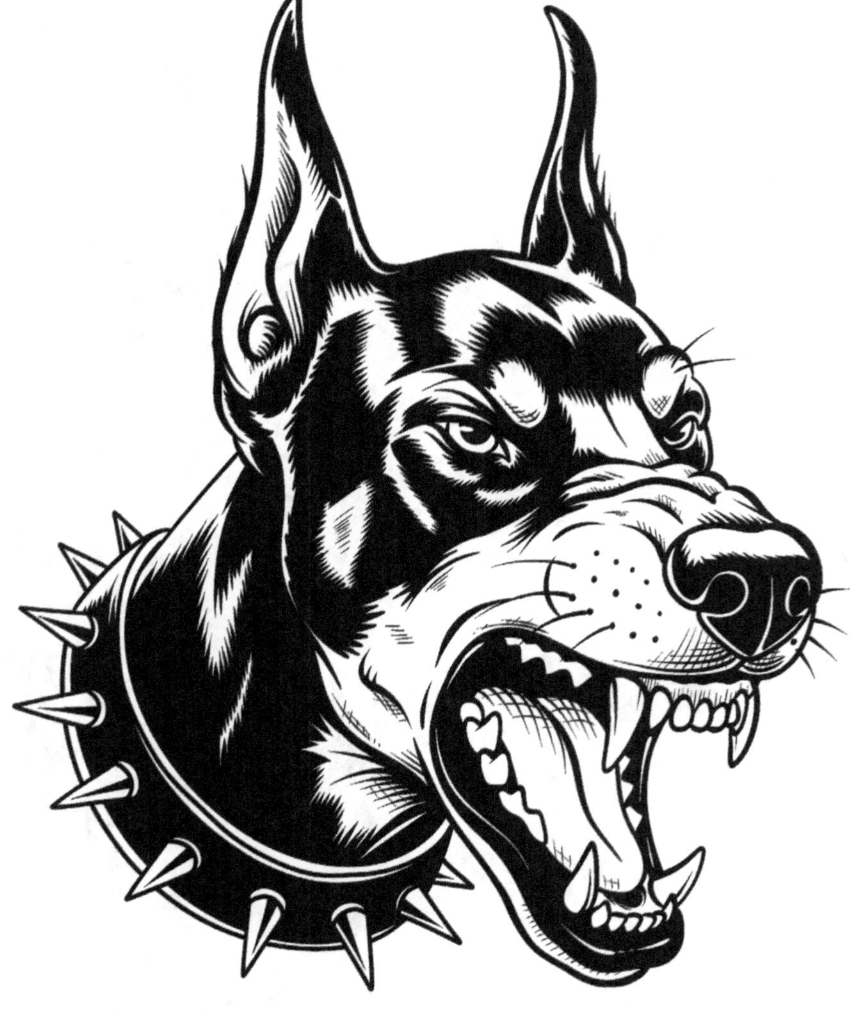

01

02

03

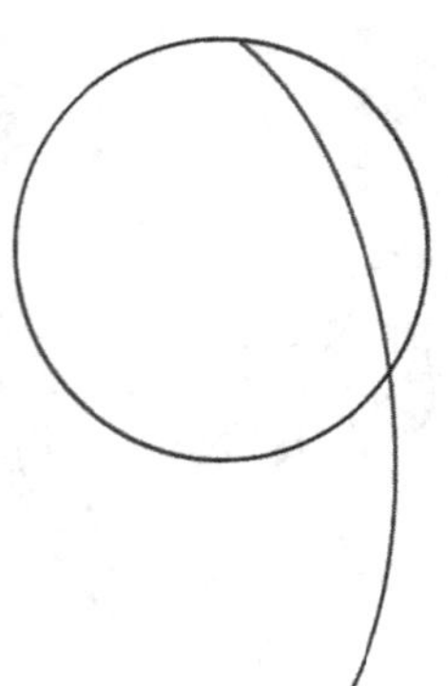

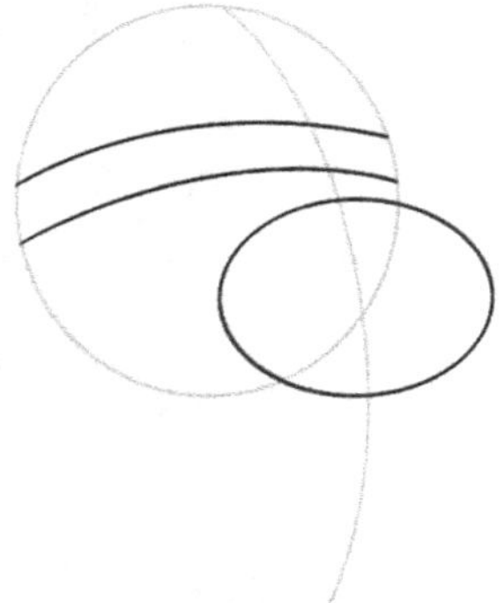

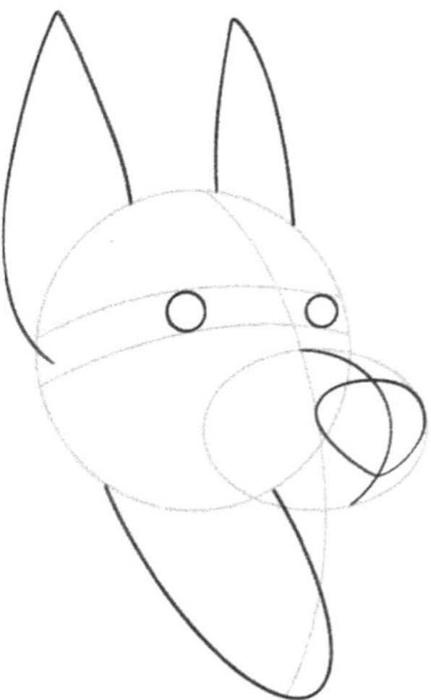

04

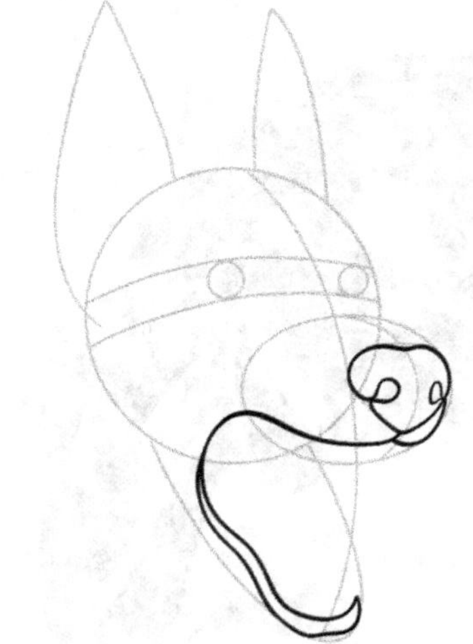

05

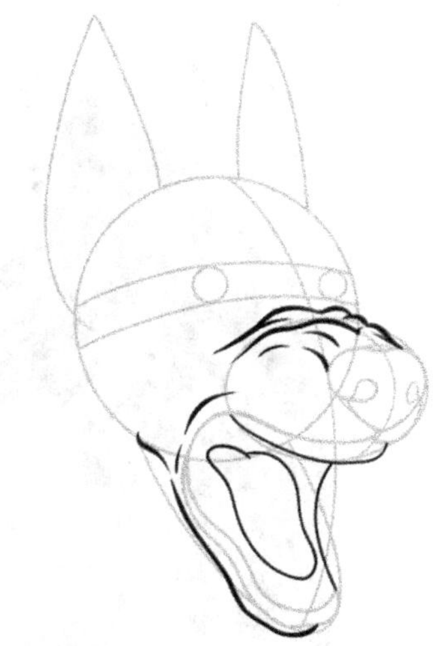

06

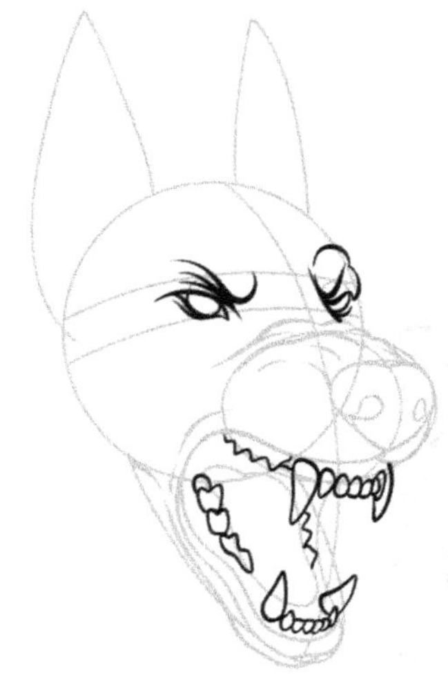

07

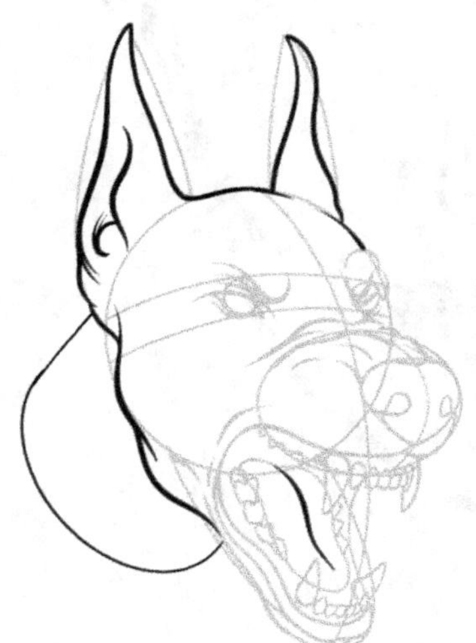

08

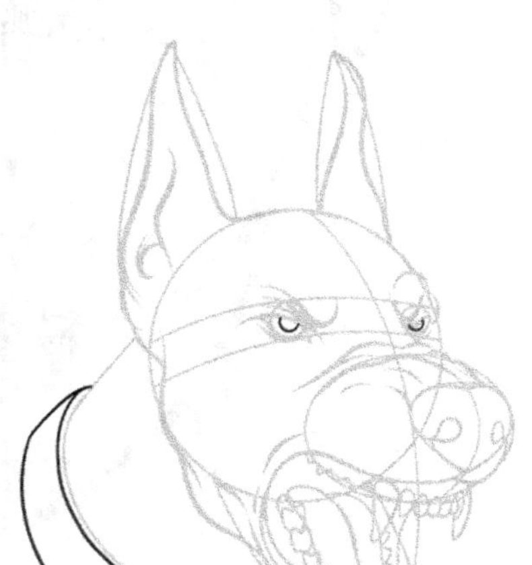

09

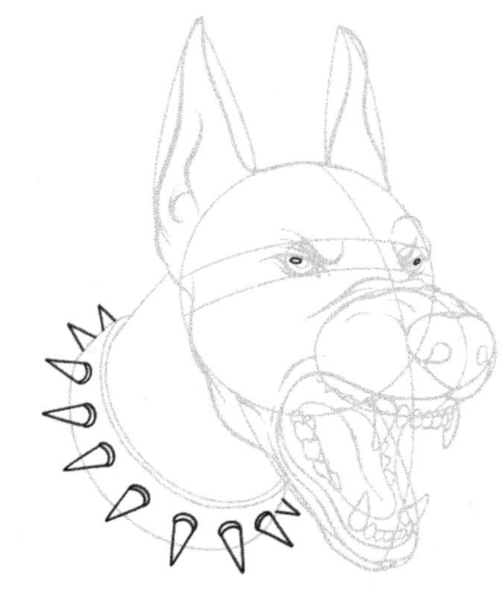

10

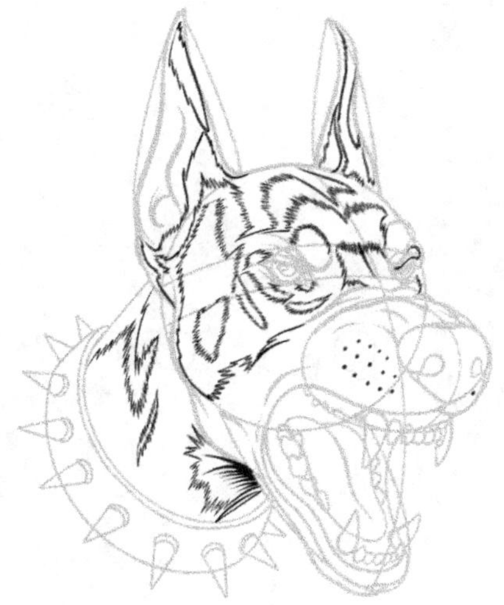

11

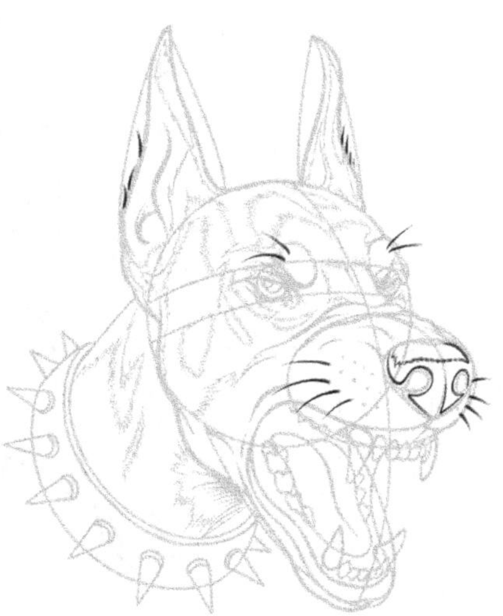

12

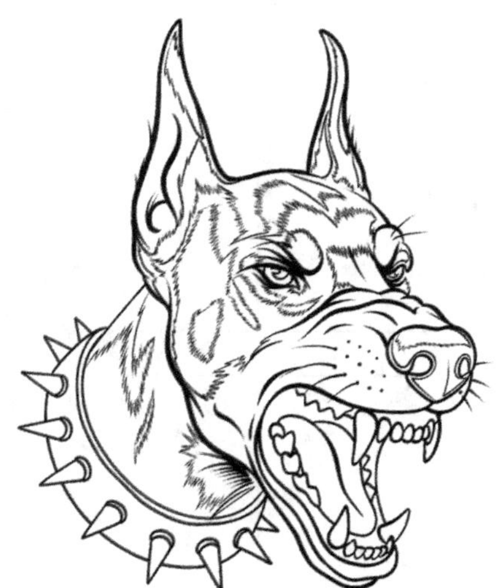

DEVIL WOMAN

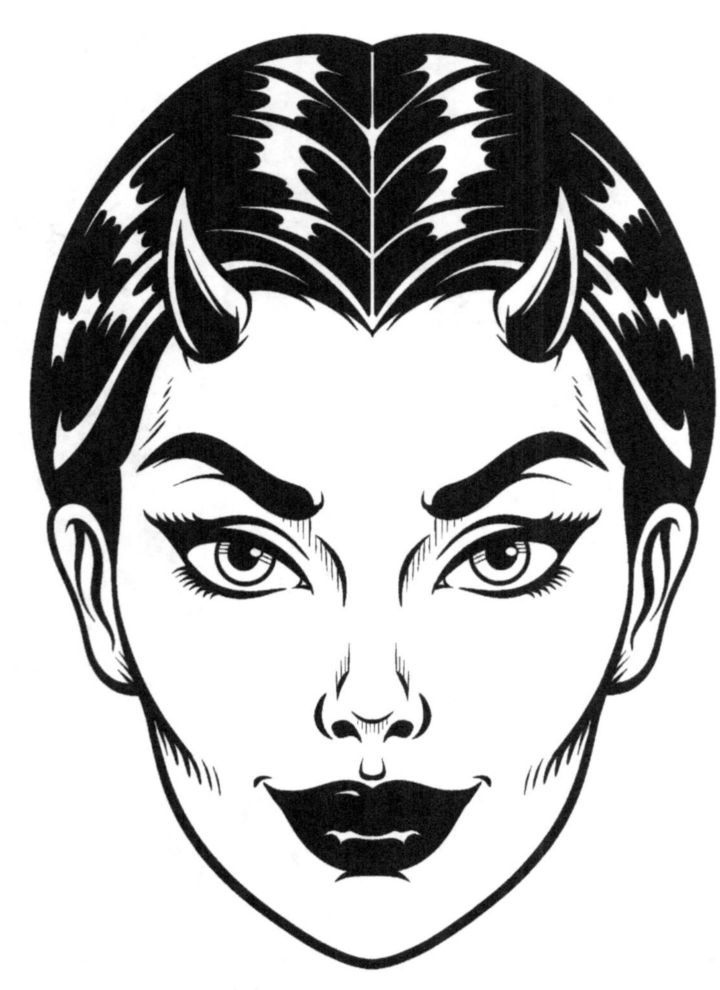

Pro tip:

Start with a head circle, then drop the
chin point about half a circle below it
and keep the jaw corners at roughly two
thirds of the circle's width for a sharp,
stylised face.

01   02   03

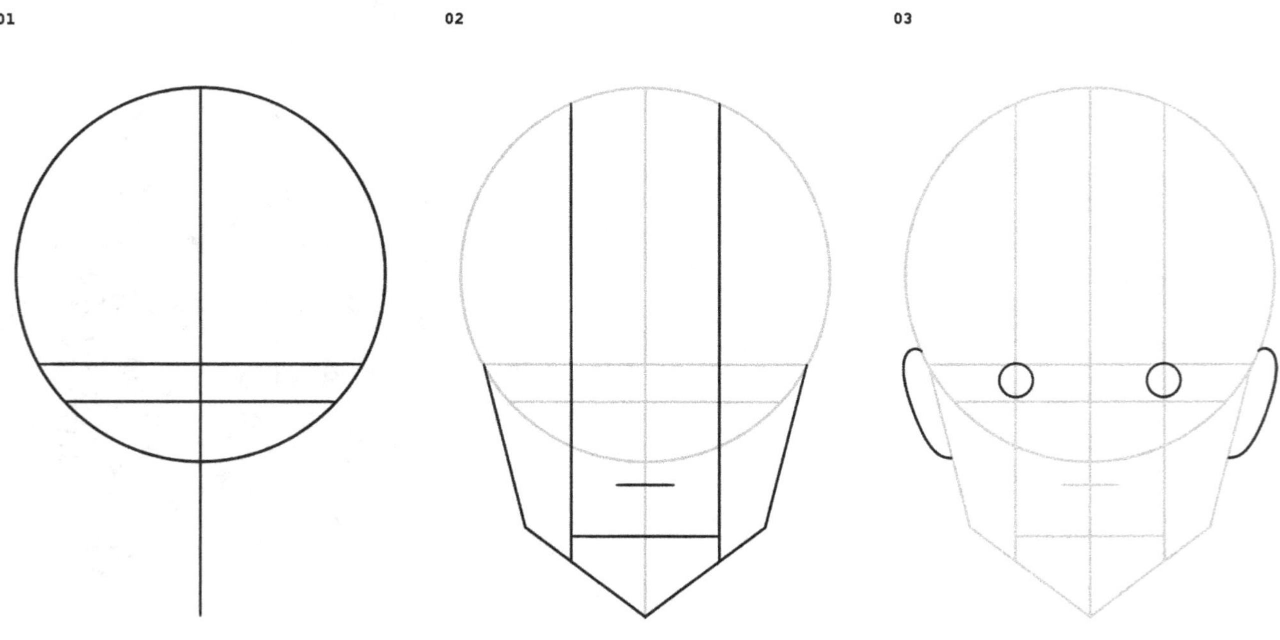

04

05

06

07

08

09

10

11

12

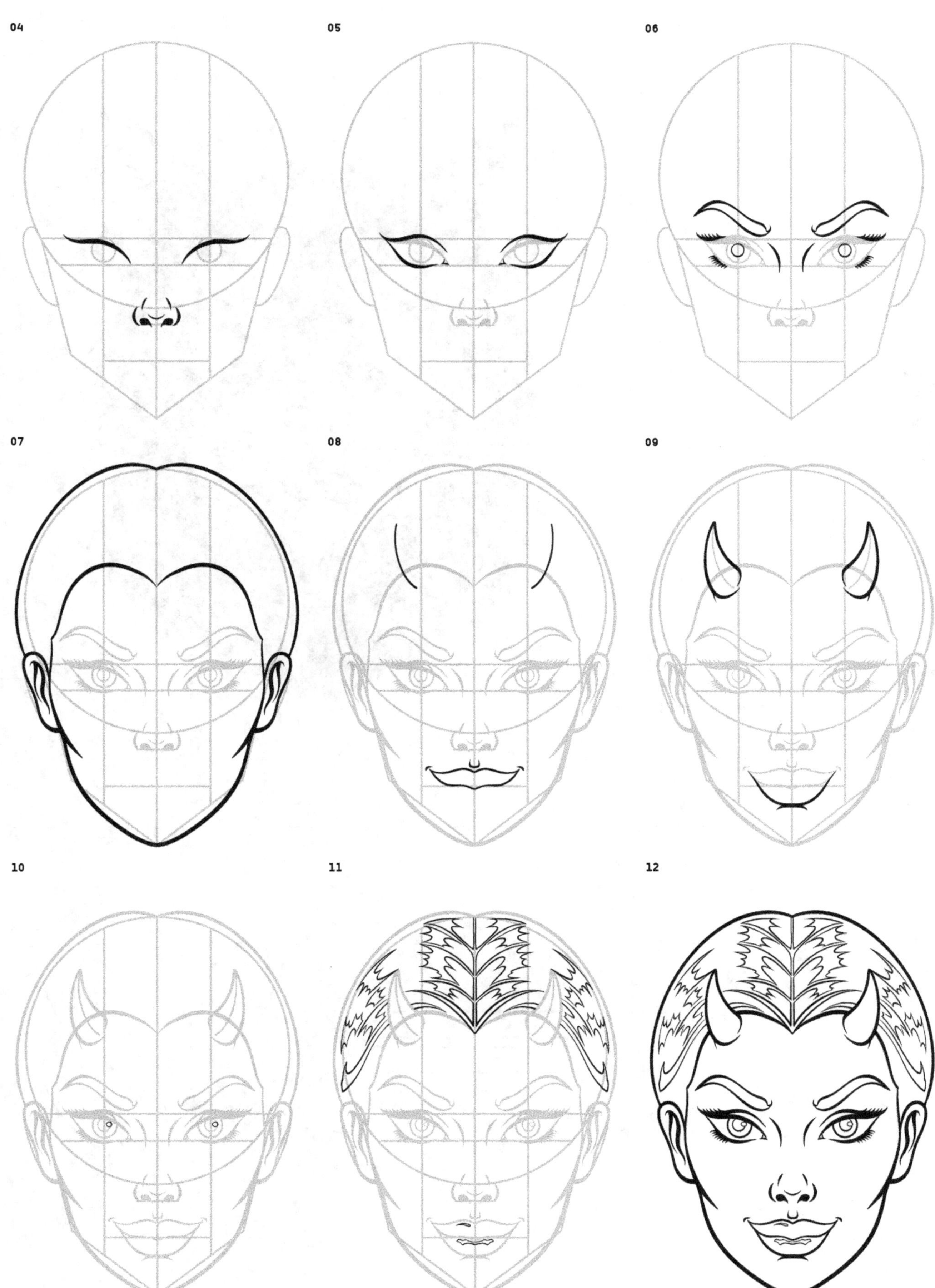

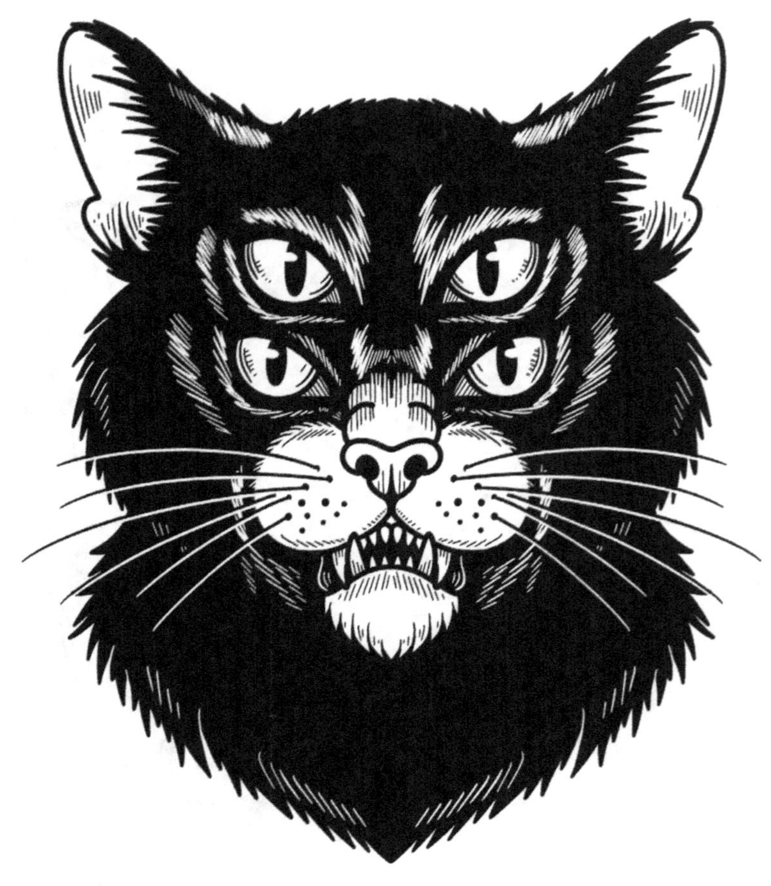

MYSTIC CAT

Pro tip:

Start by drawing both eye pairs as simple
ovals locked to the face guides, then
wrap the eyelids around the head curve
so the four eyes feel built into the skull,
not pasted on.

01

02

03

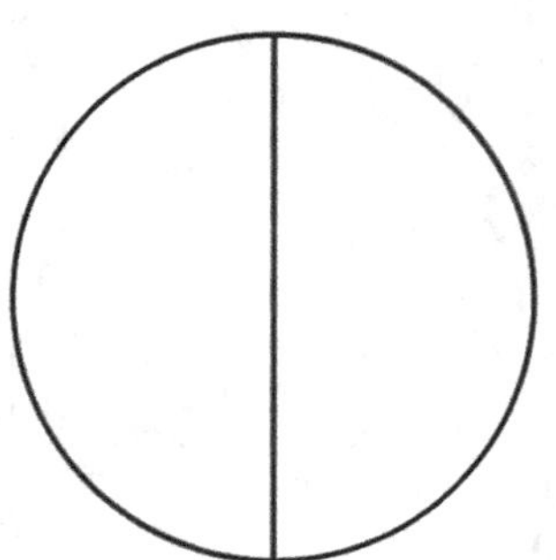

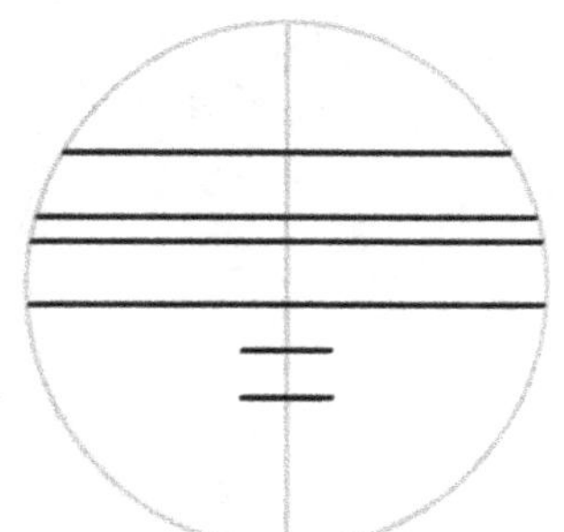

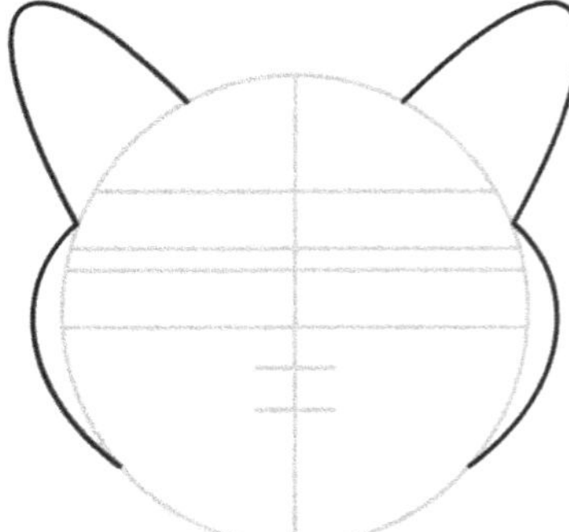

04

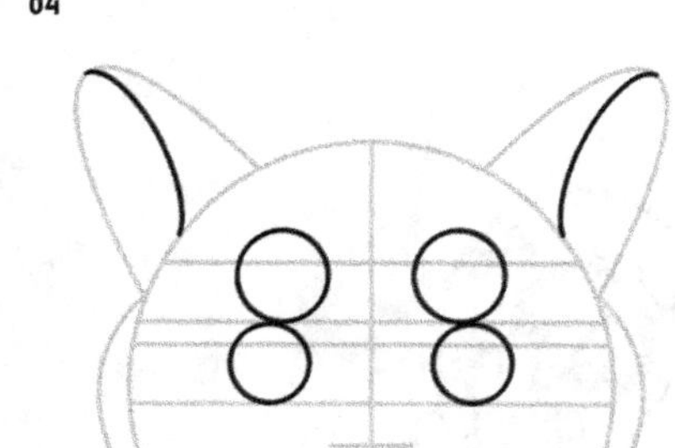

05

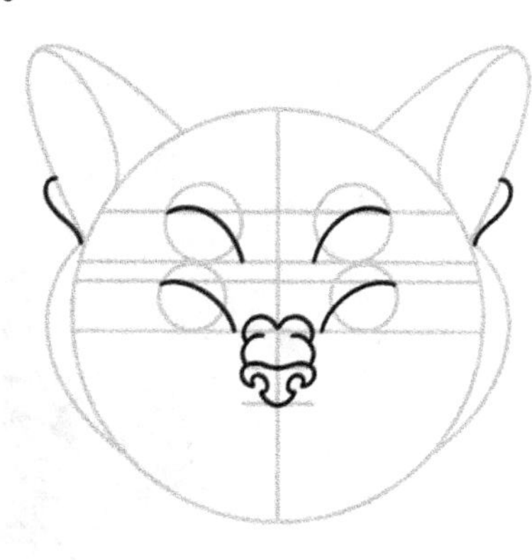

06

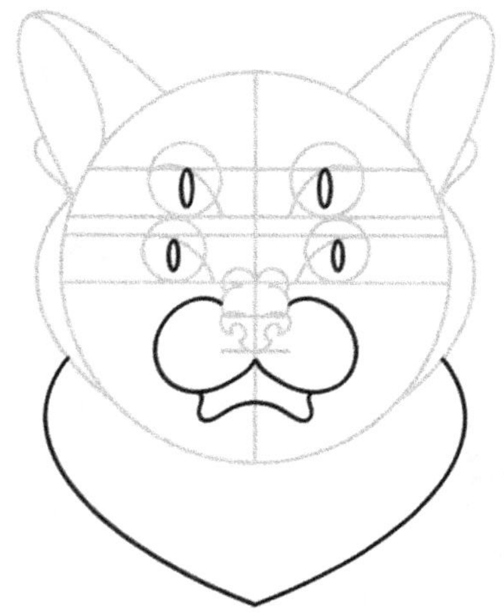

07

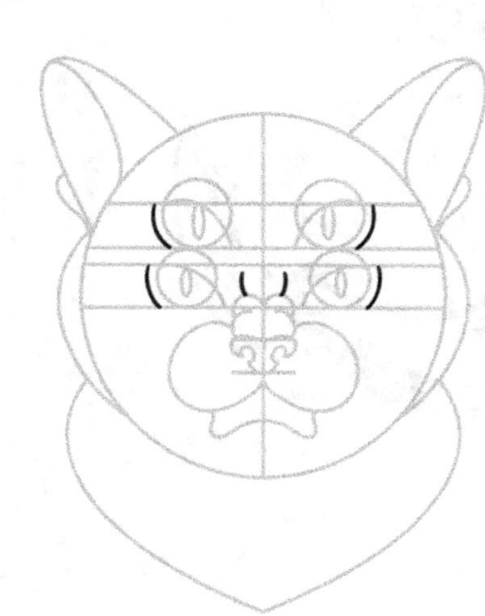

08

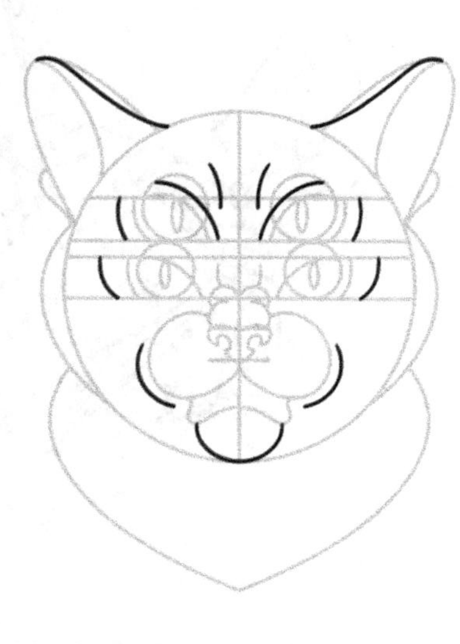

09

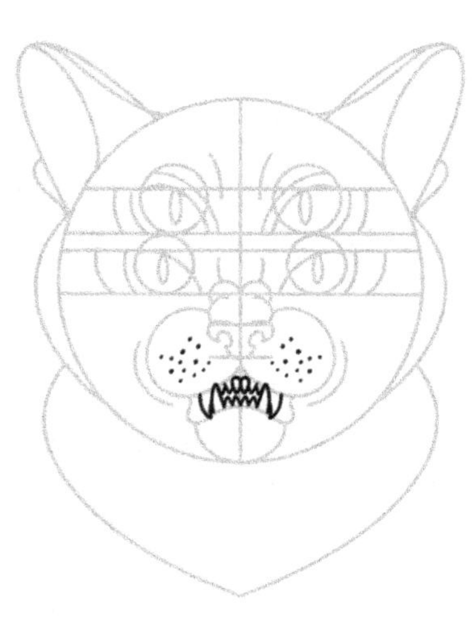

10

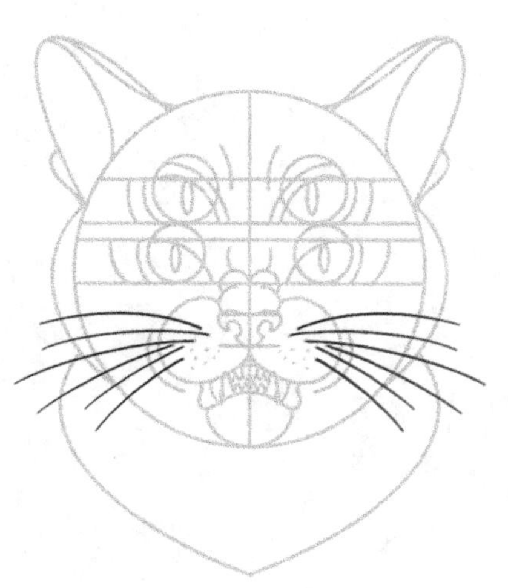

11

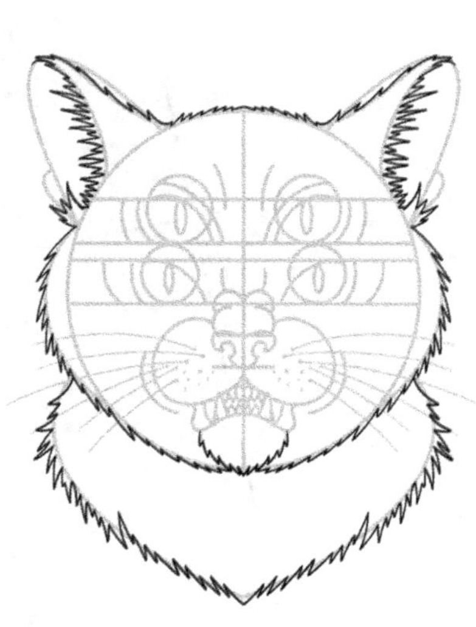

12

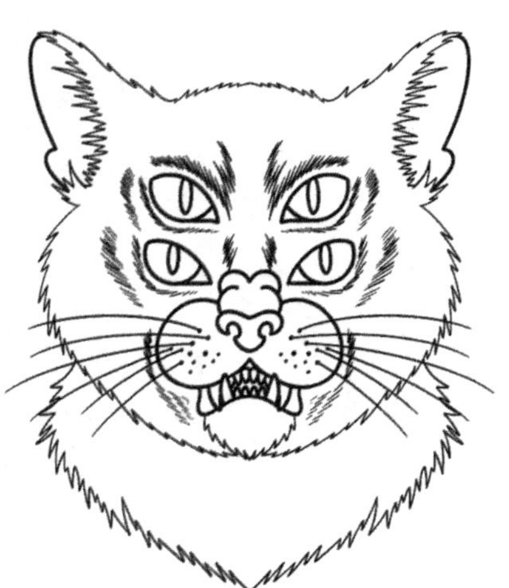

ANCHOR

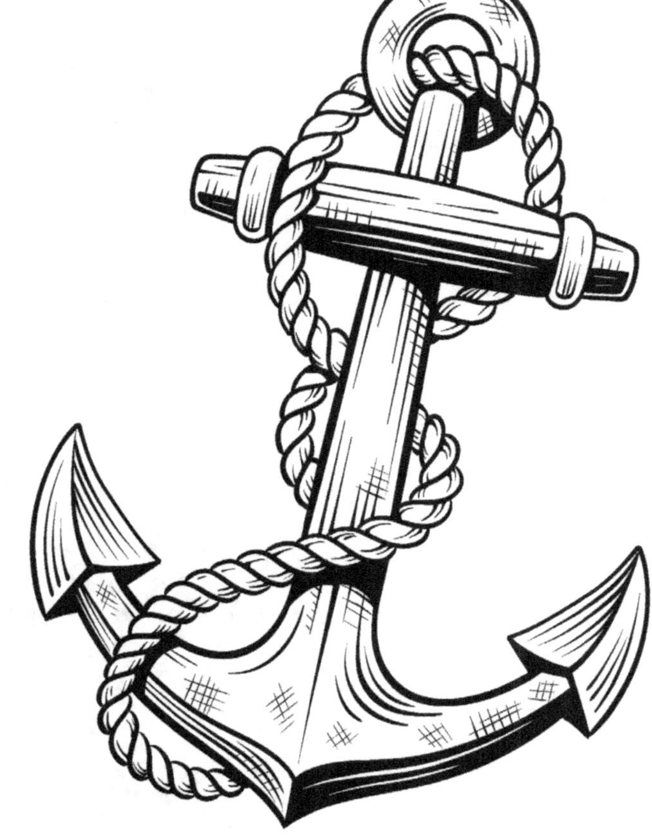

Pro tip:

Draw a centre line through the anchor
first, then mirror the two flukes from that
line so both curves match in size and
sweep perfectly.

01   02   03

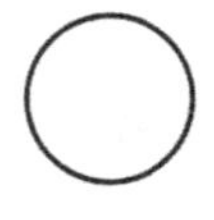

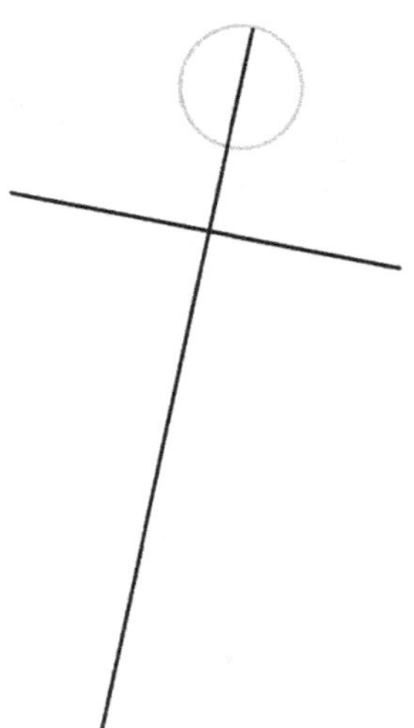

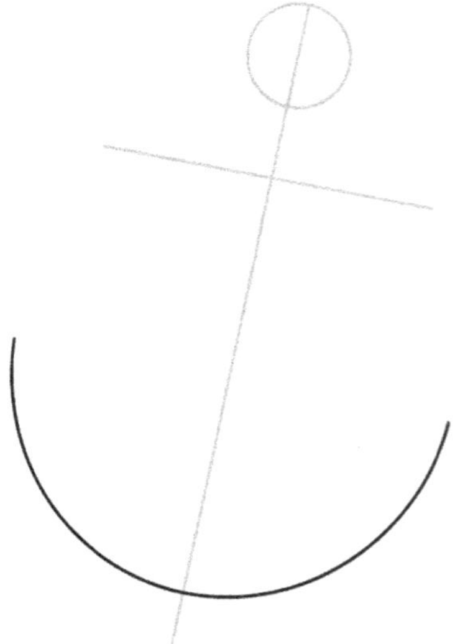

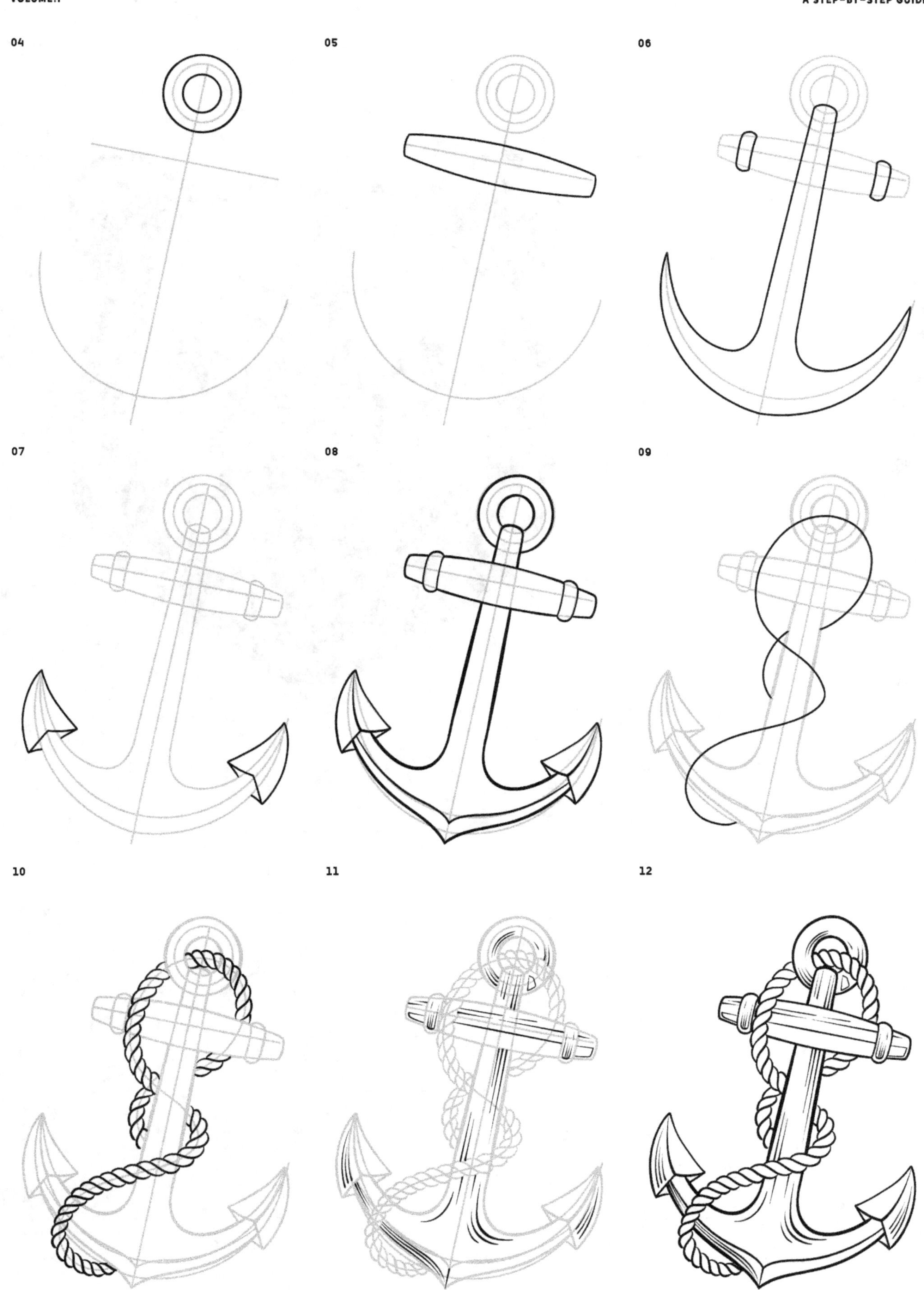
04
05
06
07
08
09
10
11
12
HOW TO DRAW COOL THINGS

GRIZZY BEAR

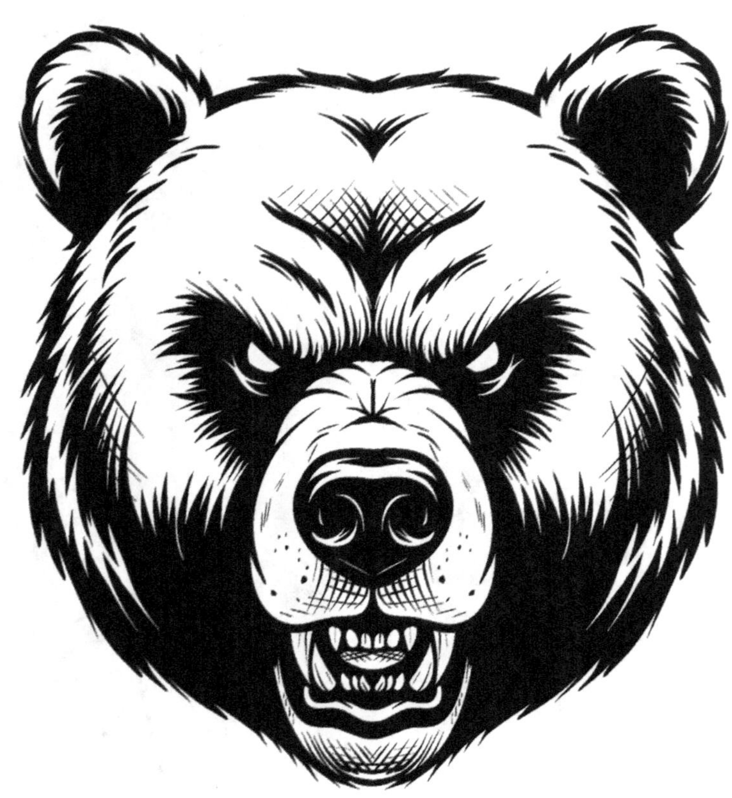

Pro tip:

Keep the muzzle oval mostly inside the
head circle, only dipping slightly below it,
and centre the nose on the vertical guide
to keep the bear's weight forward.

01   02   03

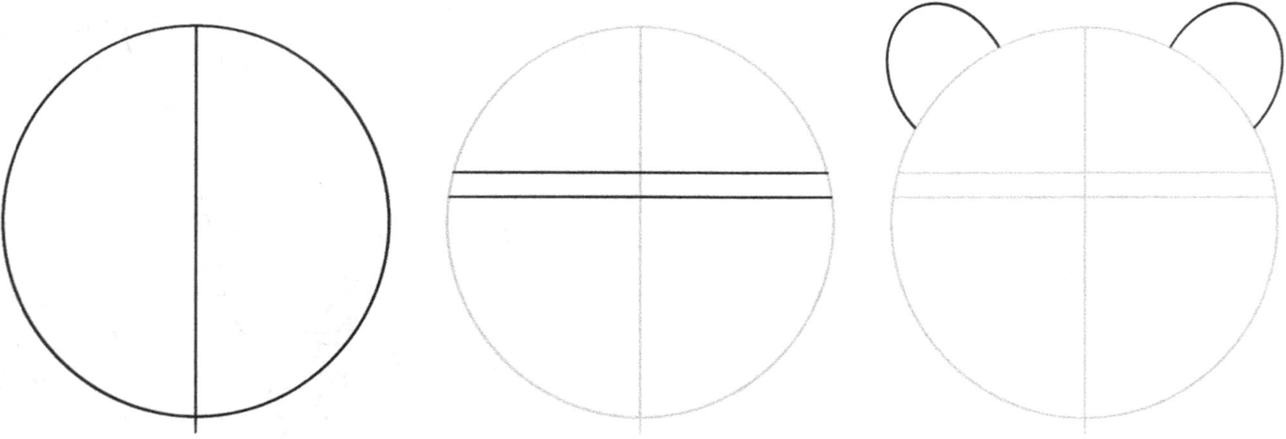

04

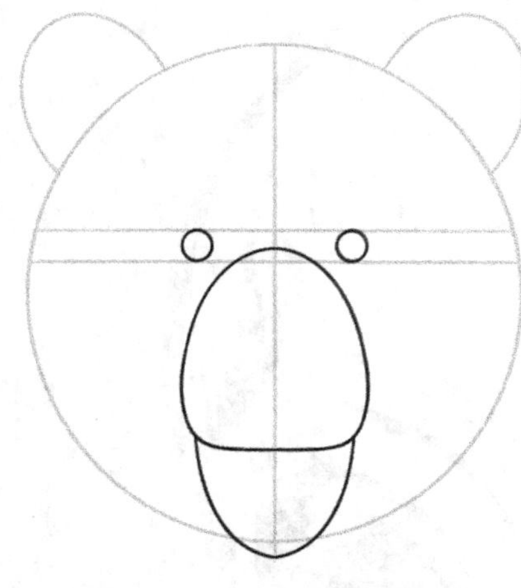

05

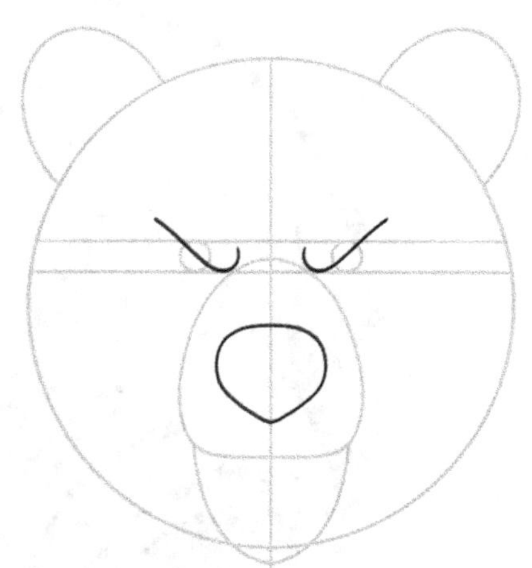

06

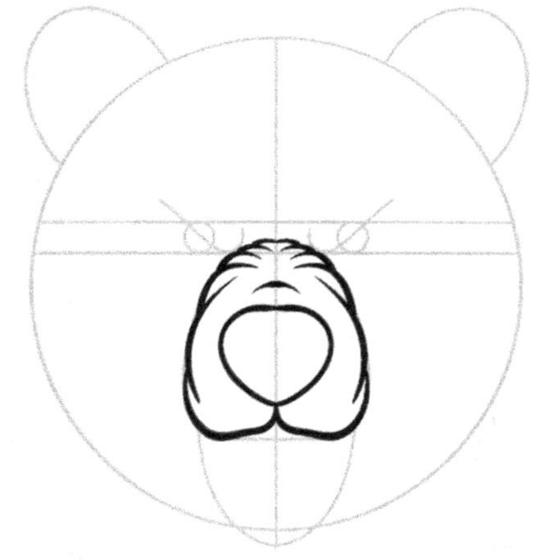

07

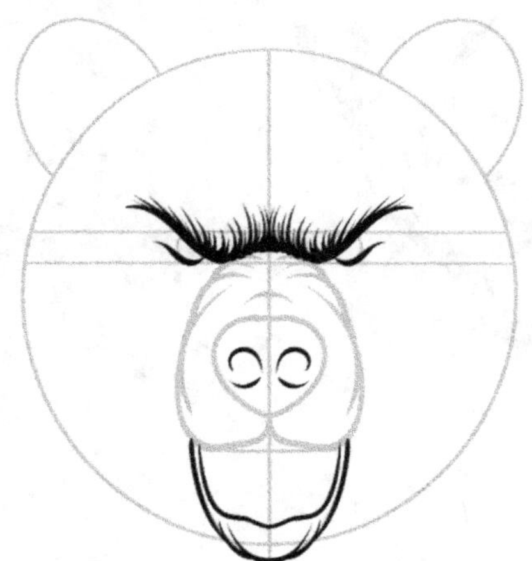

08

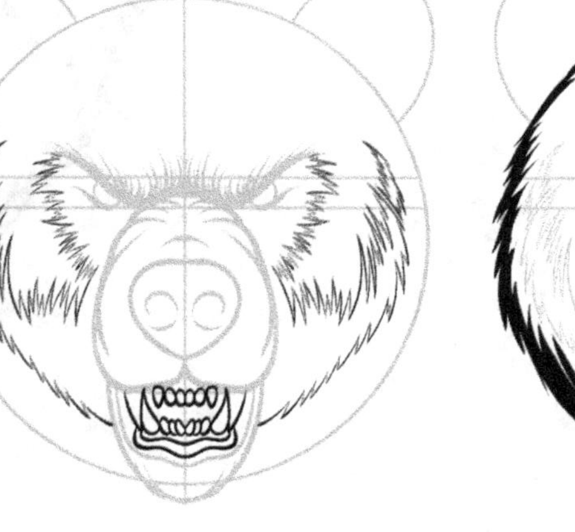

09

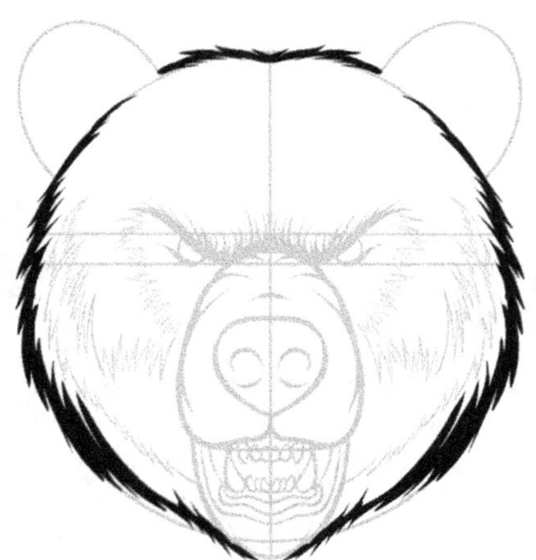

10

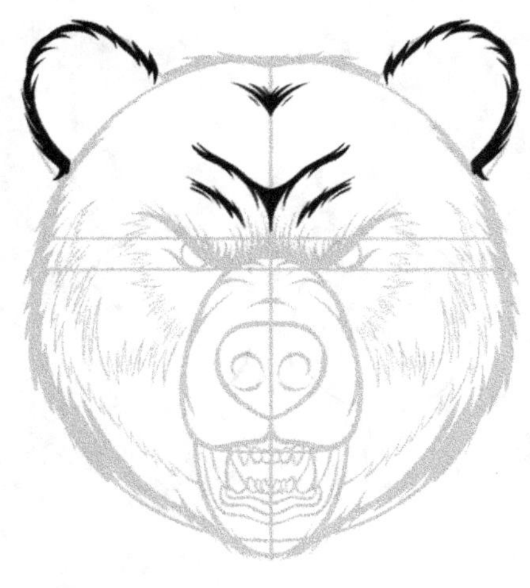

11

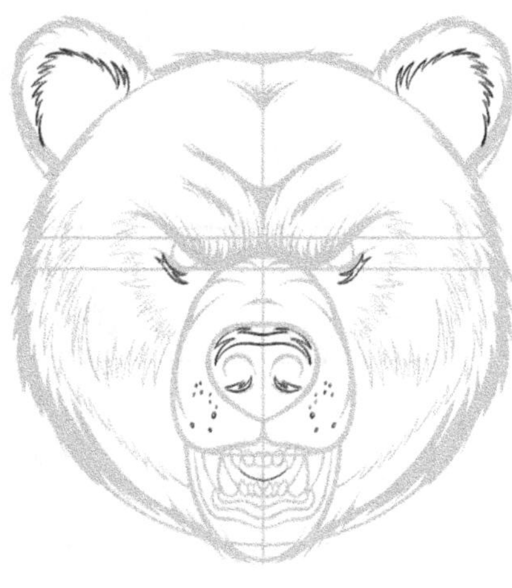

12

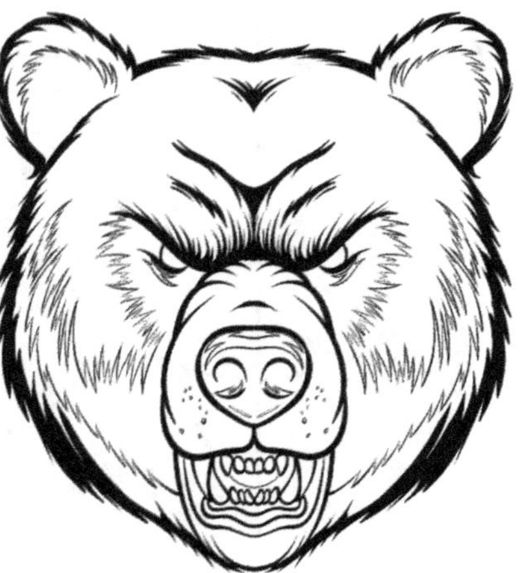

ALIEN

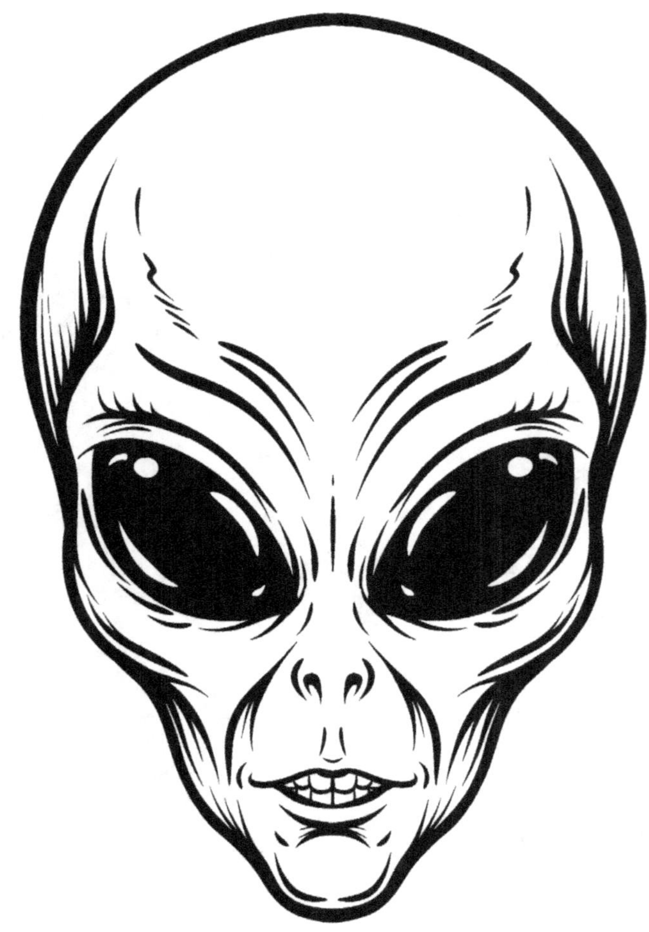

Pro tip:

Angle the eyes along the head's curve and keep their top edges parallel to the brow guide, so they feel seated in the skull rather than floating on the face.

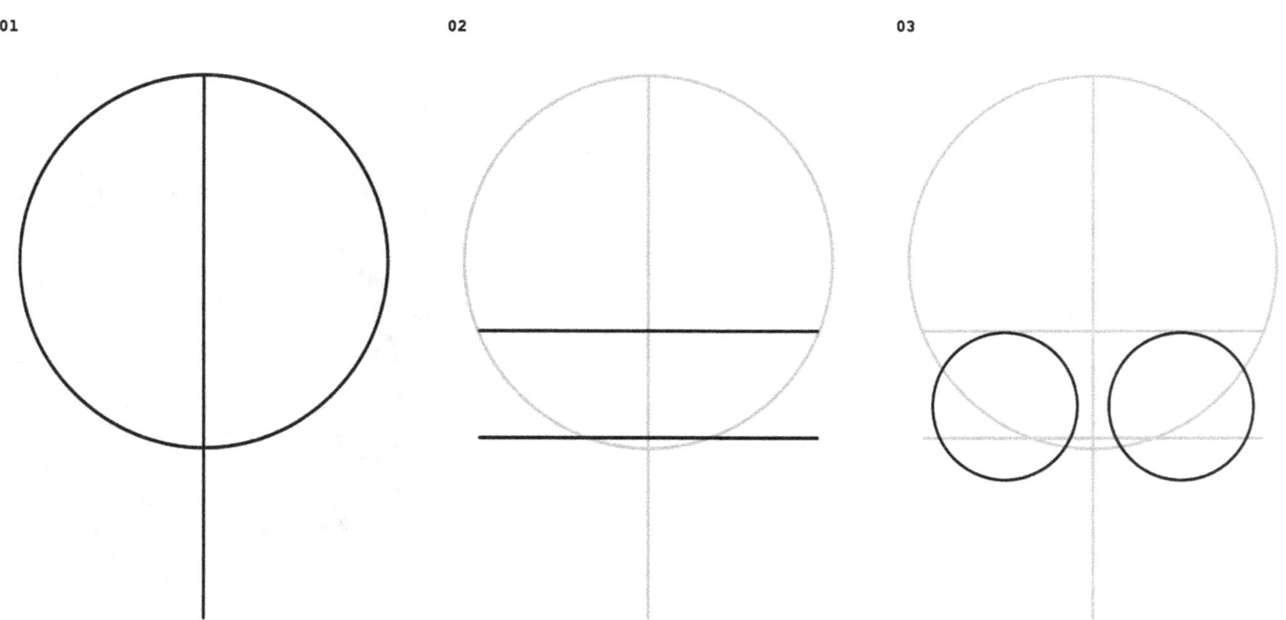

01

02

03

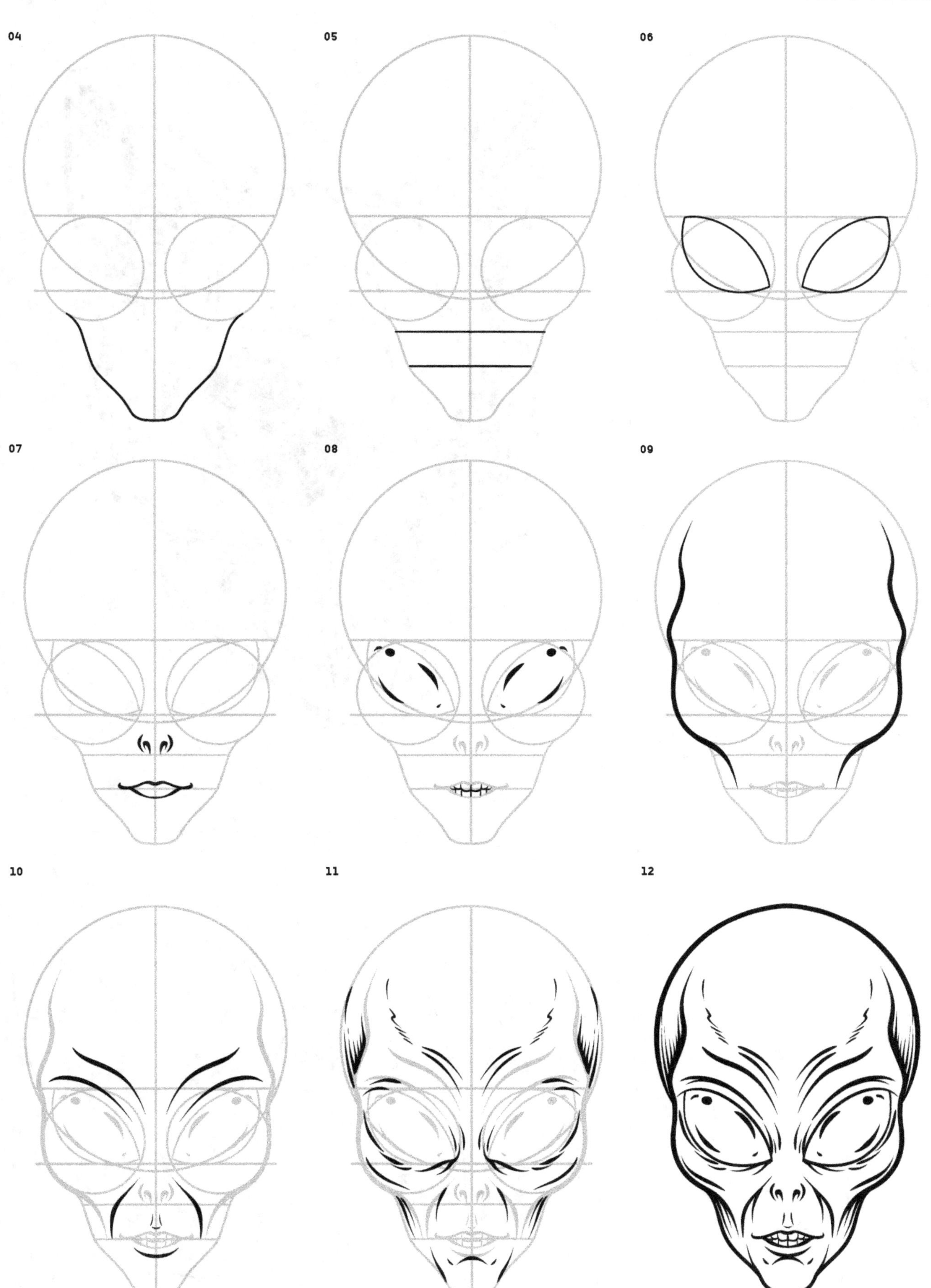

04
05
06
07
08
09
10
11
12
HOW TO DRAW COOL THINGS

CAT SKULL

Pro tip:

Treat the circle as the cranium, then
extend the jaw down by roughly one third
of the circle's diameter so the muzzle has
proper feline length.

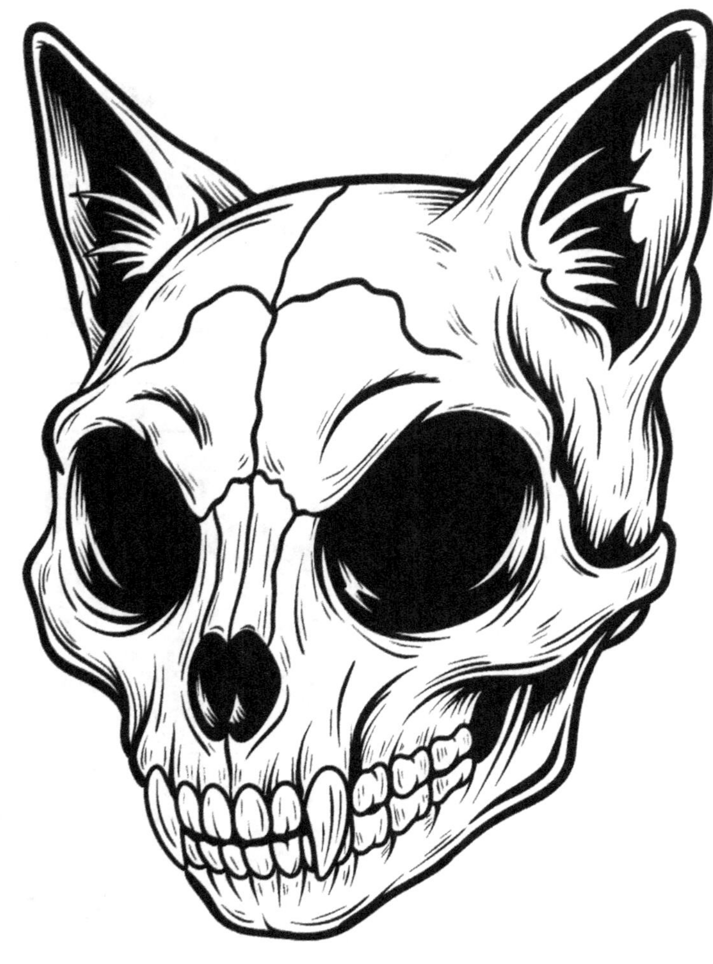

01

02

03

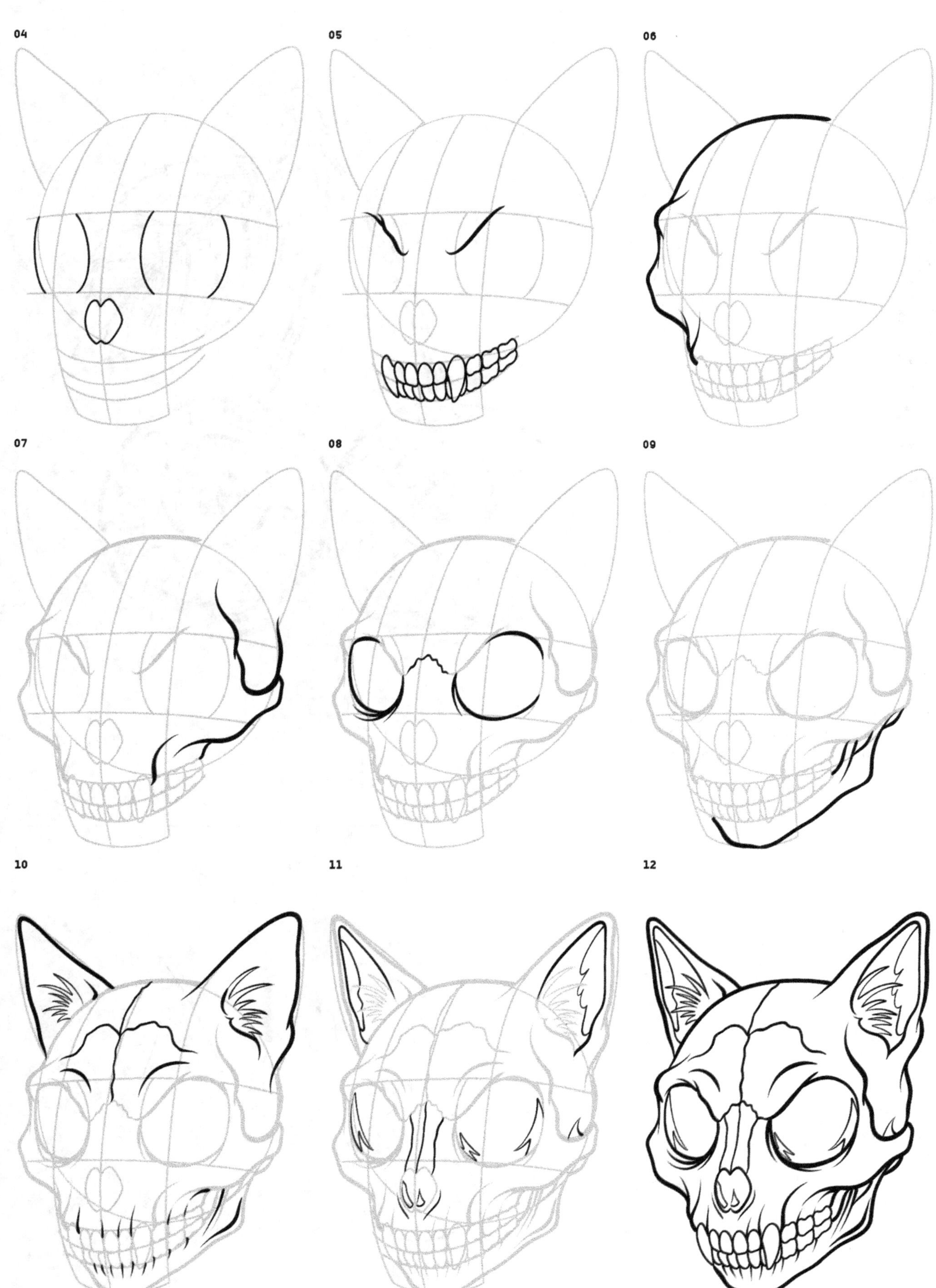

CHERRY EYEBALLS

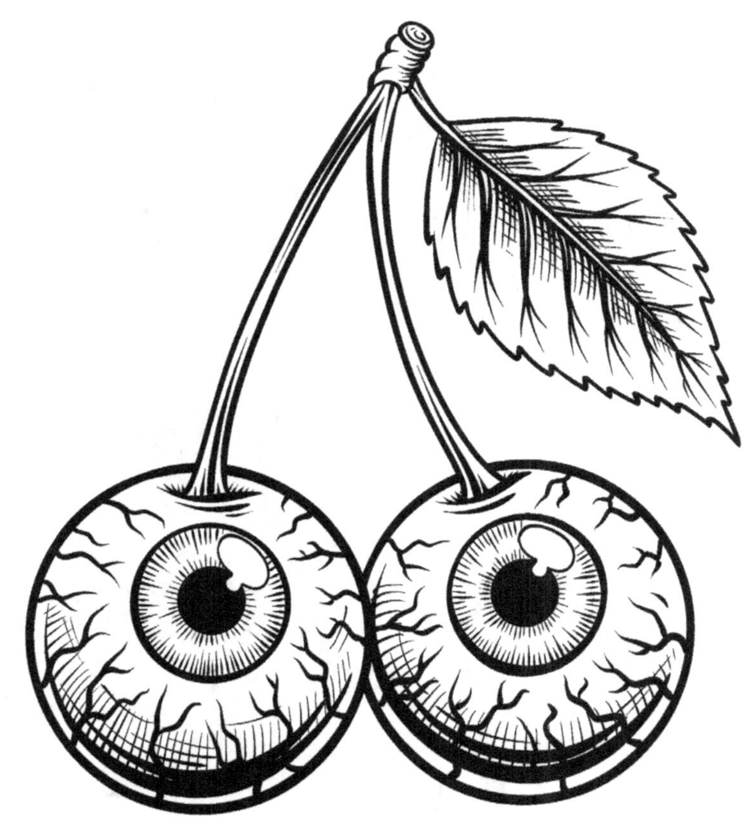

Pro tip:

Keep both cherry circles the same size
and align their highlights and pupils to
one direction, so they read as a matching
pair of eyes.

01   02   03

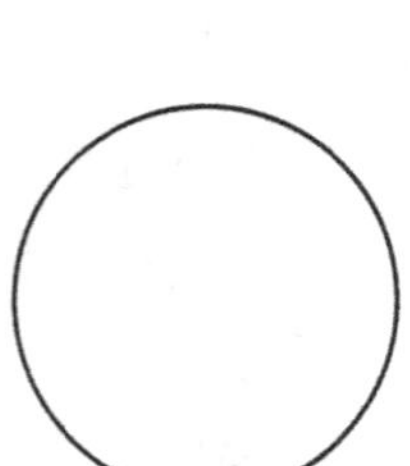

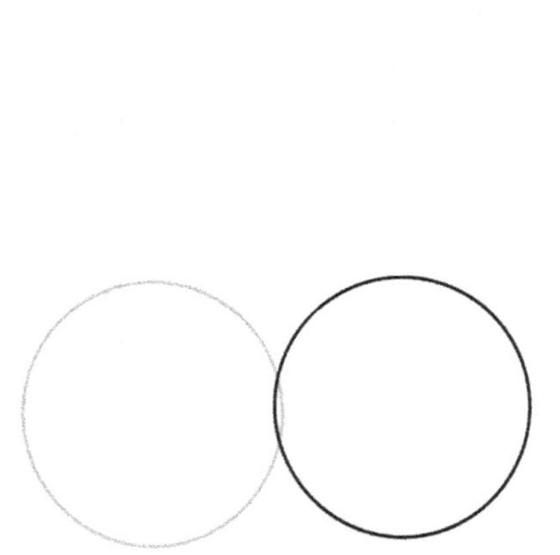

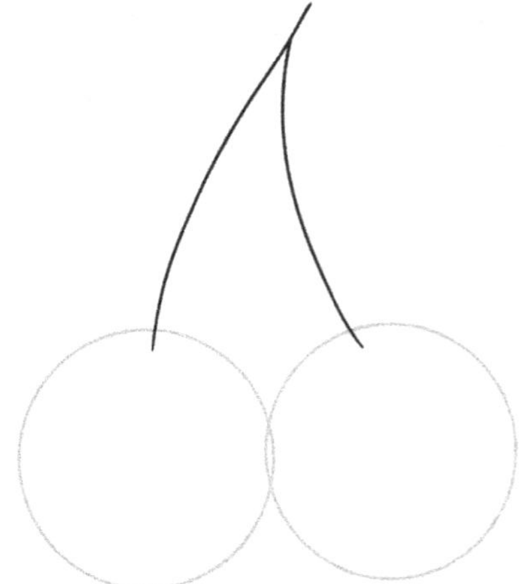

04

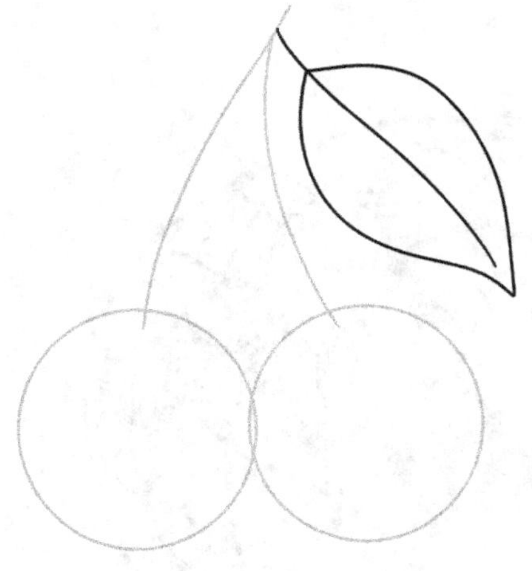

05

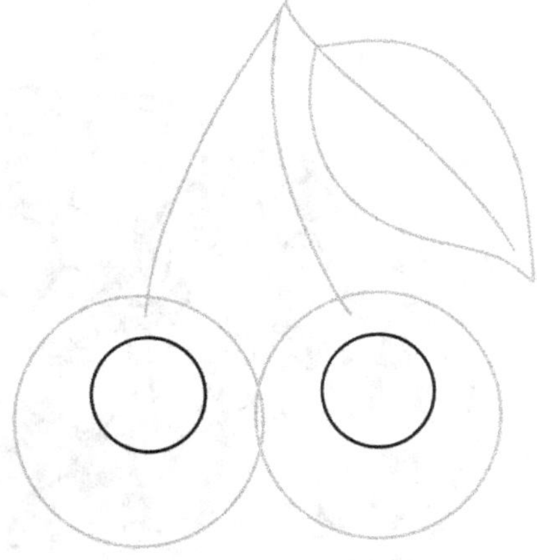

06

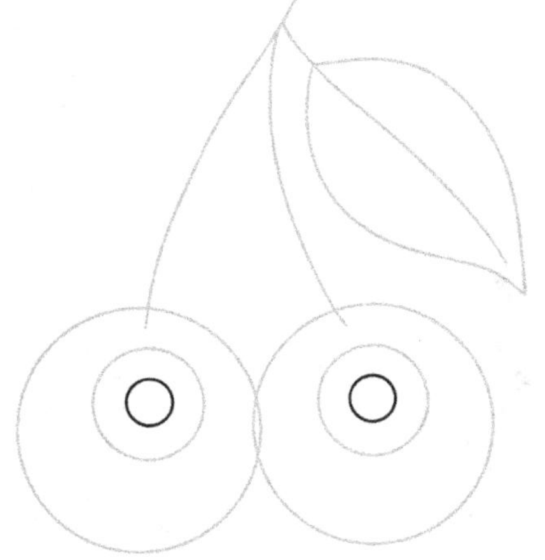

07

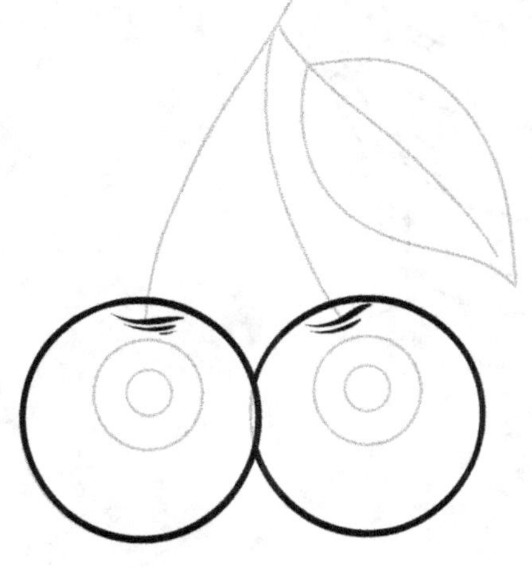

08

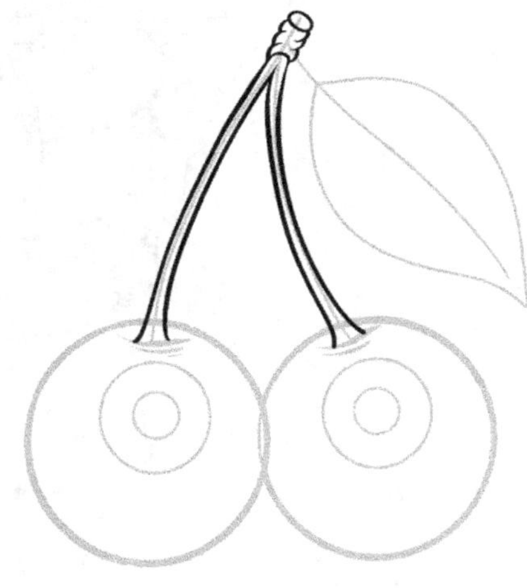

09

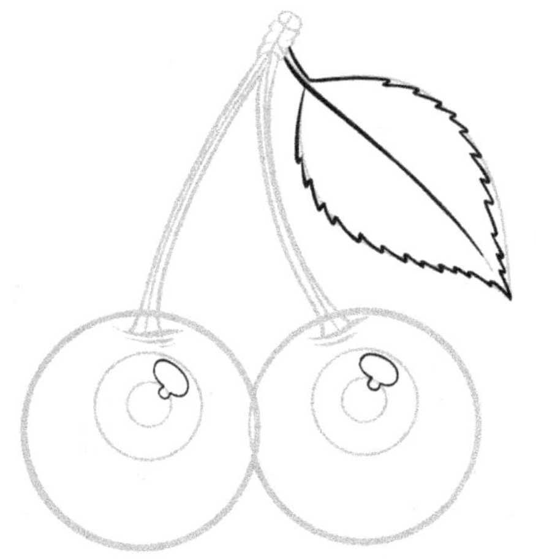

10

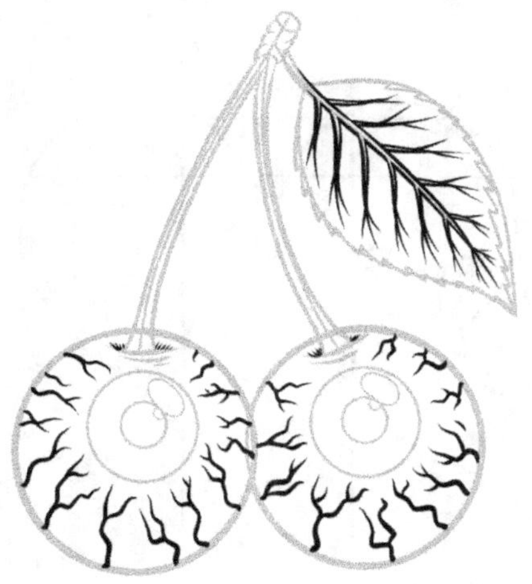

11

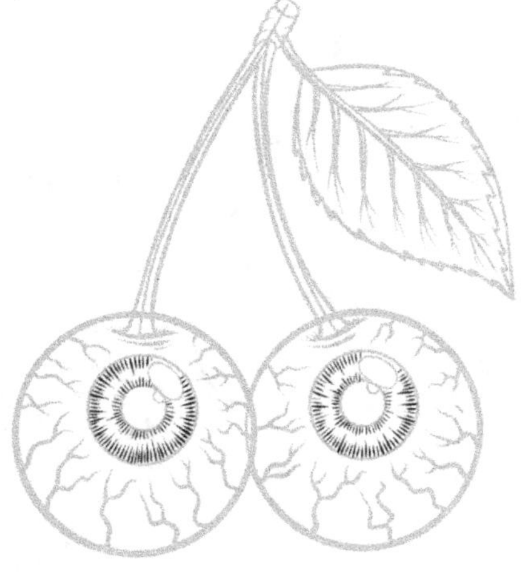

12

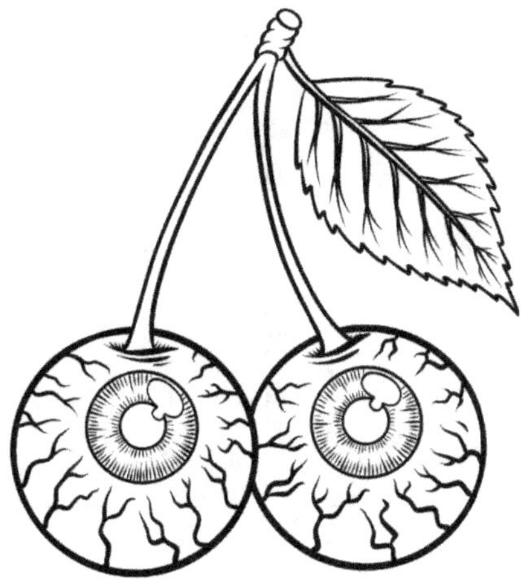

HOW TO DRAW COOL THINGS

COBRA SNAKE

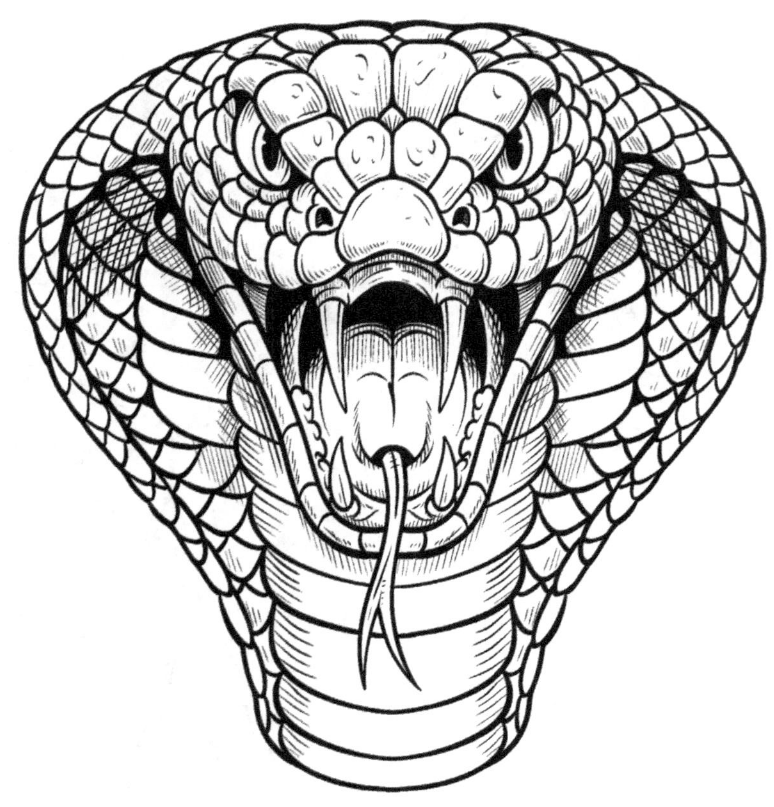

Pro tip:

Build the hood from two wide side circles, then pull the jaw into a long U-shape that stays centred on the vertical guide to keep the cobra's flare perfectly symmetrical.

01

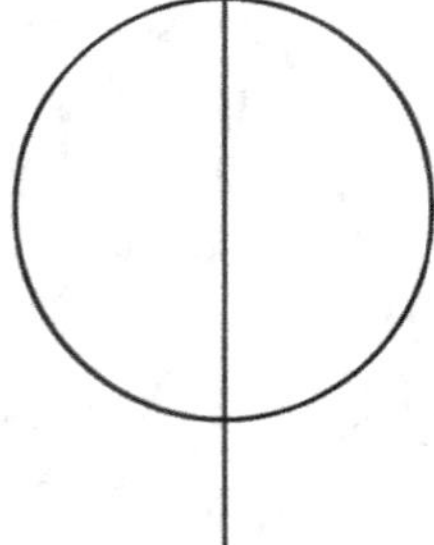

02

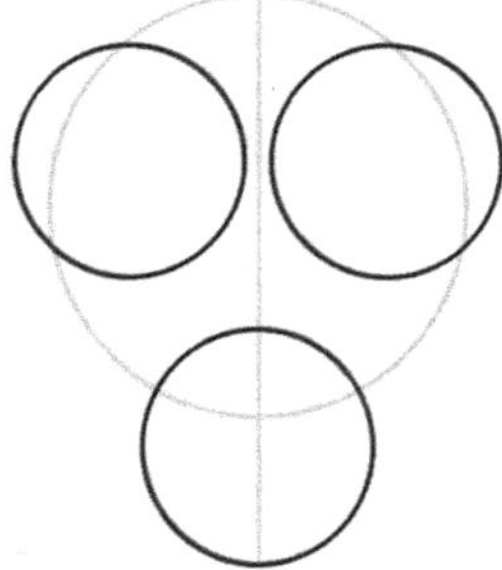

03

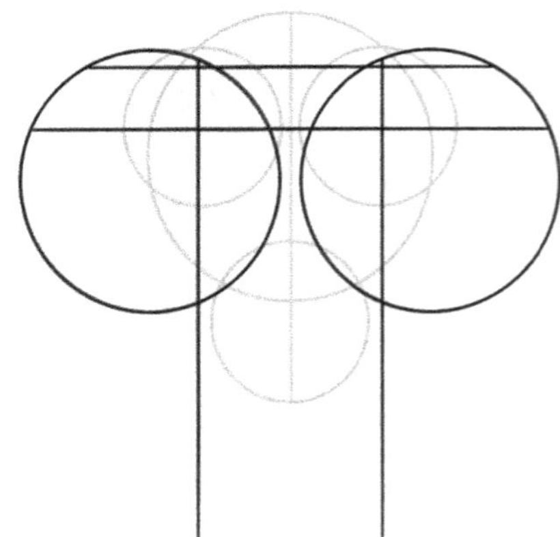

04

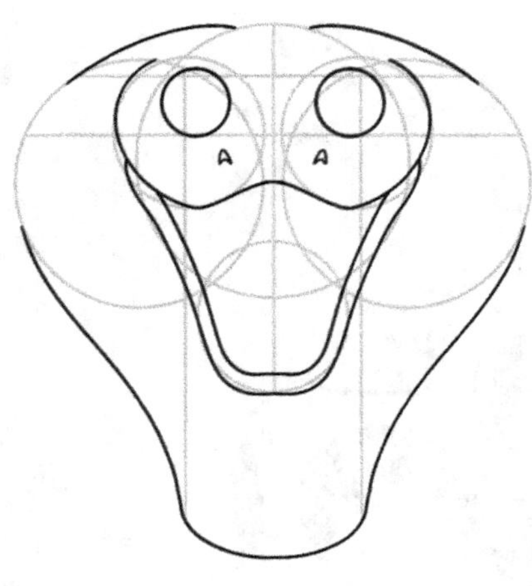

05

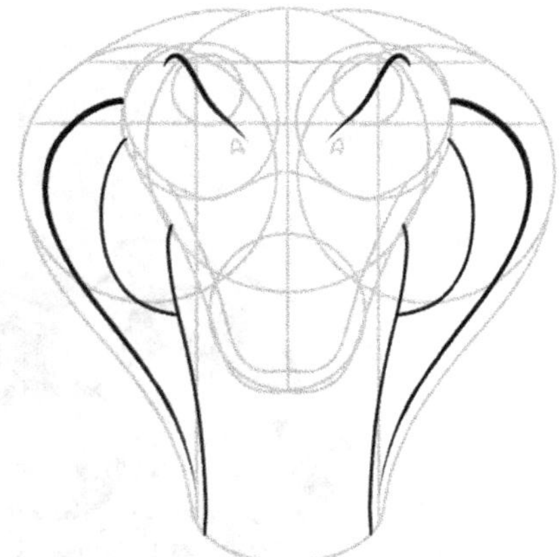

06

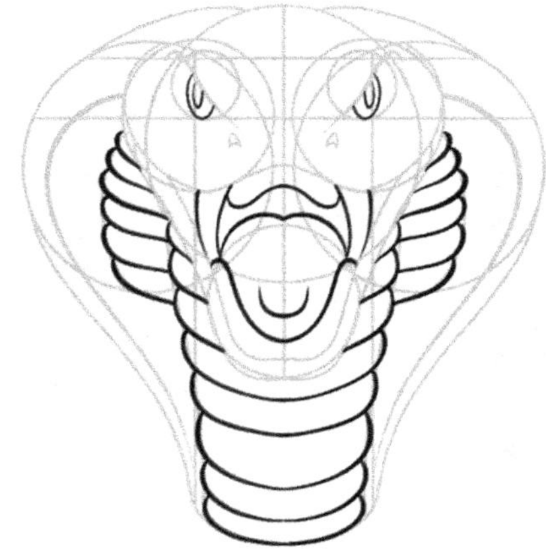

07

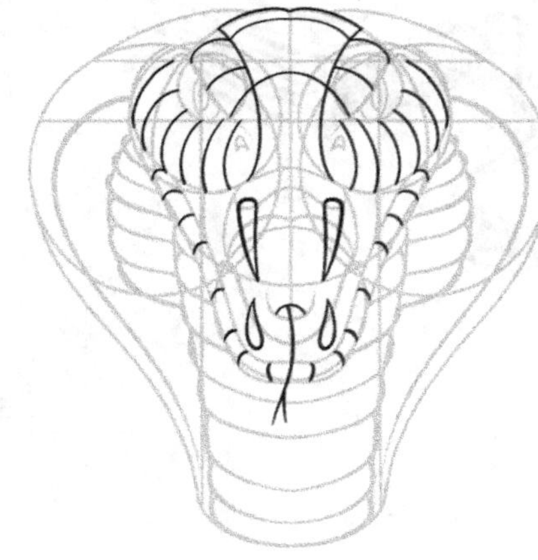

08

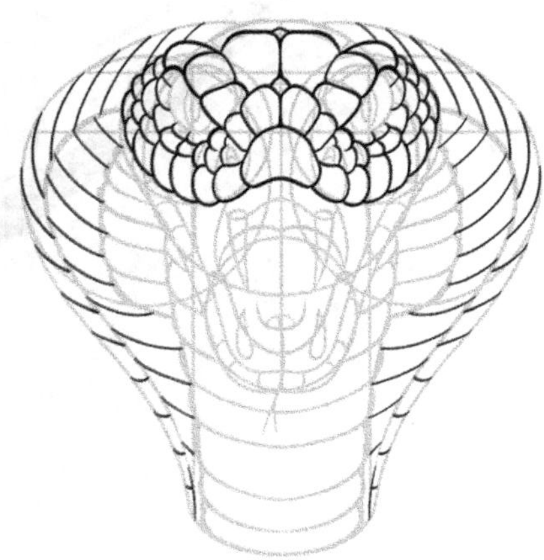

09

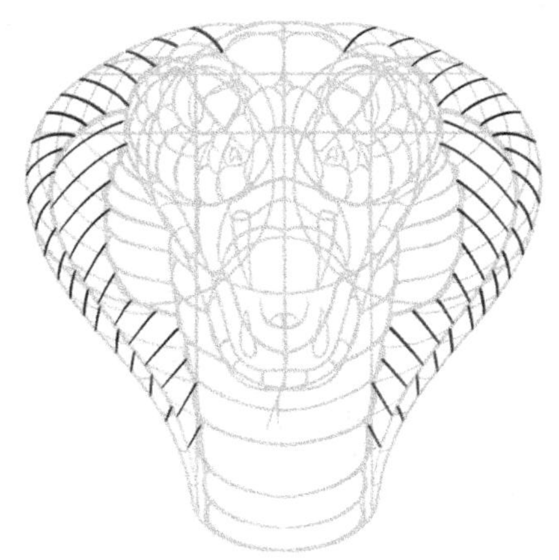

10

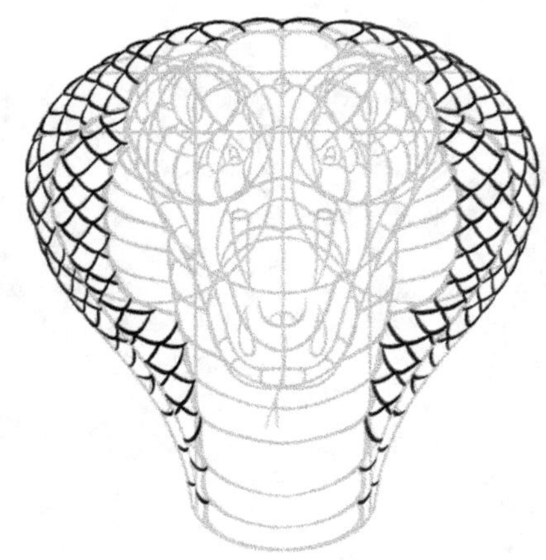

11

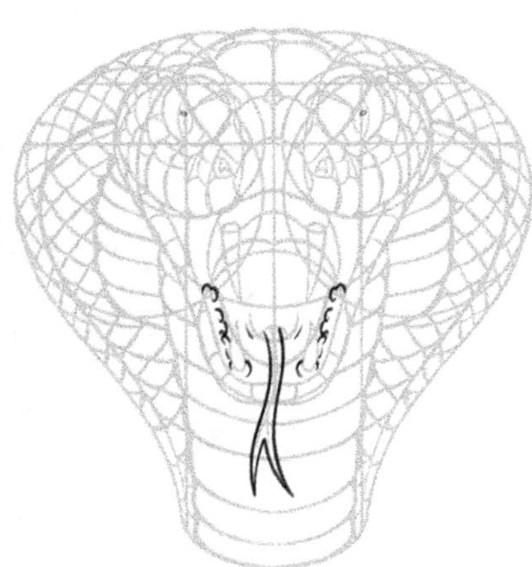

12

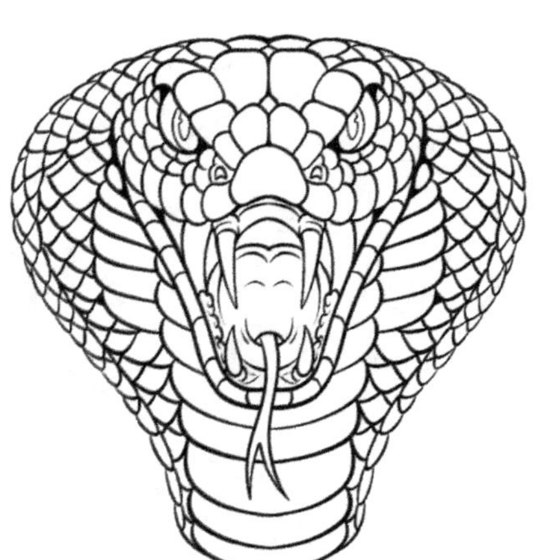

BRASS KNUCKLES

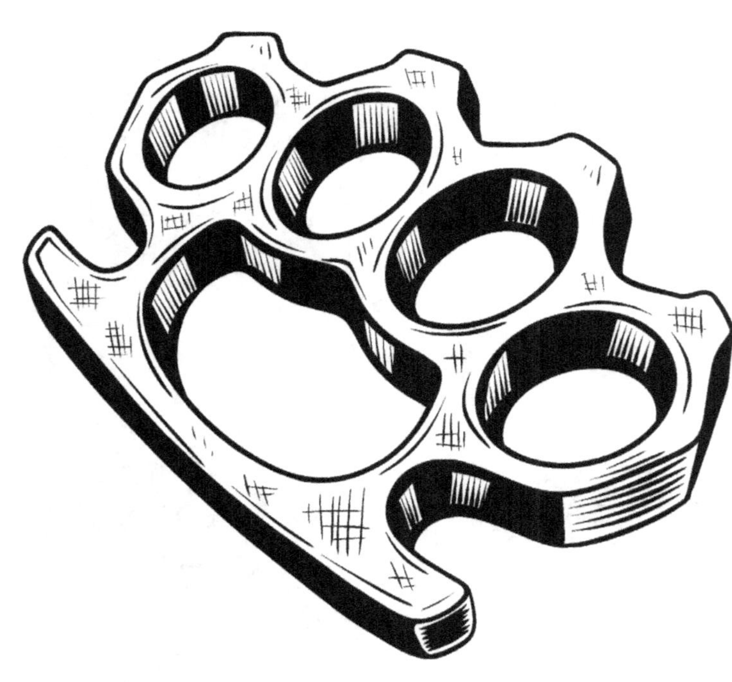

Pro tip:

Block in the four finger holes first as evenly spaced ovals, then draw the grip oval beneath them to lock in the angle and thickness.

01

02

03

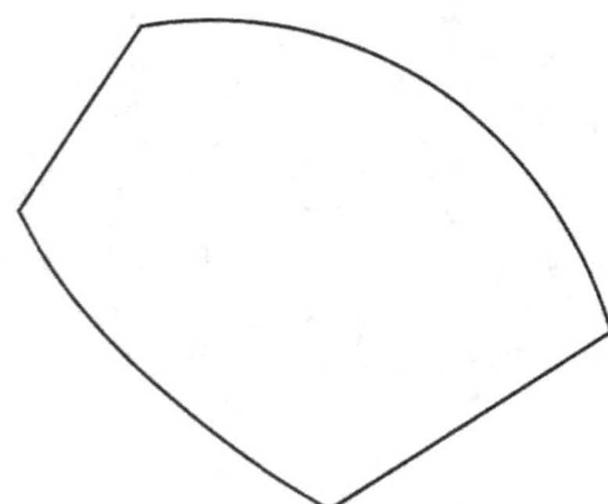

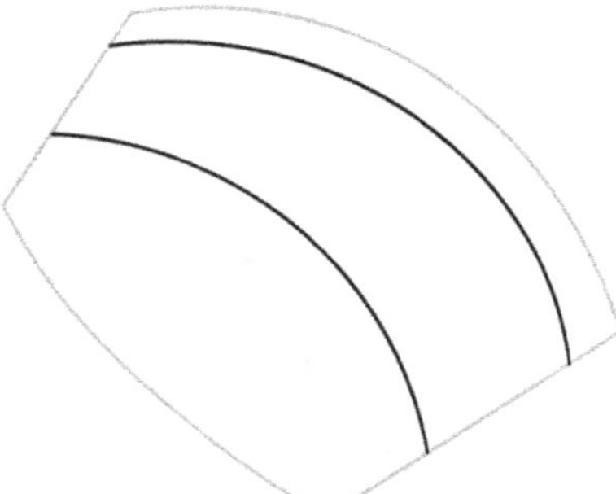

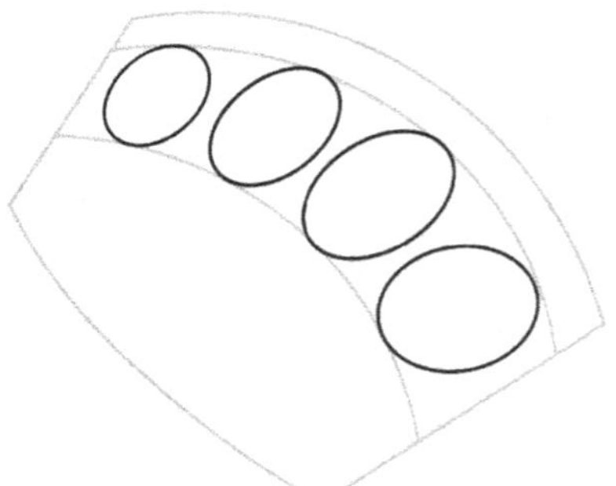

04

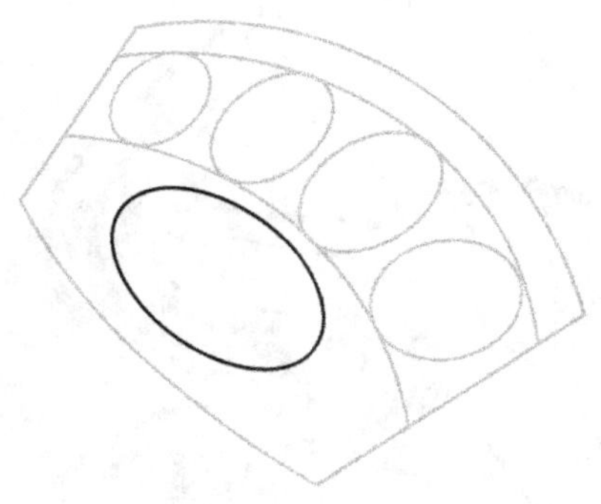

05

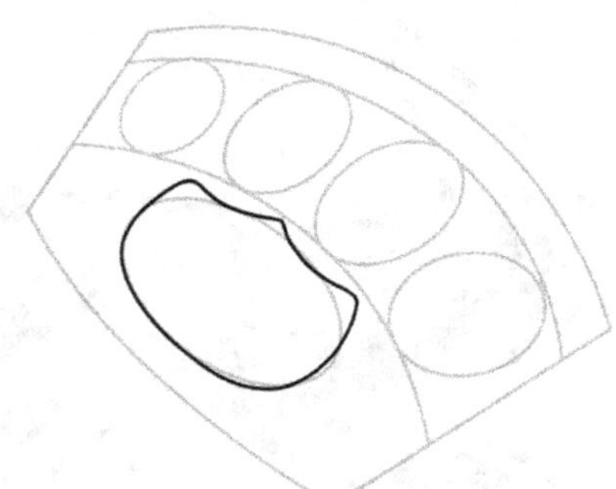

06

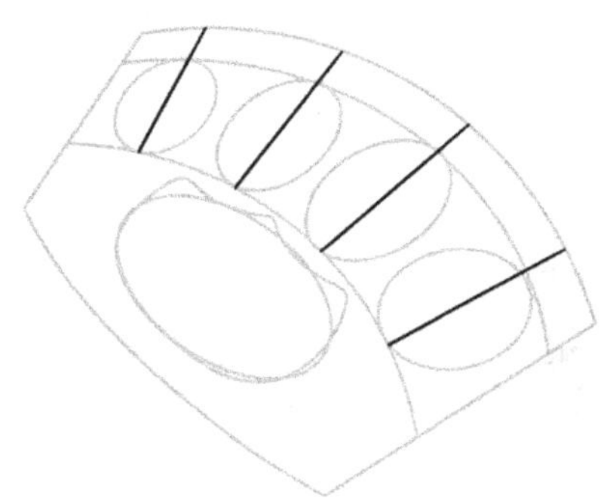

07

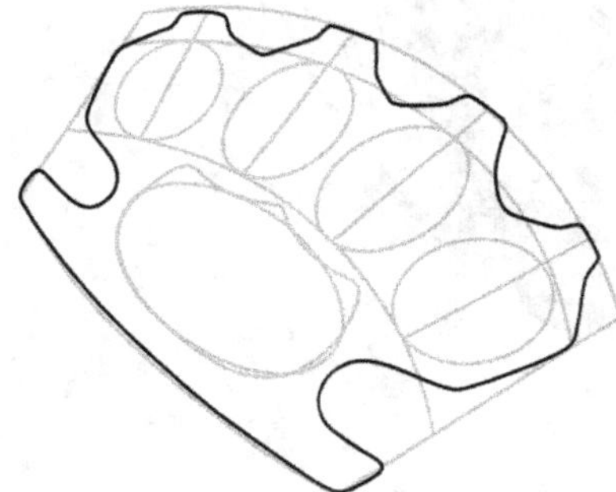

08

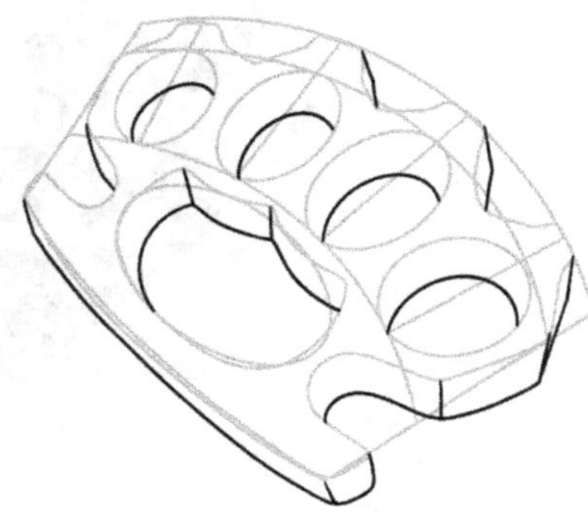

09

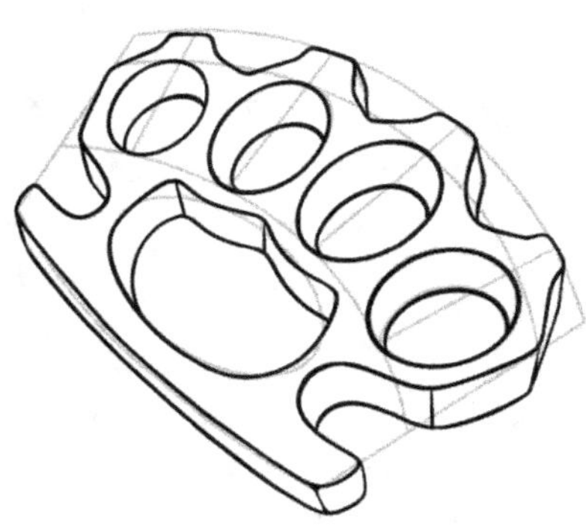

10

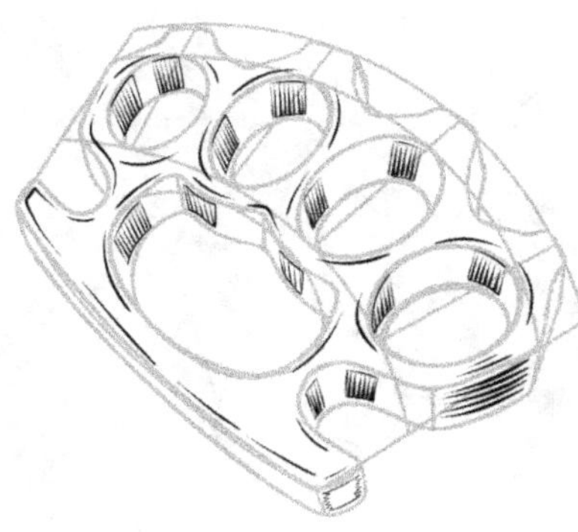

11

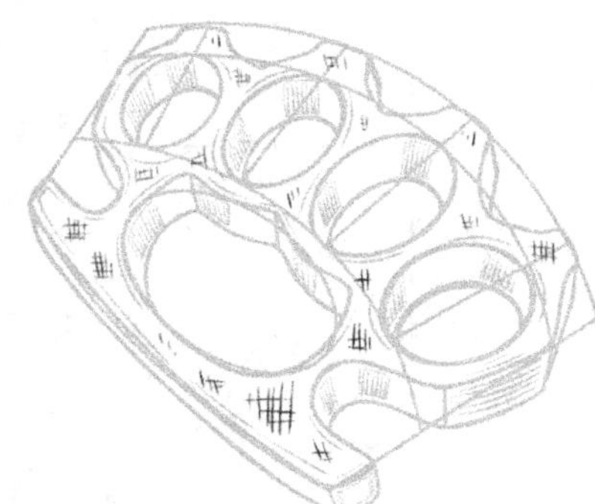

12

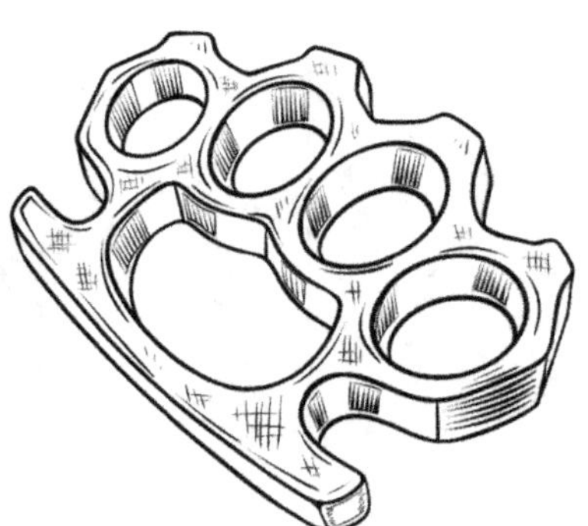

RAGING BULL

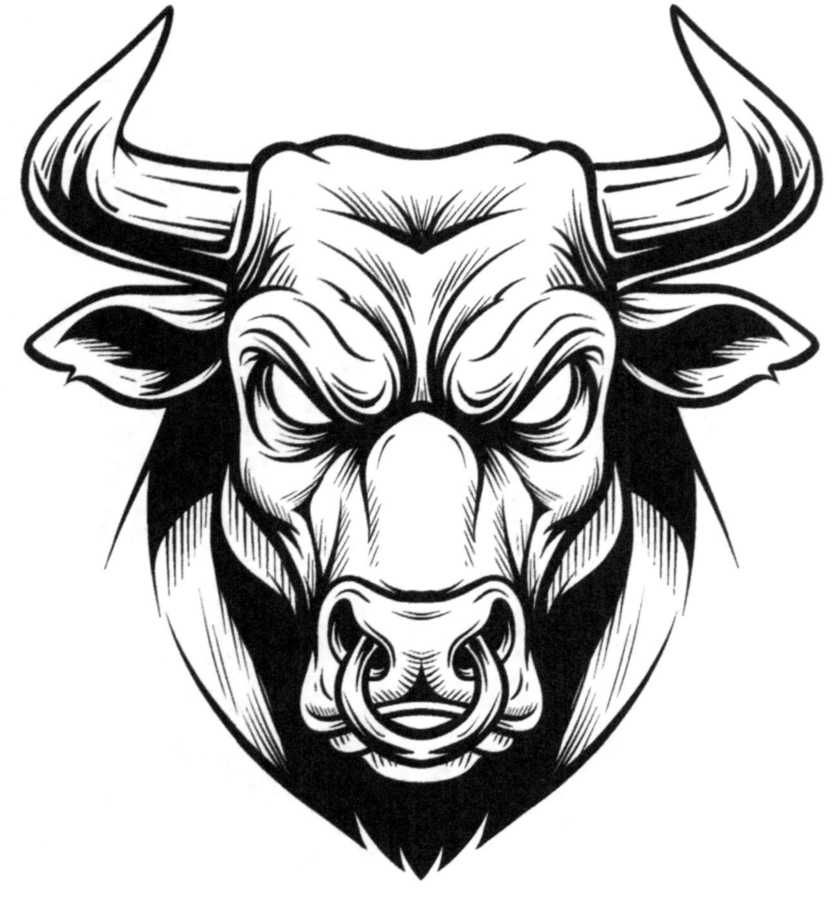

Pro tip:

Place the muzzle as an oval half the head circle's width, centred on the midline, with its top edge touching the circle bottom and dropping another half-circle below it.

01

02

03

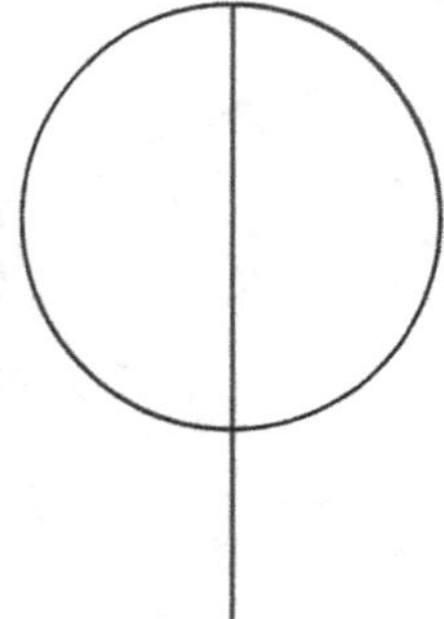

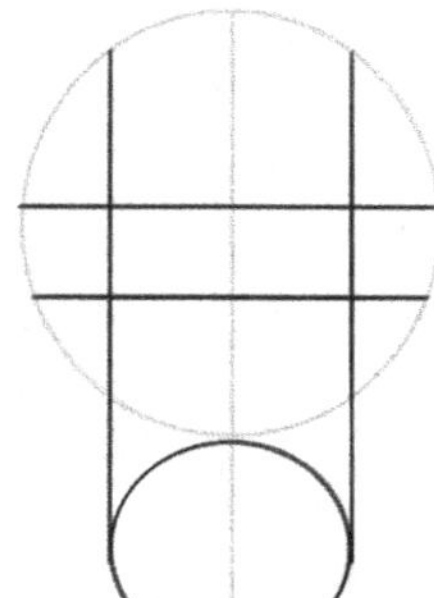

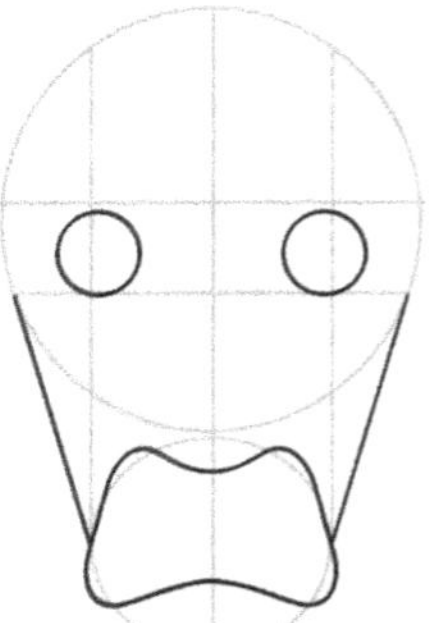

04

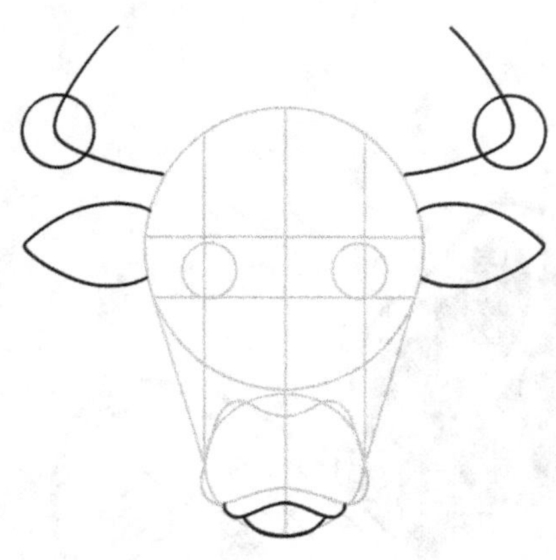

05

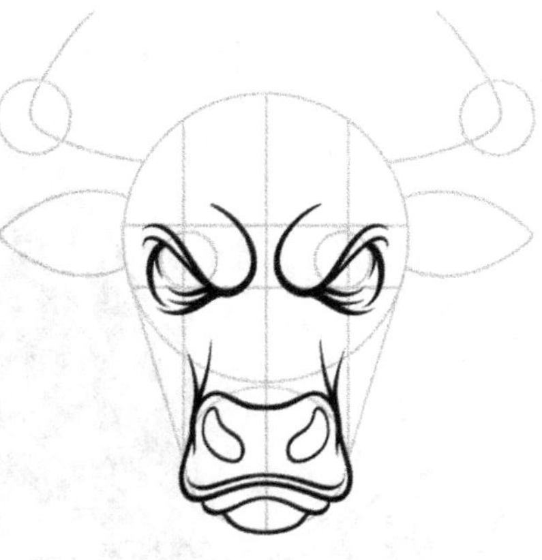

06

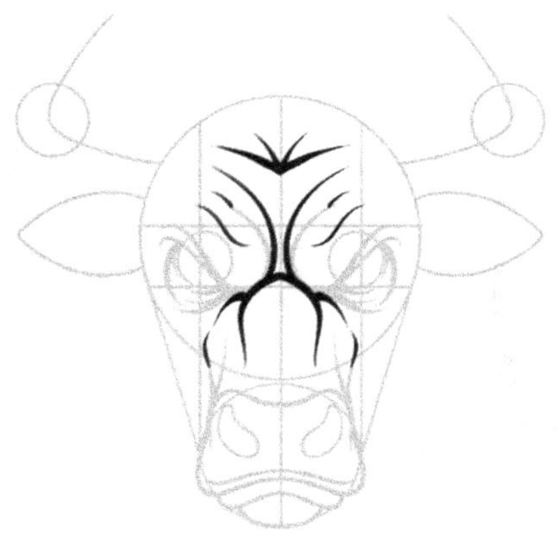

07

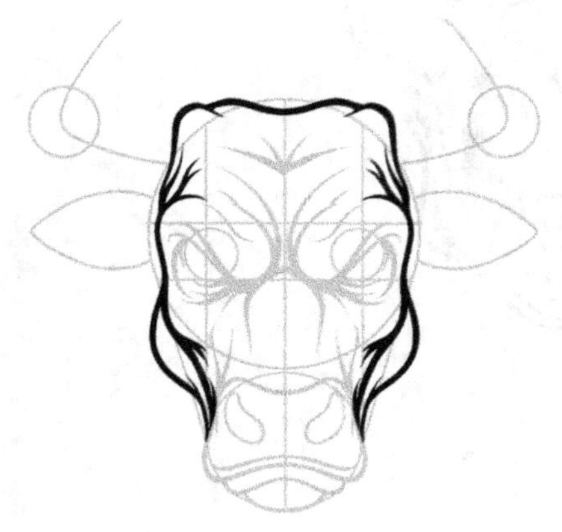

08

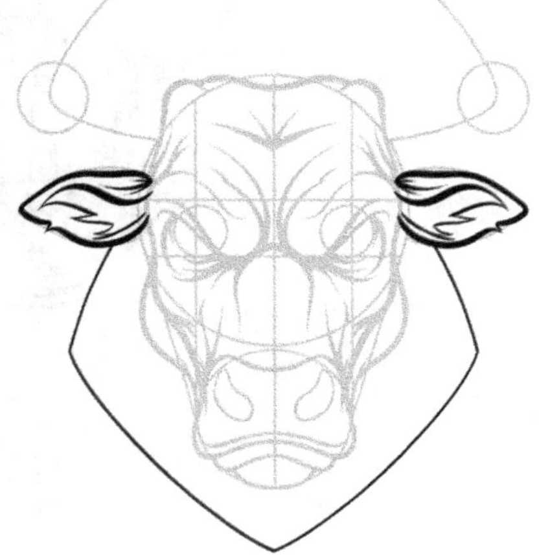

09

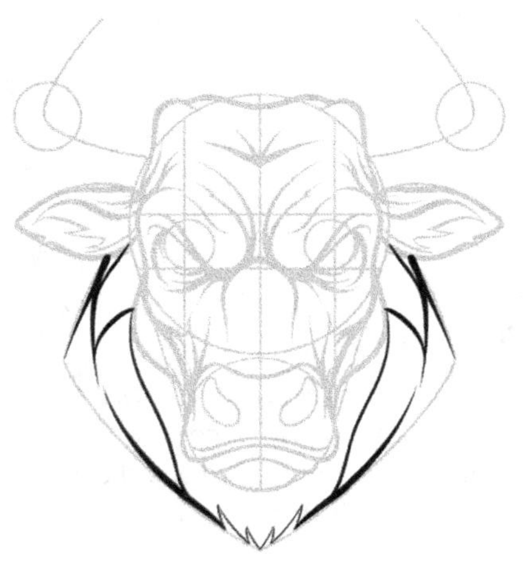

10

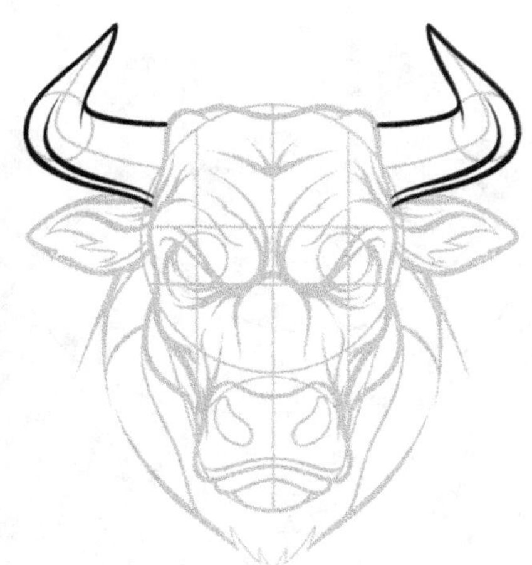

11

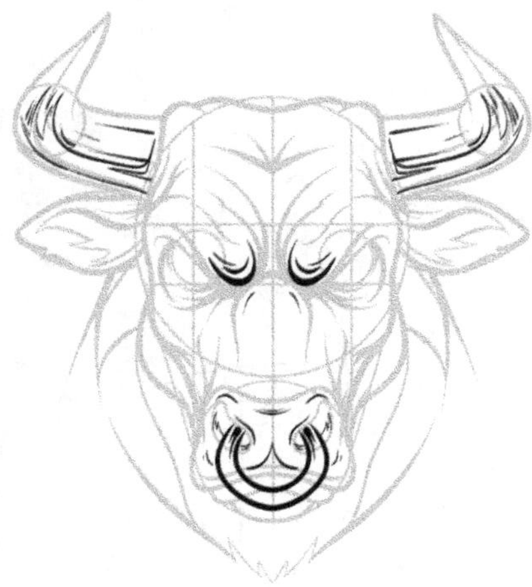

12

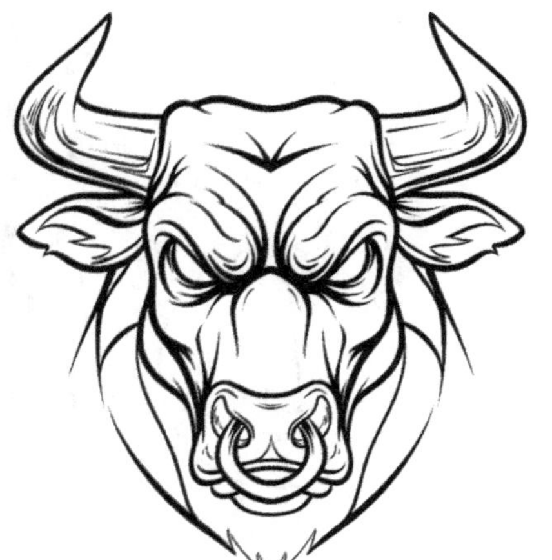

COWBOY SKULL

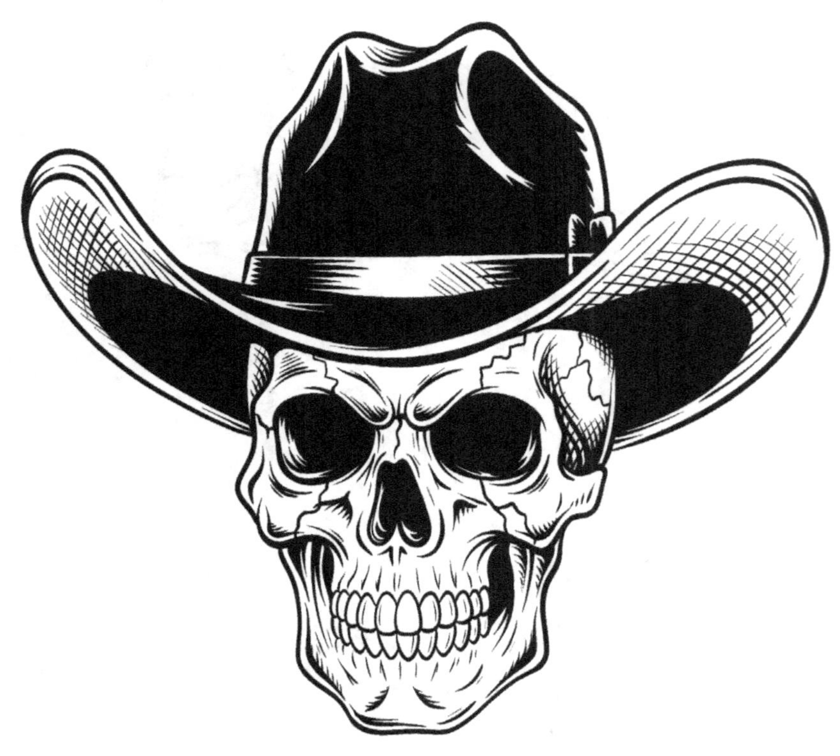

Pro tip:

Set the hat brim to span about 2× the
skull circle's width, with the crown
centred and rising roughly one circle
height above the top of the circle.

01

02

03

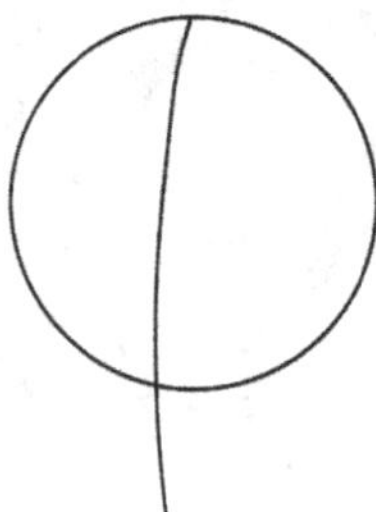

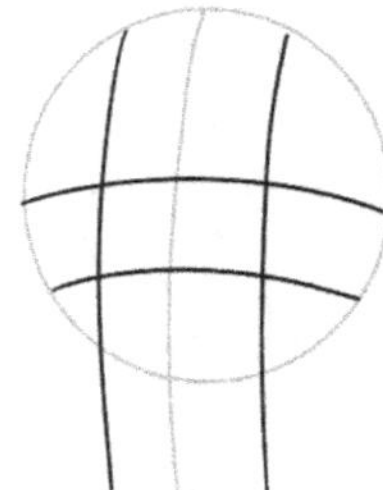

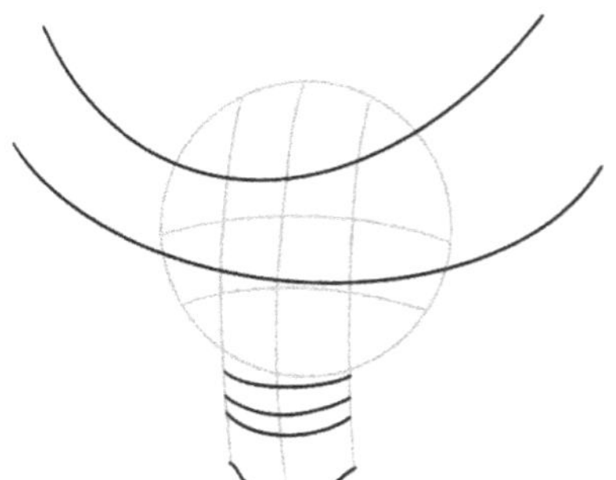

04
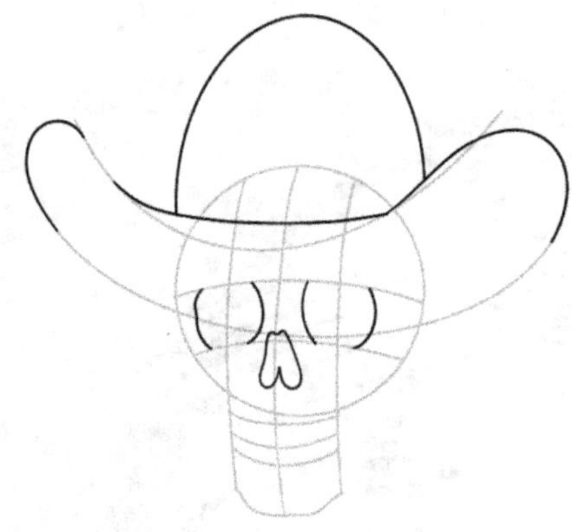

05
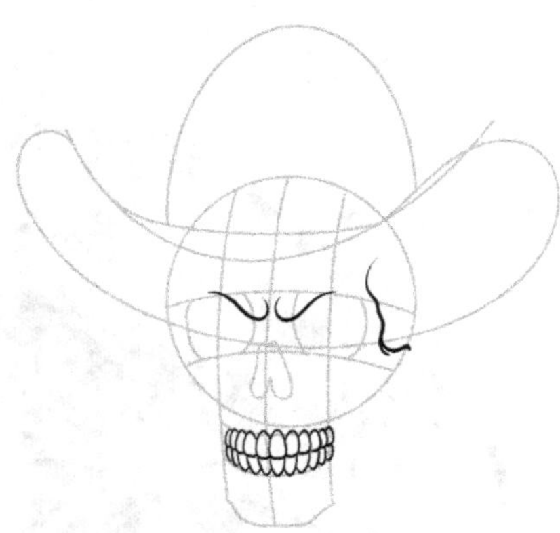

06
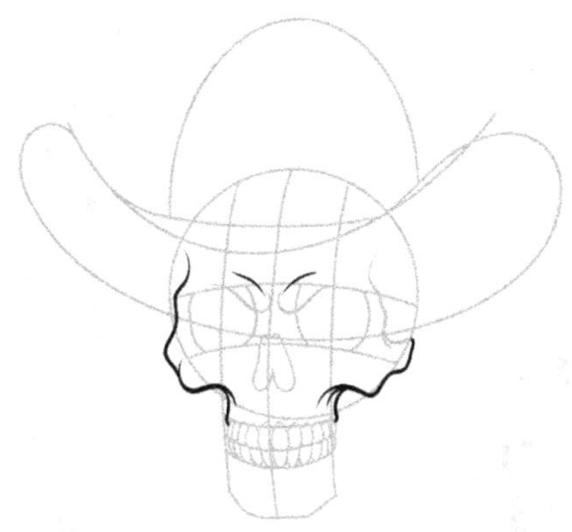

07
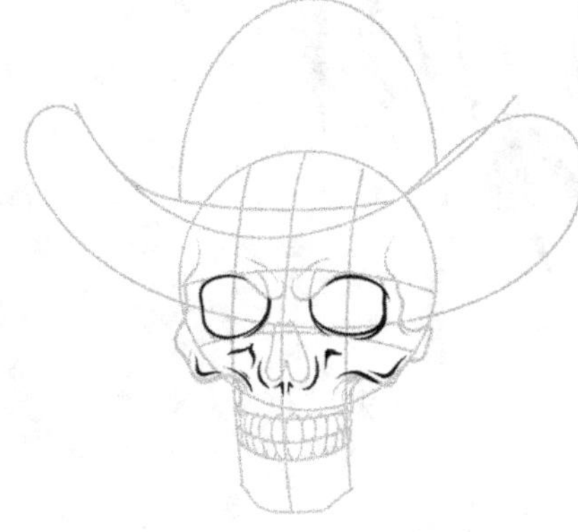

08
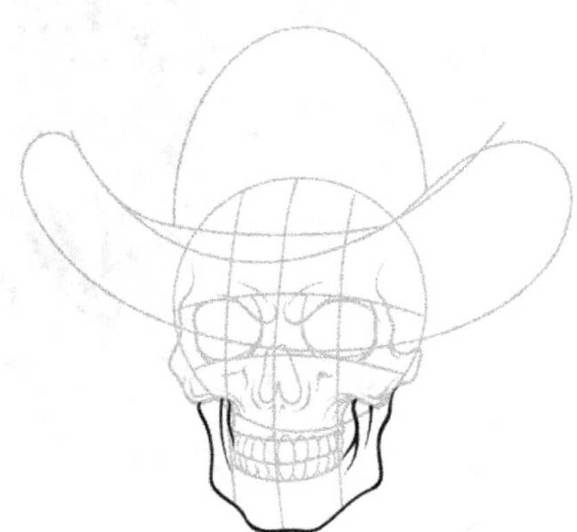

09
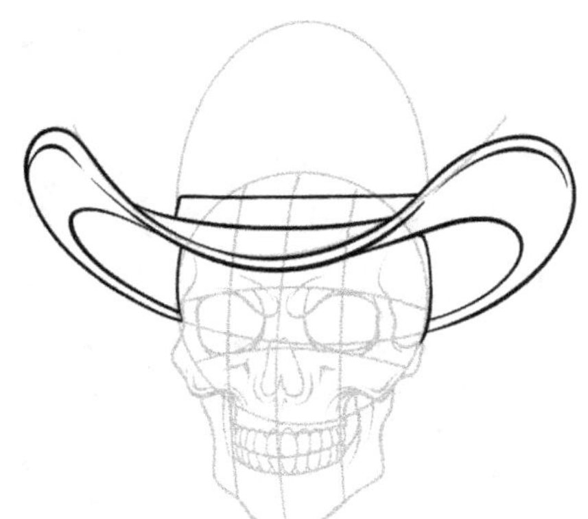

10
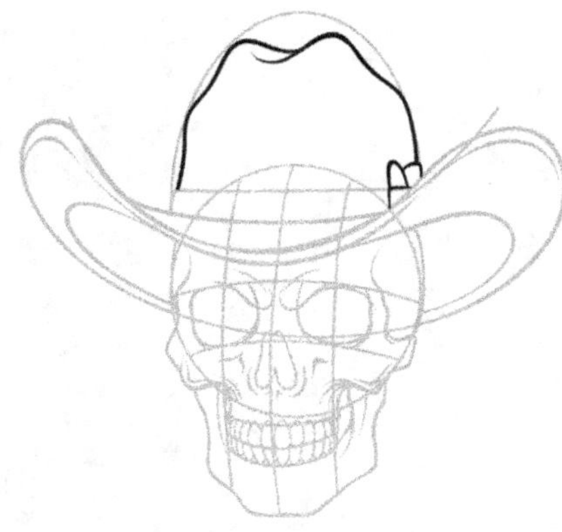

11
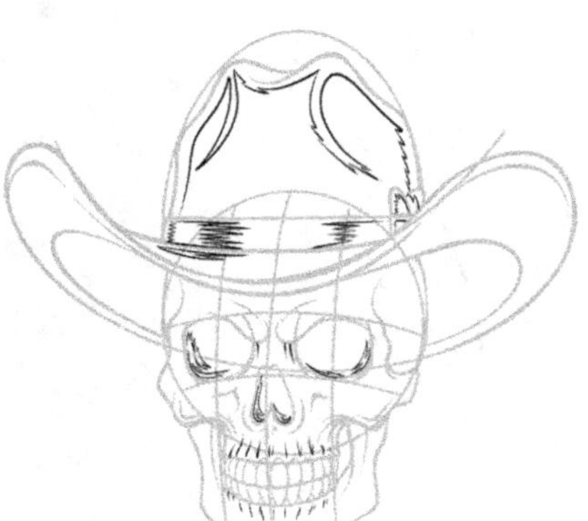

12
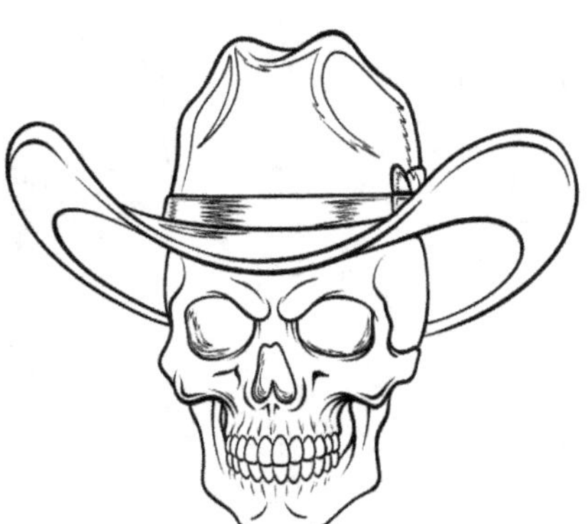

EAGLE

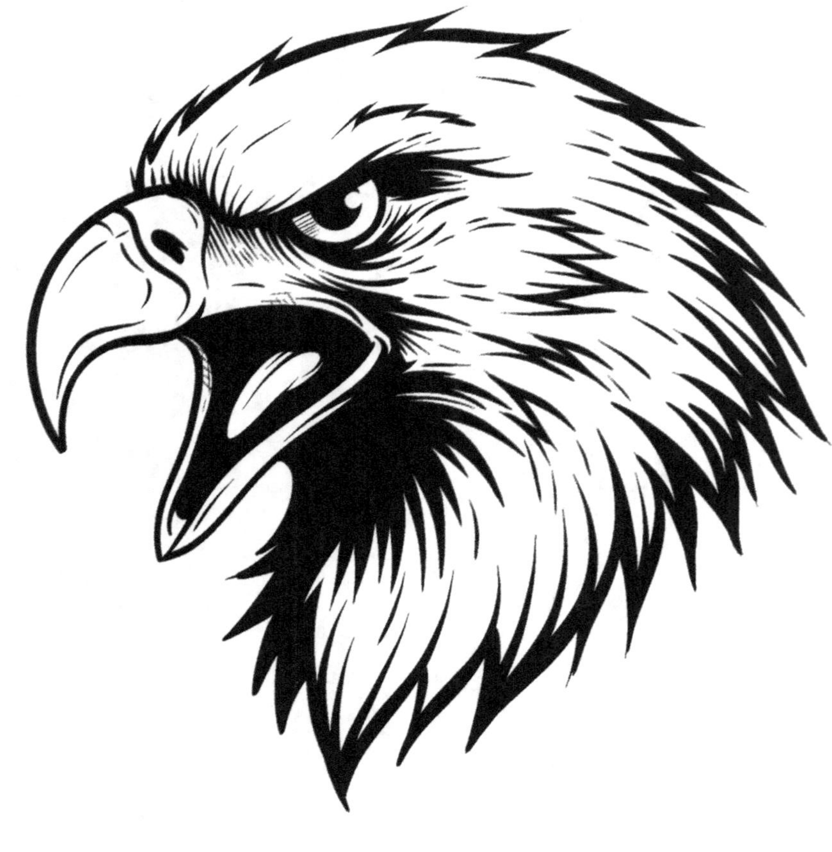

Pro tip:

Use the head circle as the anchor, then pull the neck and chest into a teardrop that's about 2× the circle's height, tapering to a point below.

01

02

03

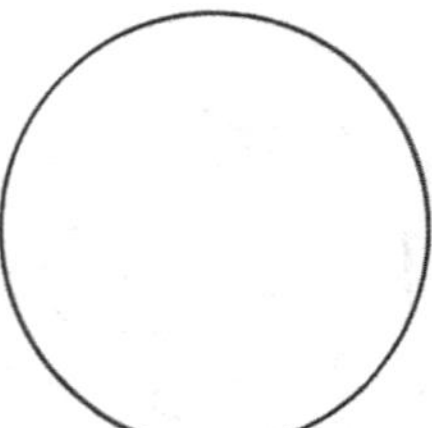

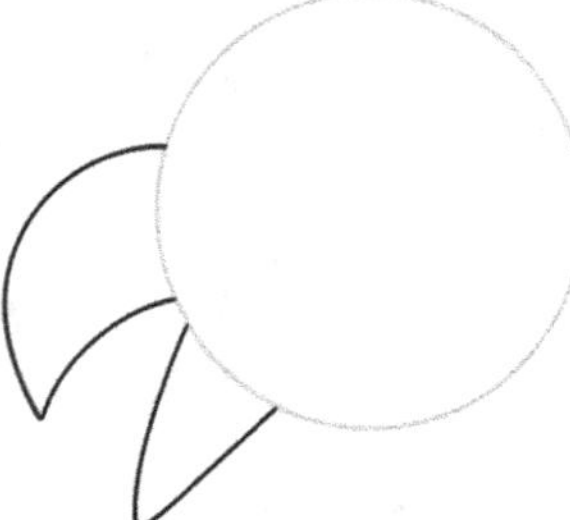

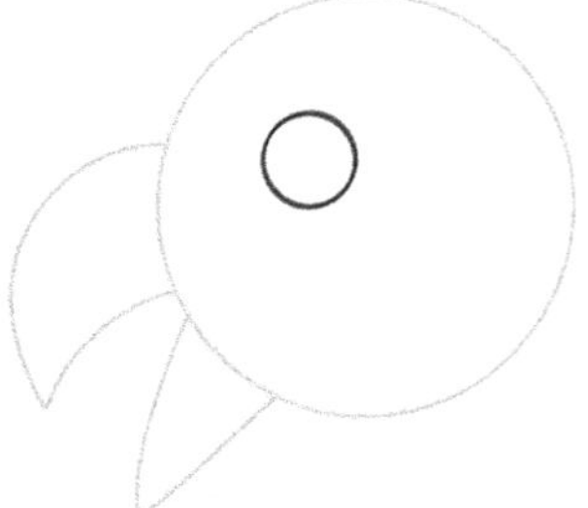

04

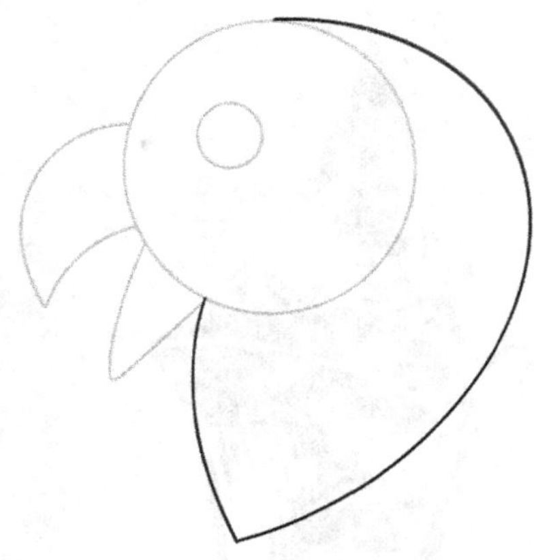

05

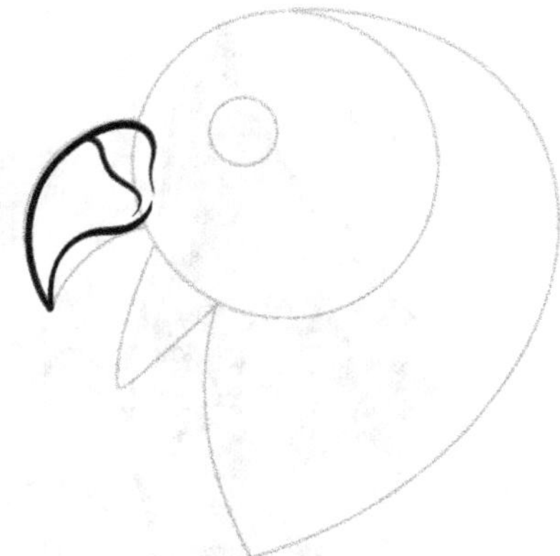

06

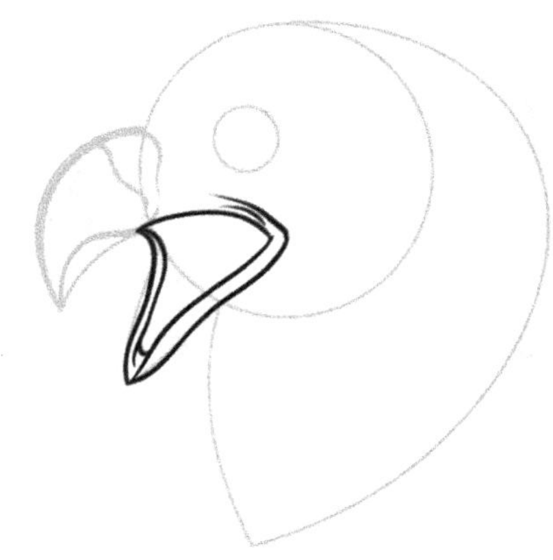

07

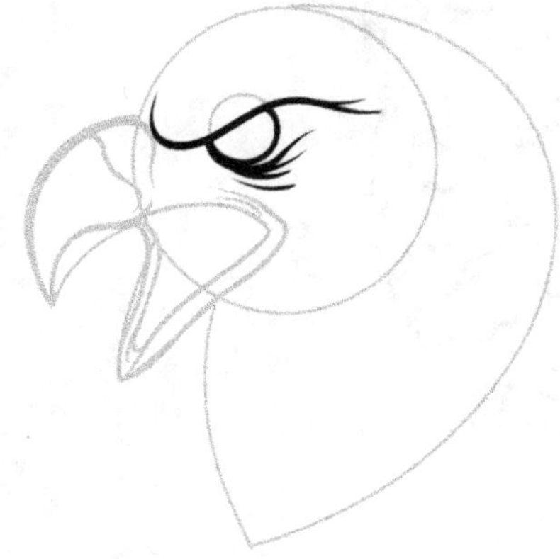

08

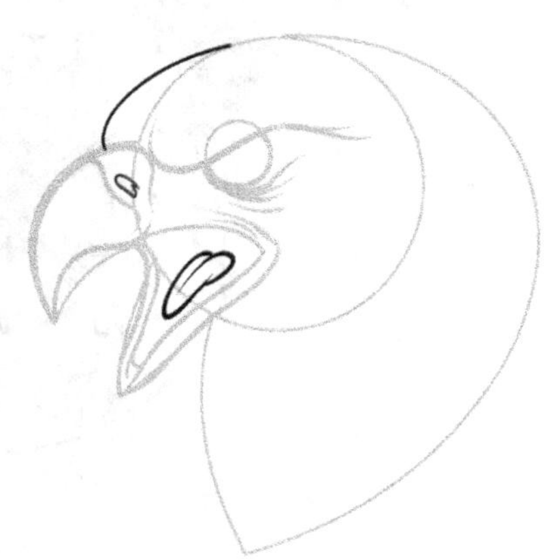

09

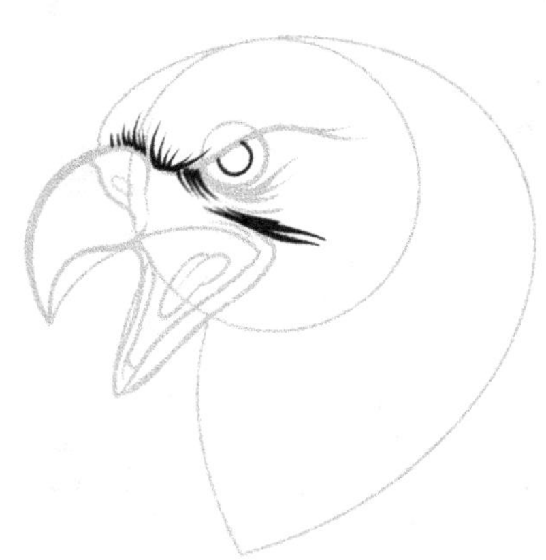

10

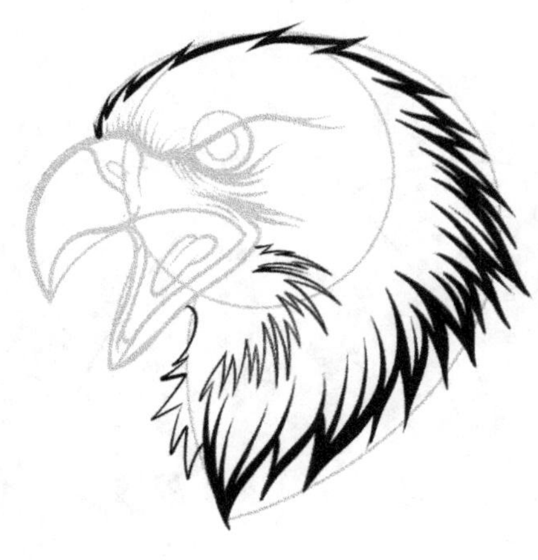

11

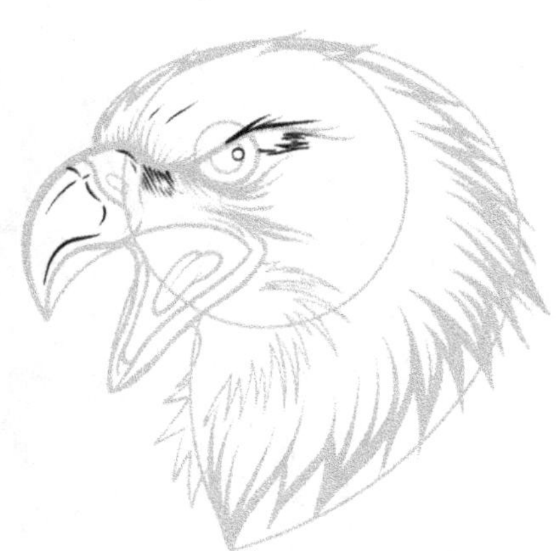

12

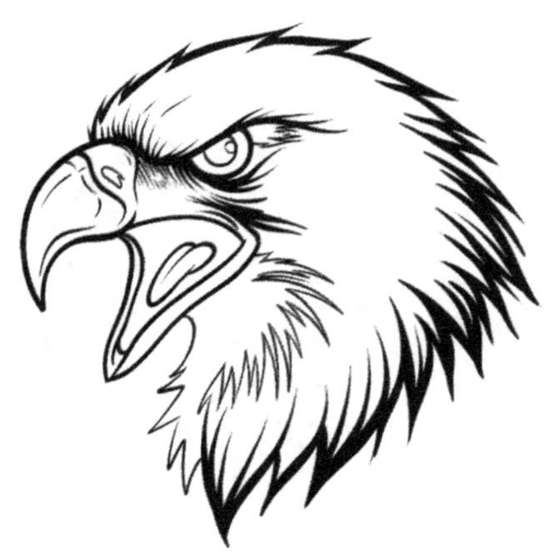

HOW TO DRAW COOL THINGS

EYEBALL WITH BAT WINGS

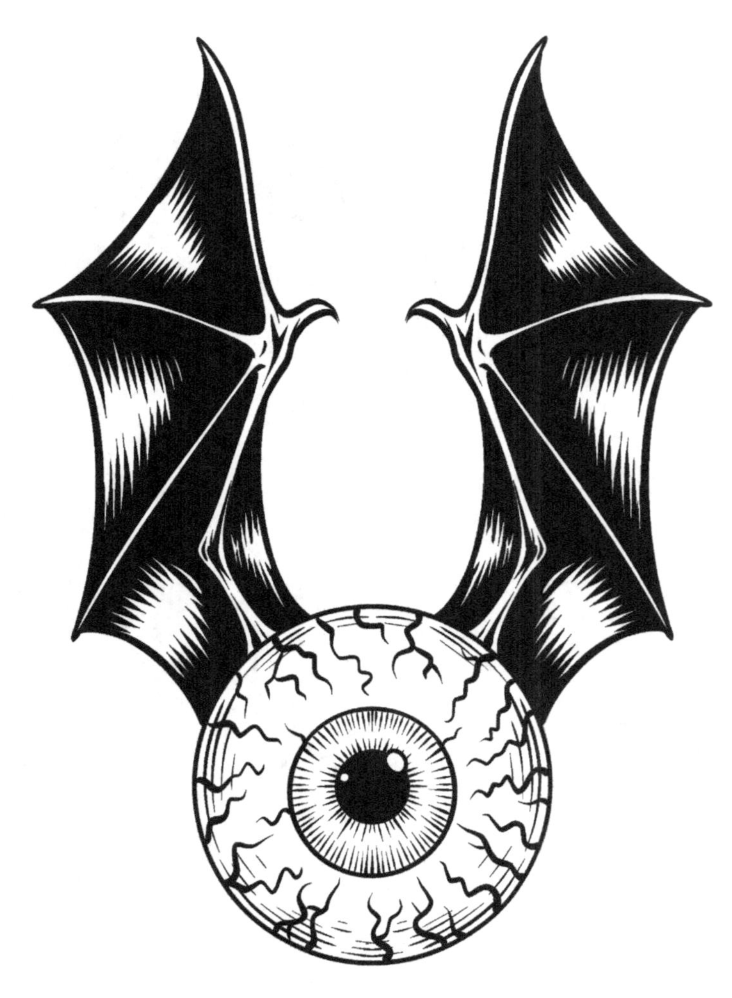

Pro tip:

Make each wing about one and a half eyeballs diameter tall and one diameter wide. Attach the inner wing bones to the eyeball's outer edge at mid-height.

01   02   03

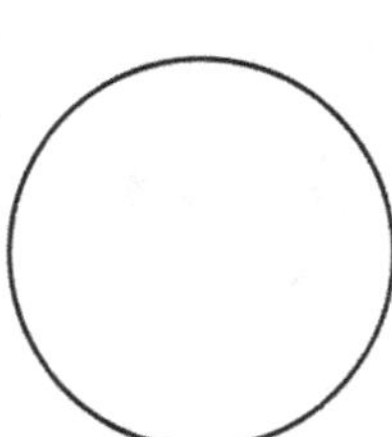

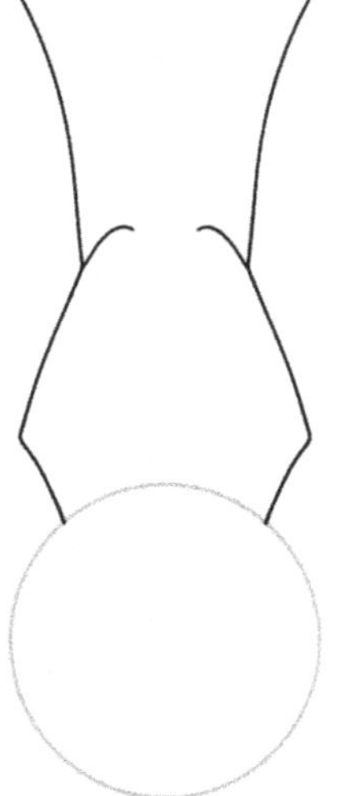

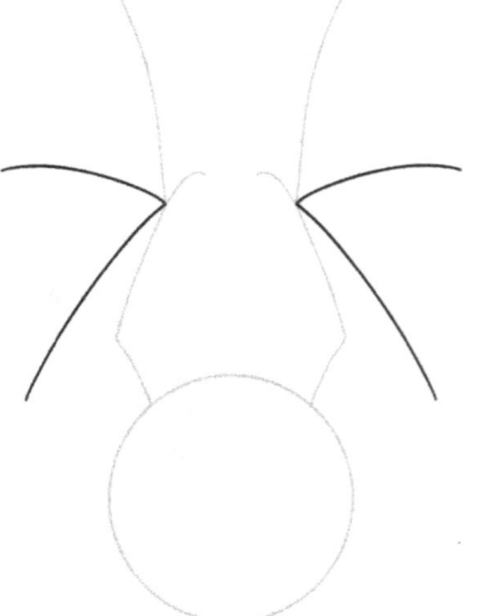

04

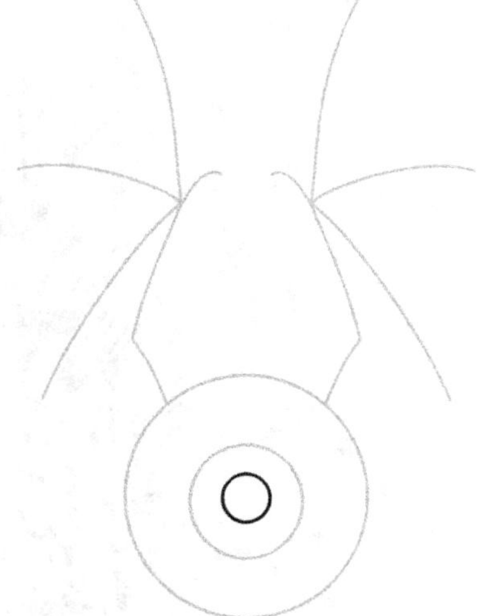

05

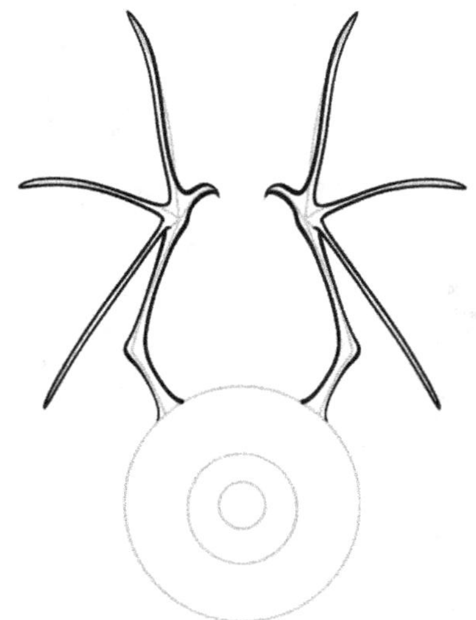

06

07

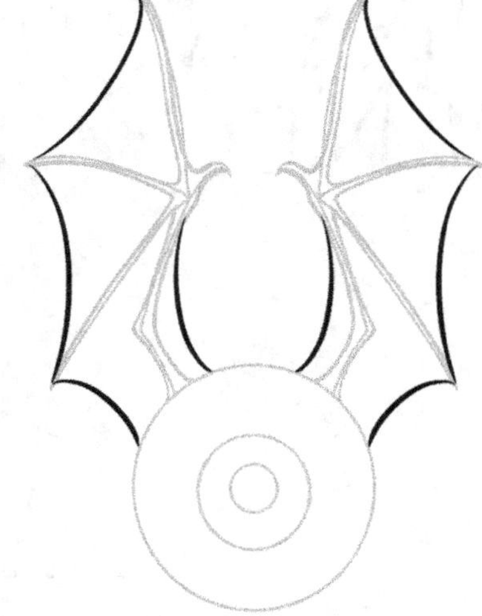

08

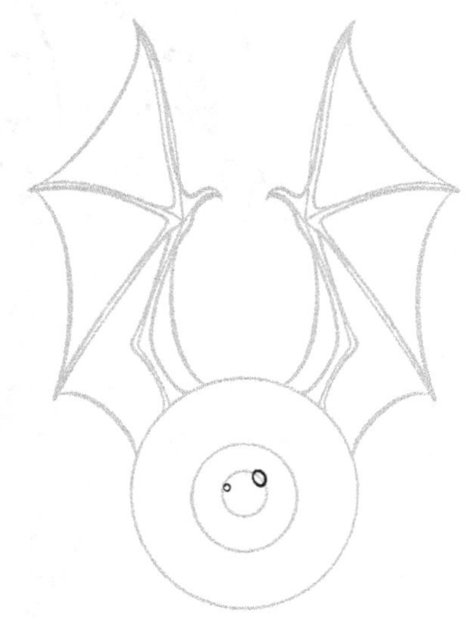

09

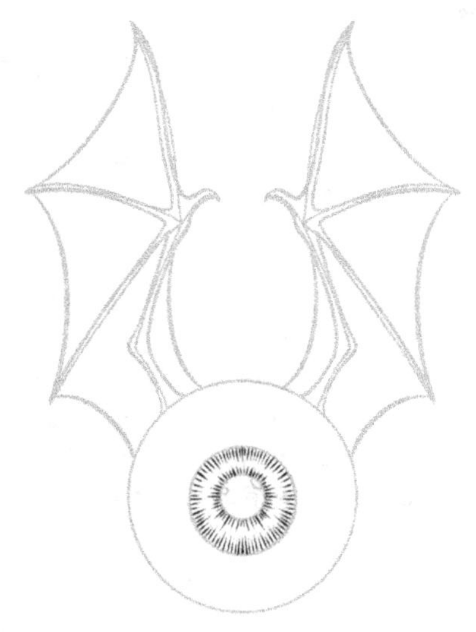

10

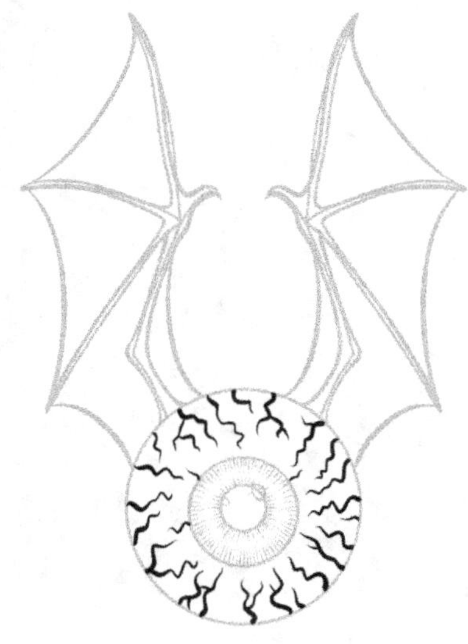

11

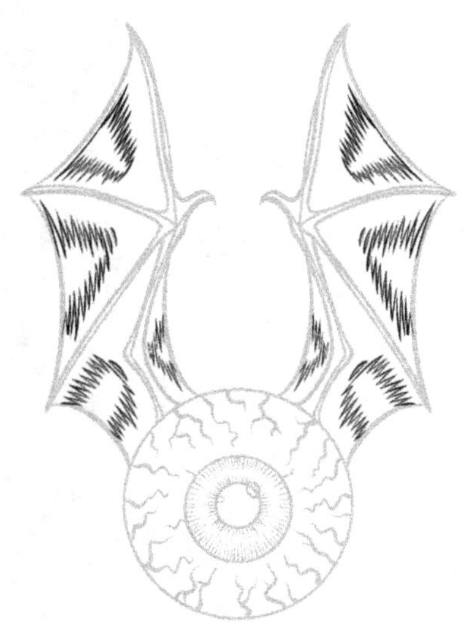

12

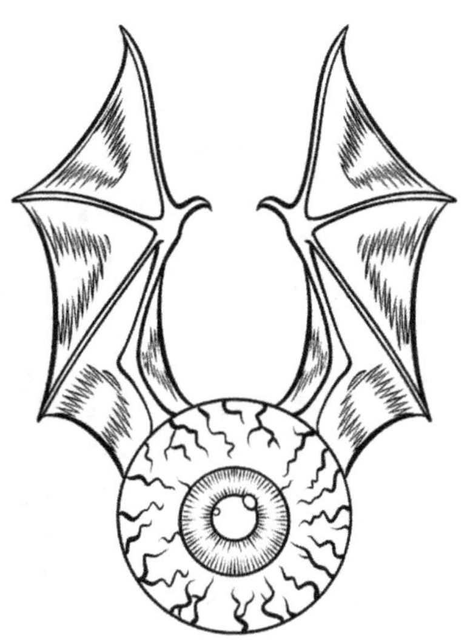

HOW TO DRAW COOL THINGS

FLOWER & EYEBALL

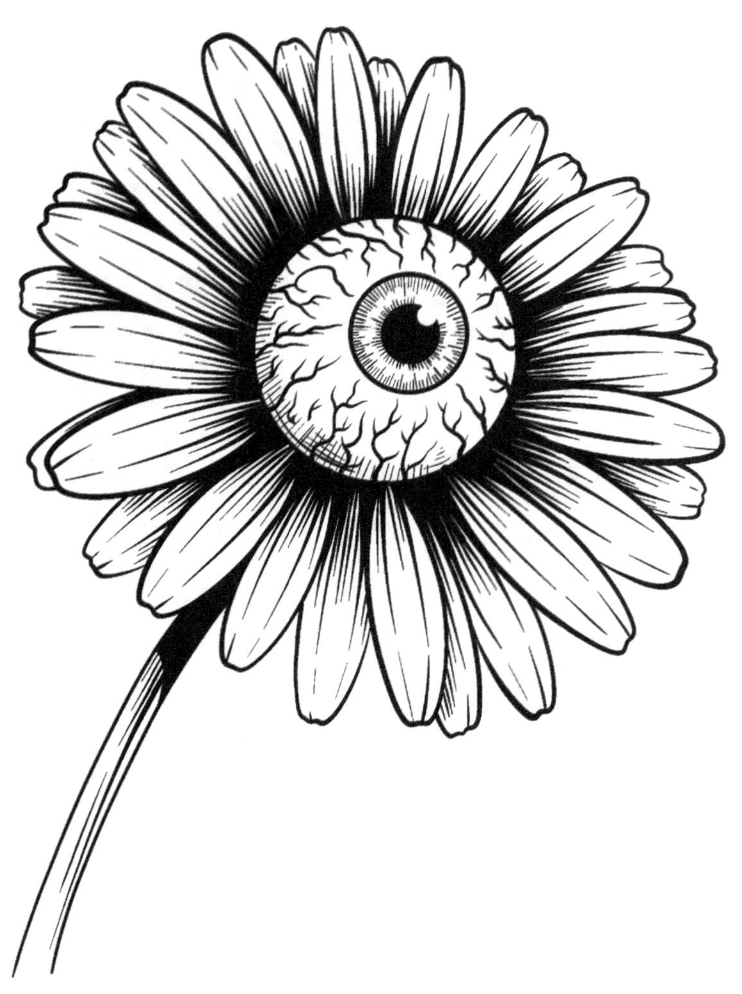

Pro tip:

Use the eyeball circle as the centre, then make each petal about 1–1.5× the circle's radius and space them evenly like clock points before refining the overlaps.

01　　　　　　　　　　　　　　　　02　　　　　　　　　　　　　　　　03

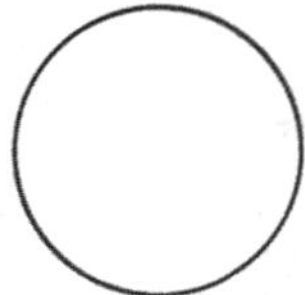

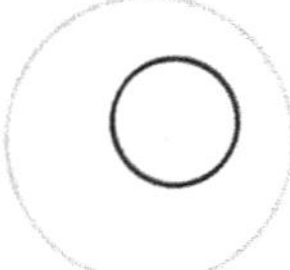

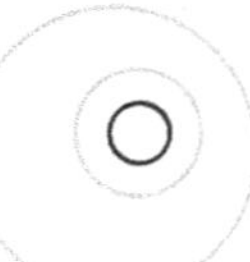

04

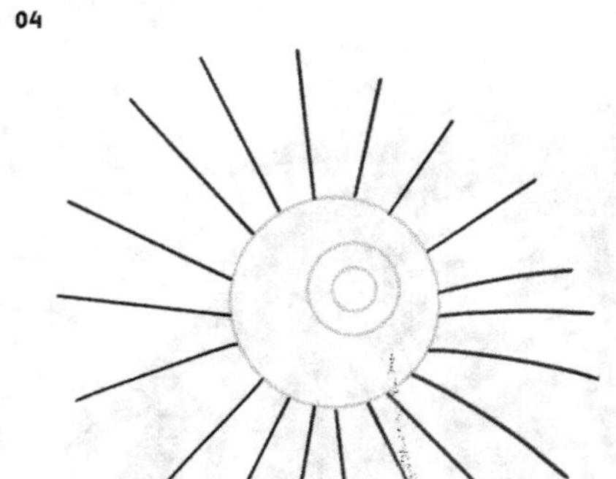

05

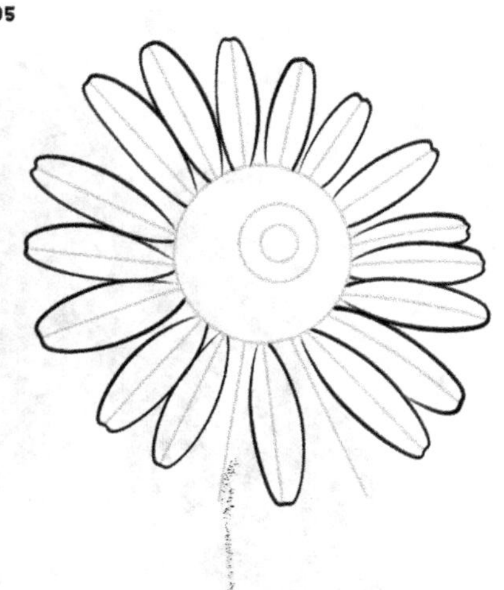

06

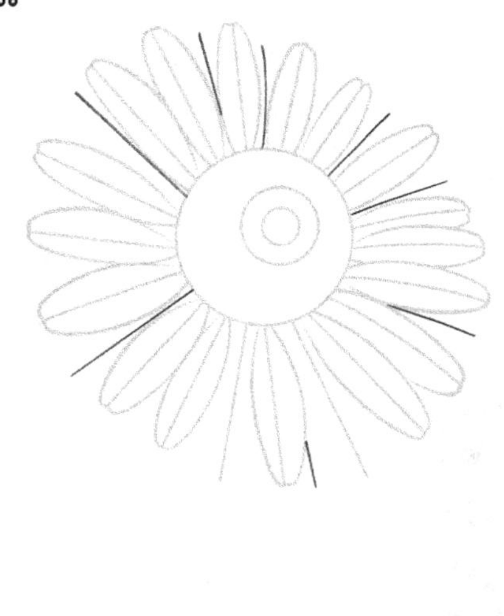

07

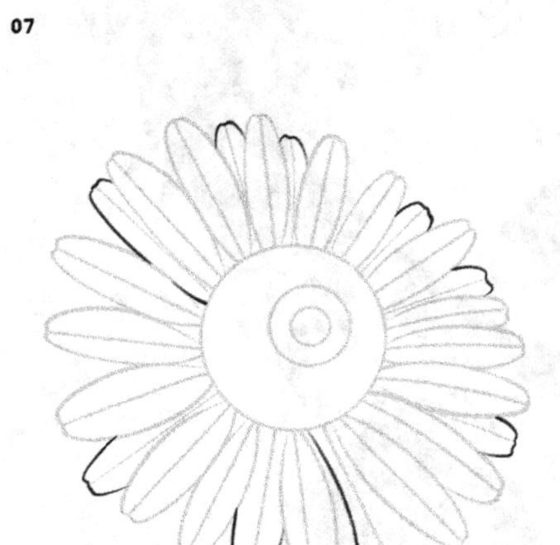

08

09

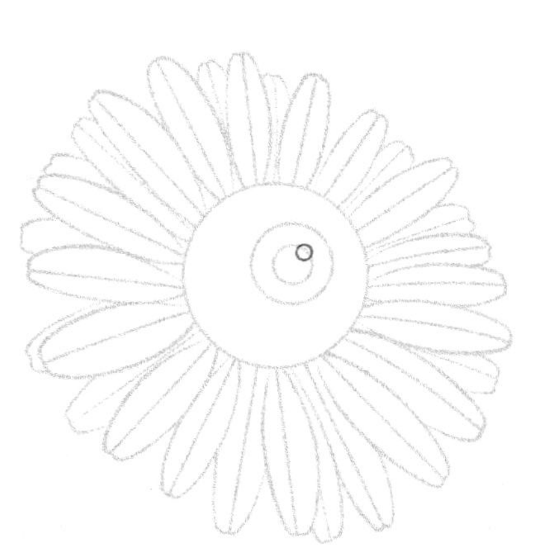

10

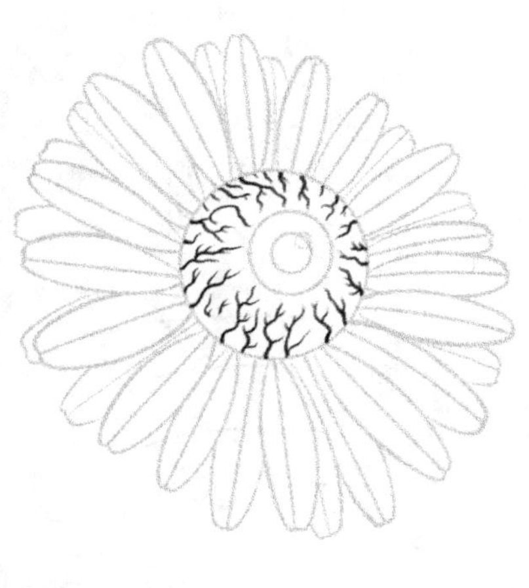

11

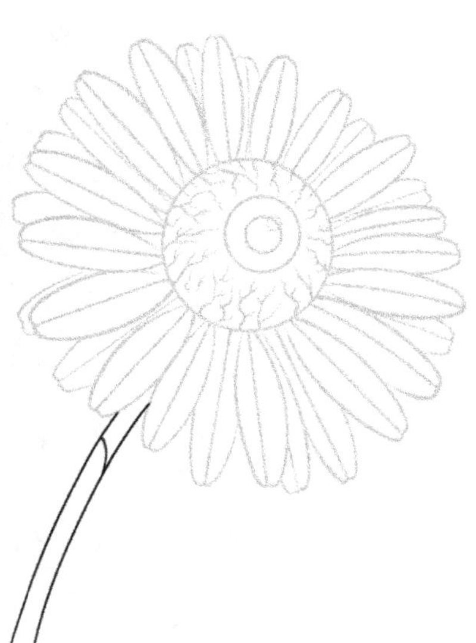

12

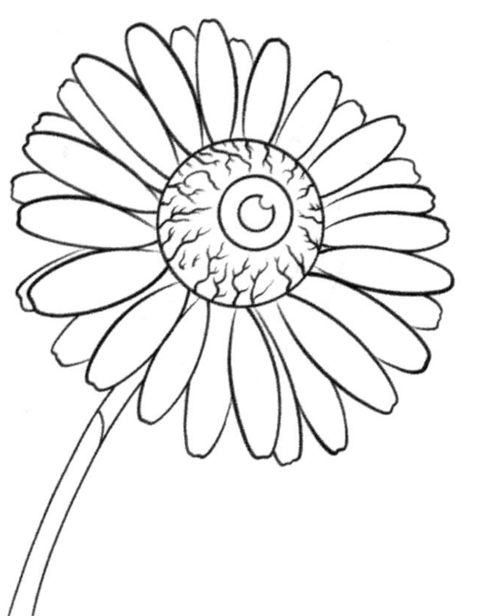

GOTH GIRL

Pro tip:

Pull the jaw into a V that narrows to about half the head circle's width, with the chin landing roughly one third of a circle below the eye line.

01   02   03

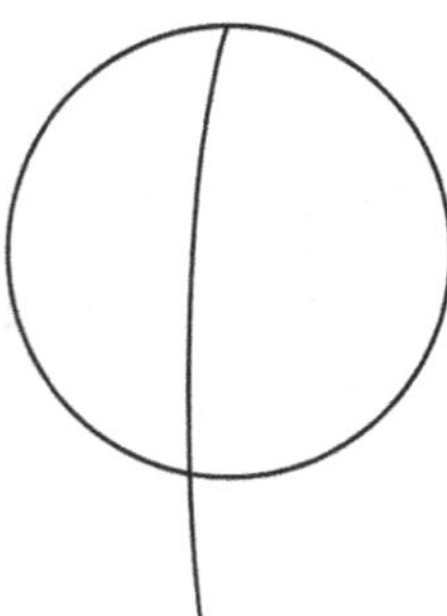

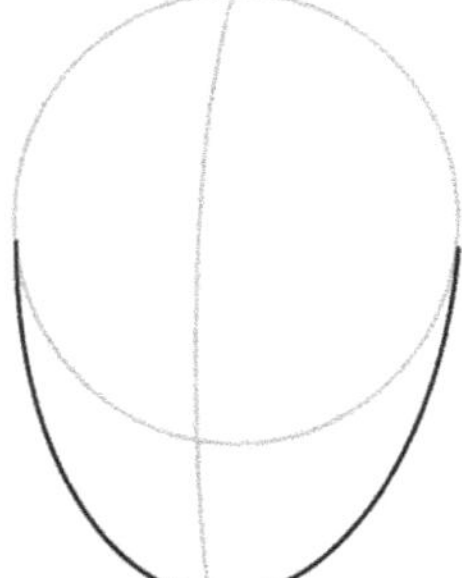

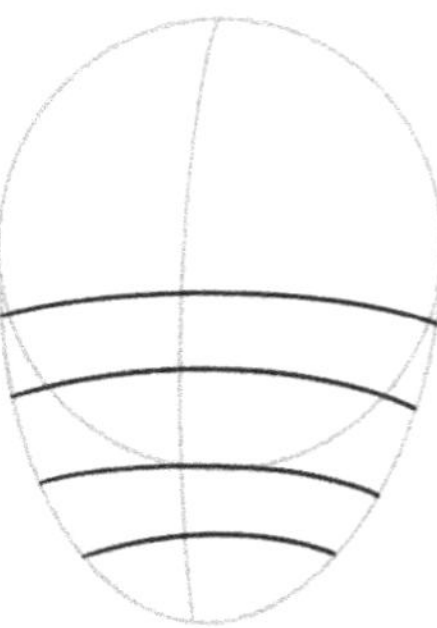

04

05

06

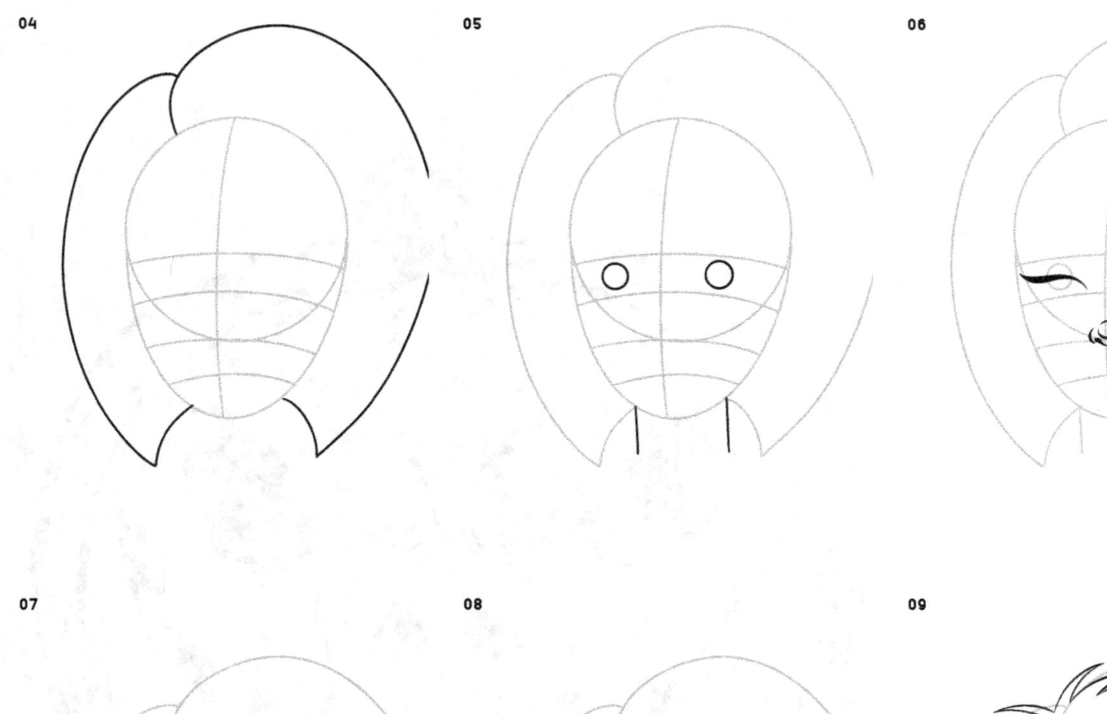

07

08

09

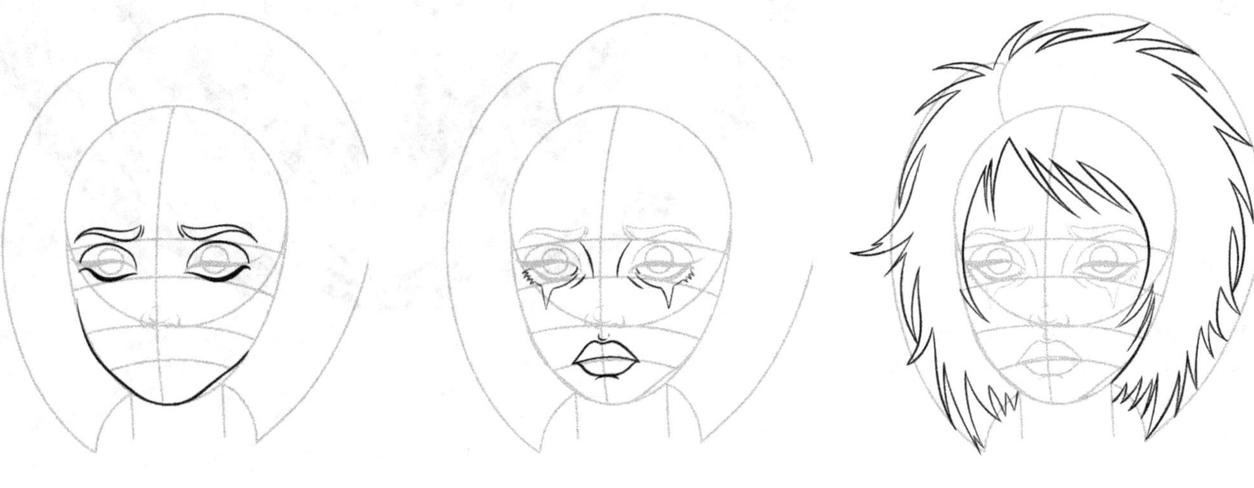

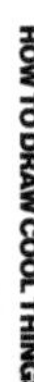

10

11

12

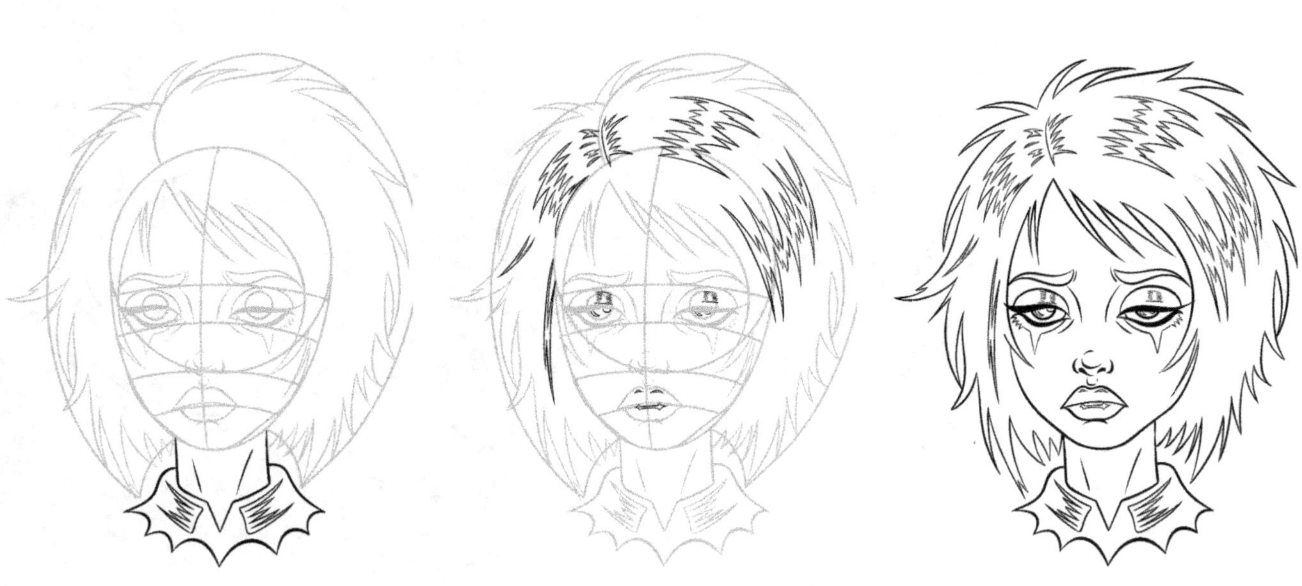

JACK O'LANTERN

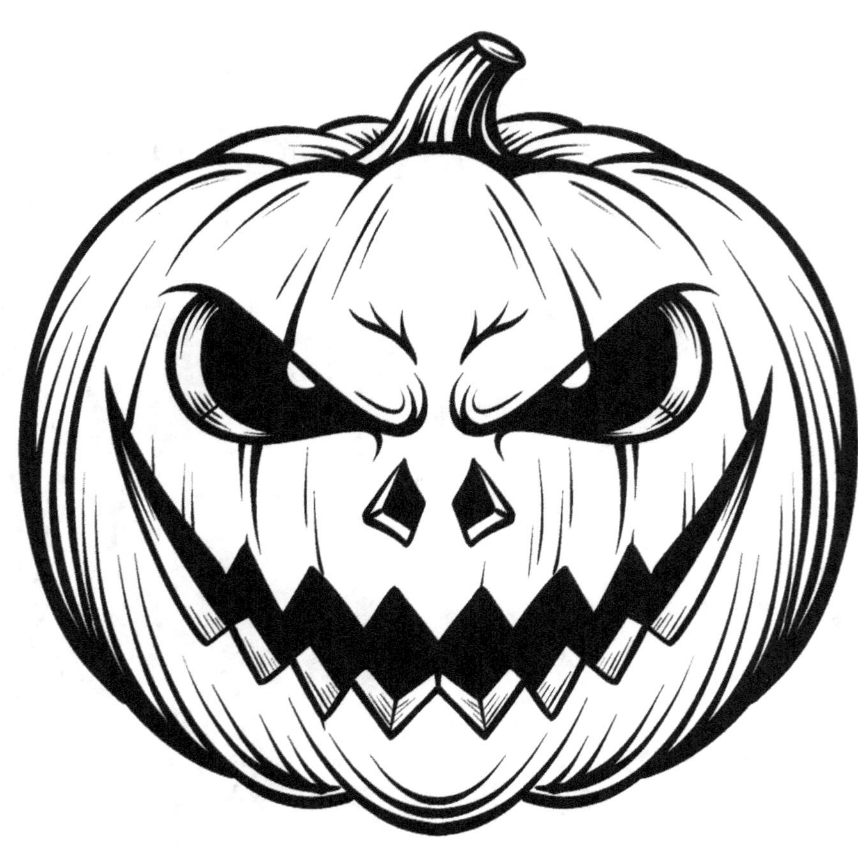

Pro tip:

Block the eyes as angled wedges about half the pumpkin circle's width, sitting on the upper guide line with roughly one sixth of the circle between them.

01   02   03

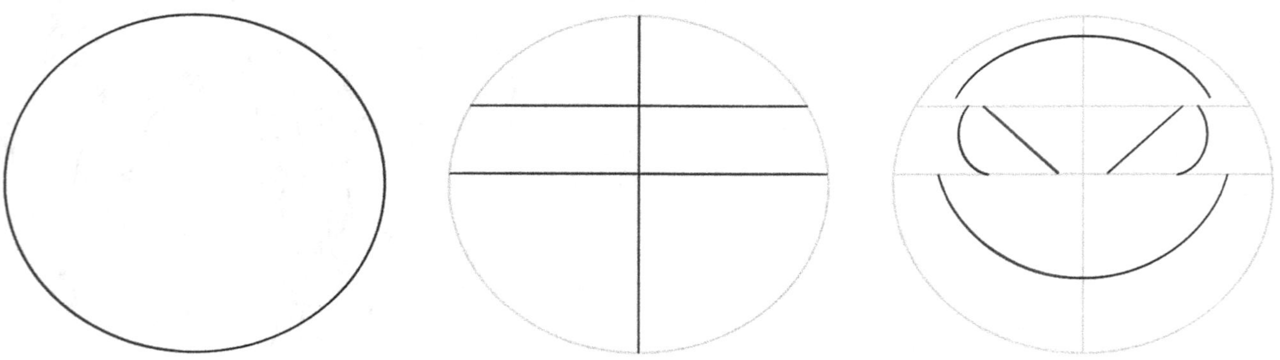

04

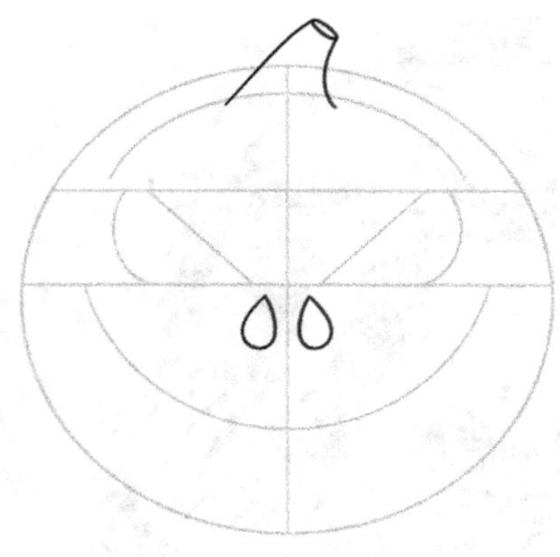

05

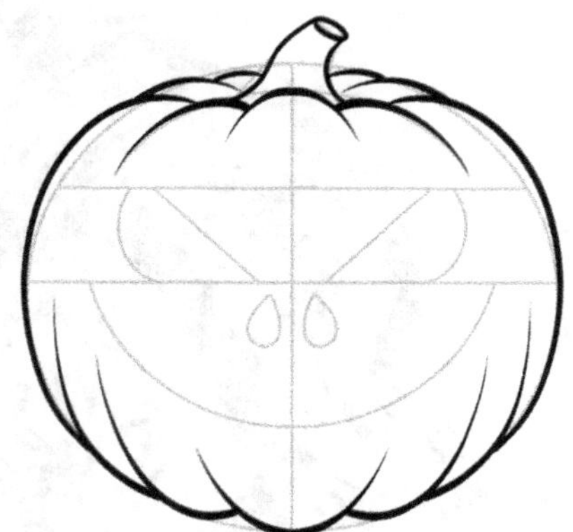

06

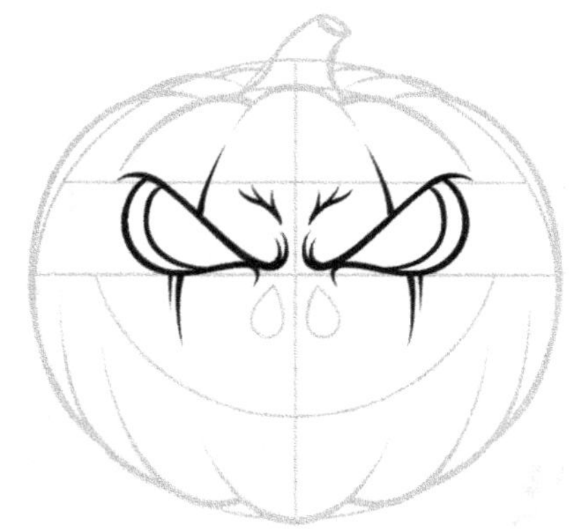

07

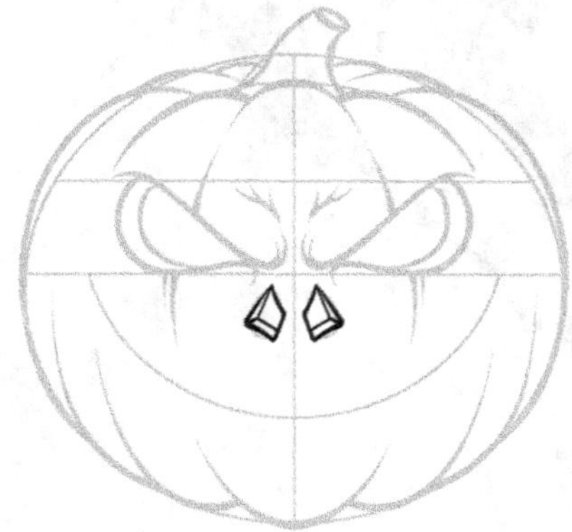

08

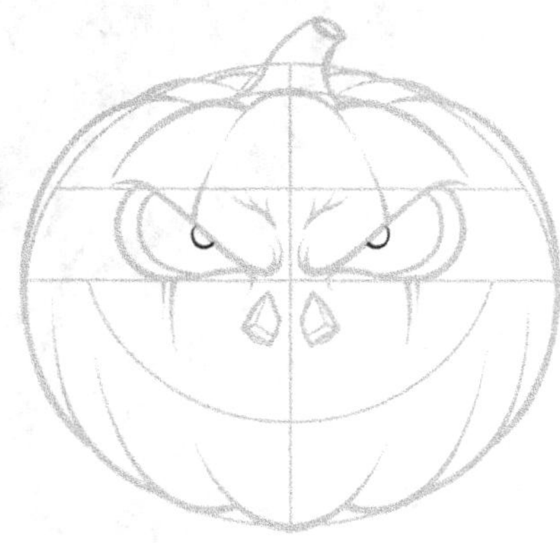

09

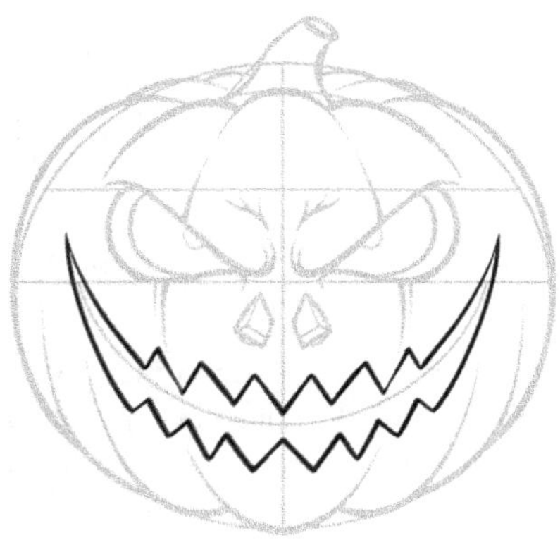

10

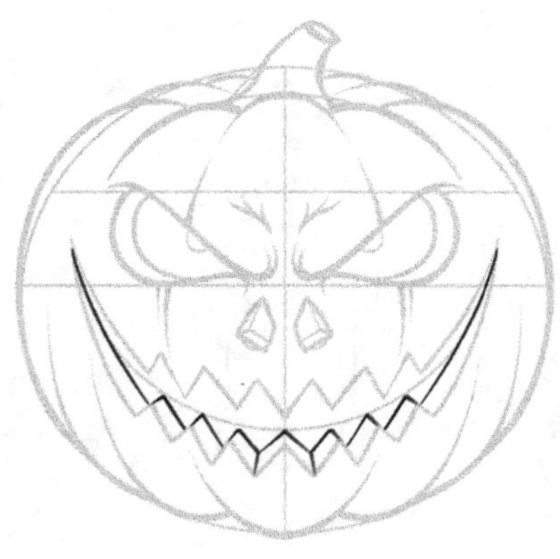

11

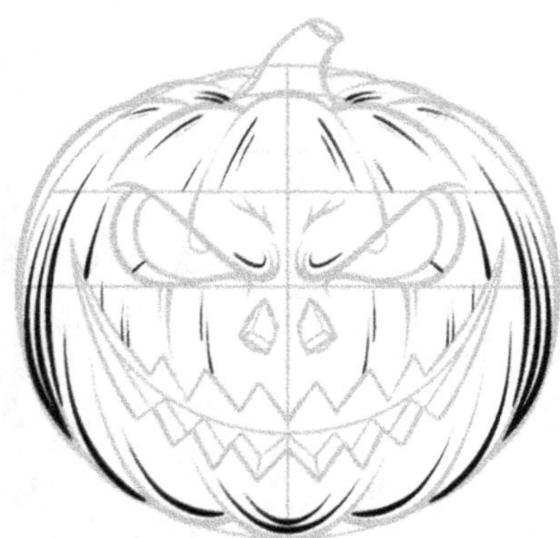

12

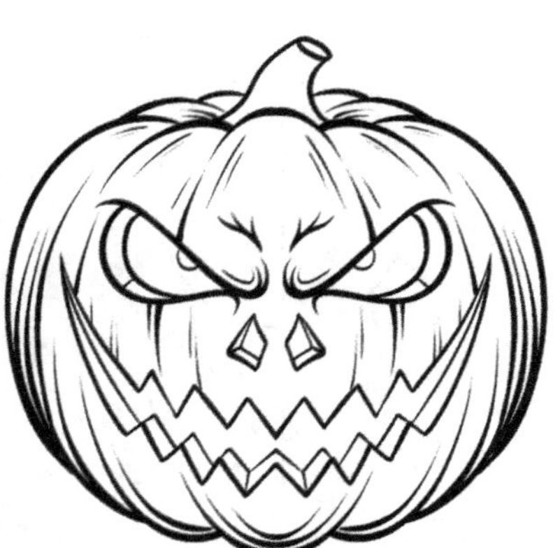

LION

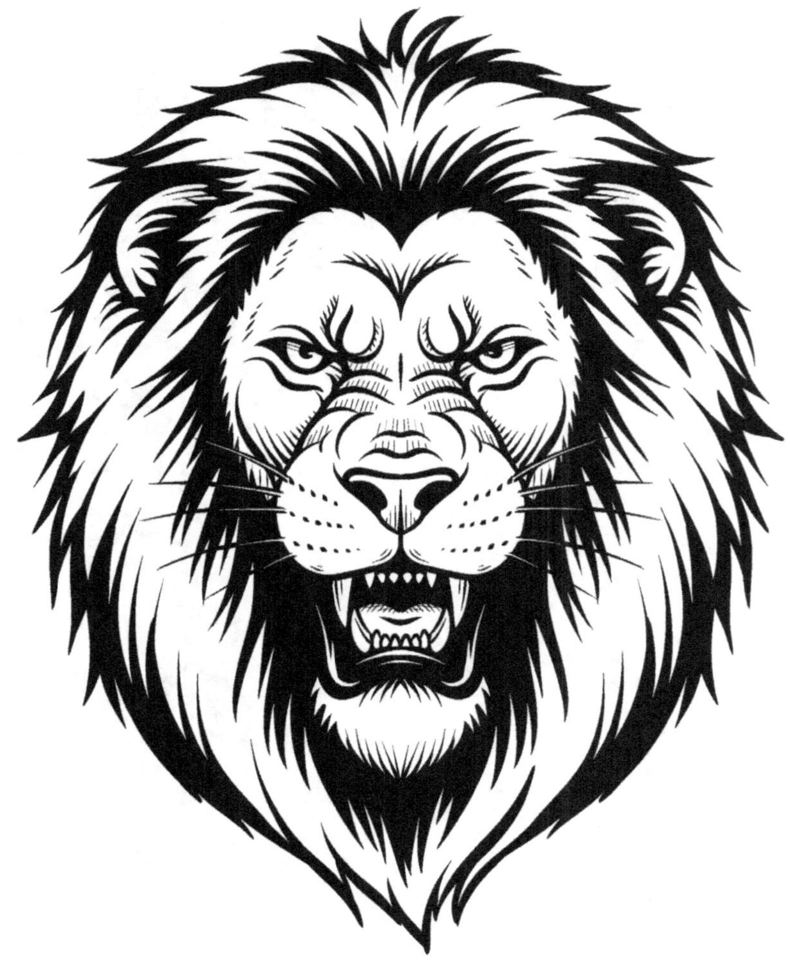

Pro tip:

Build the mane as a teardrop about 2×
the head circle's height and 1.5× its width,
tapering to a point one circle below the
lion's chin.

---

01   **02**   **03**

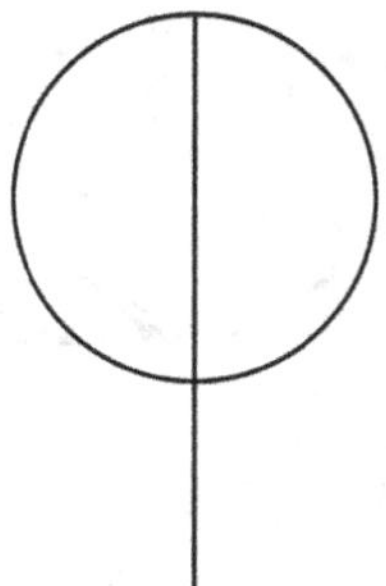

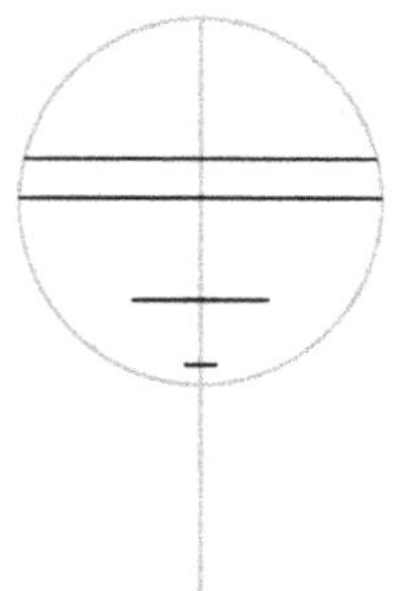

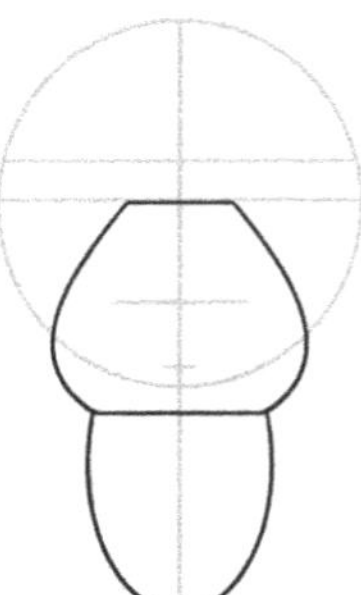

04

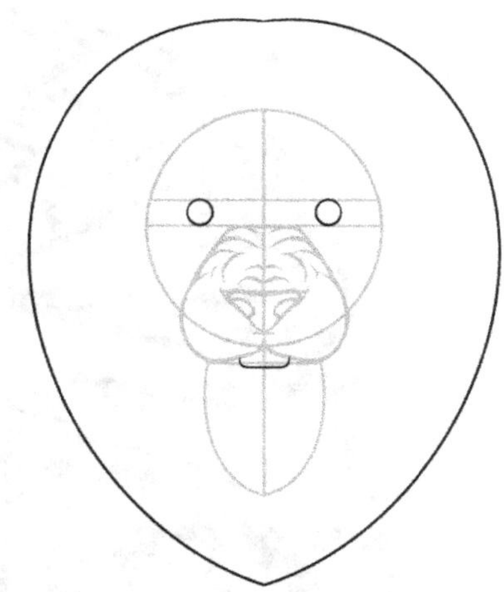

05

06

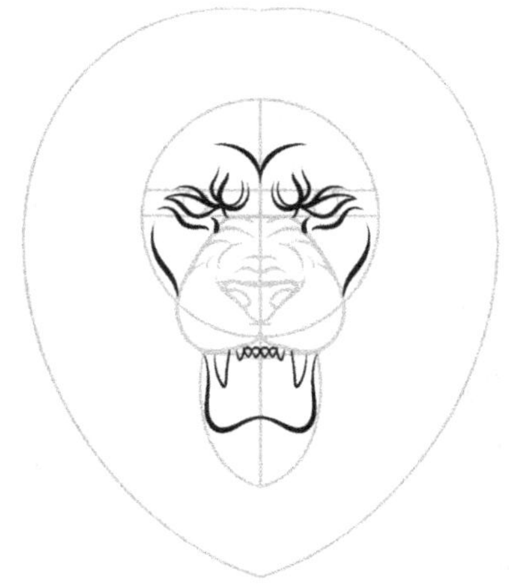

07

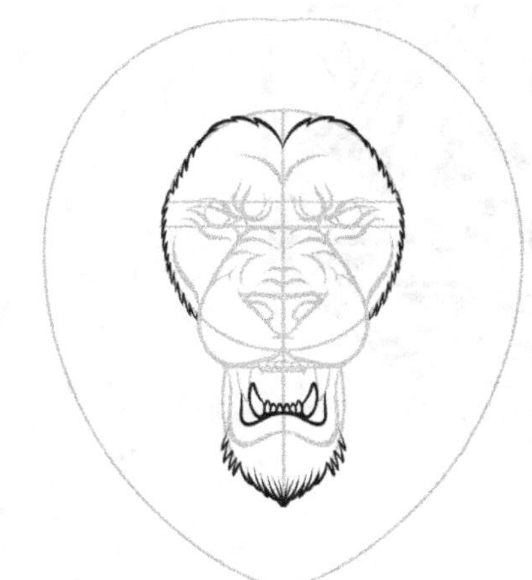

08

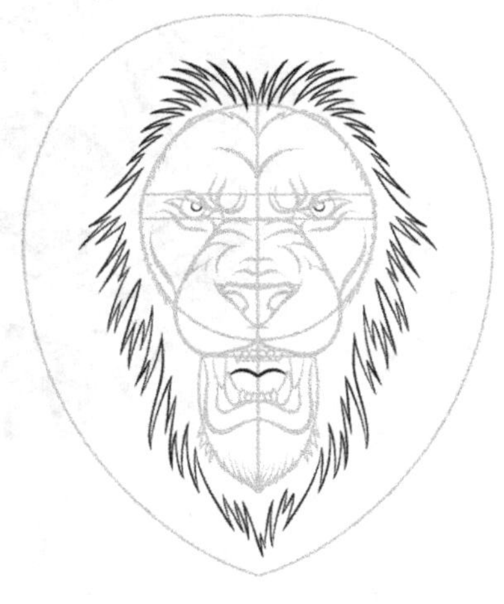

09

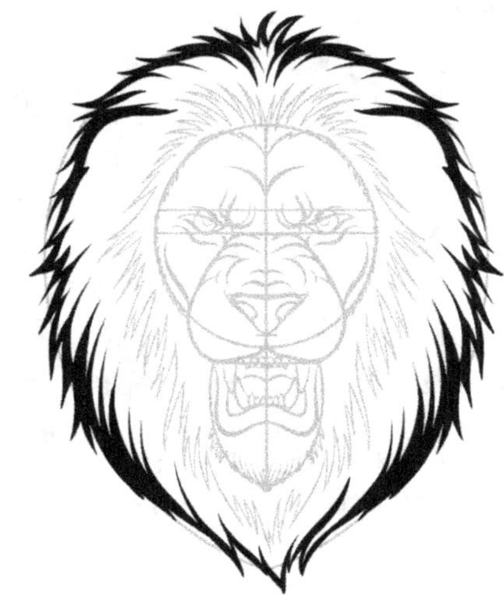

10

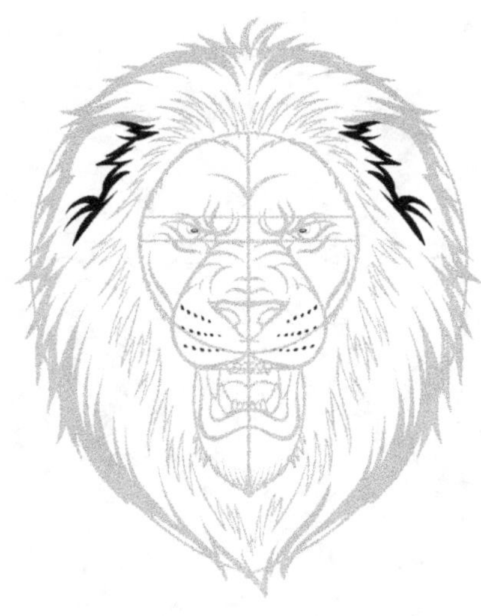

11

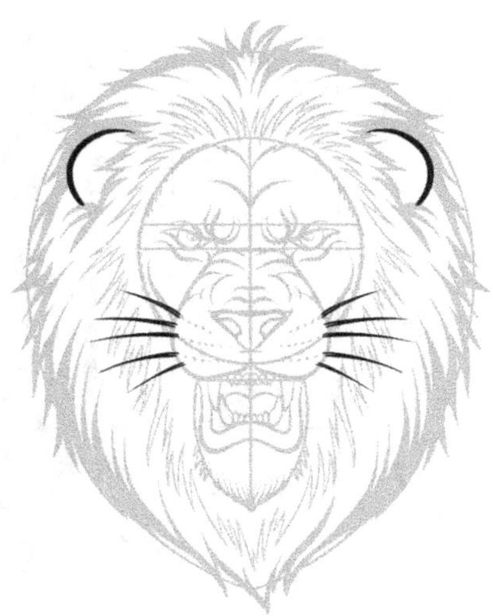

12

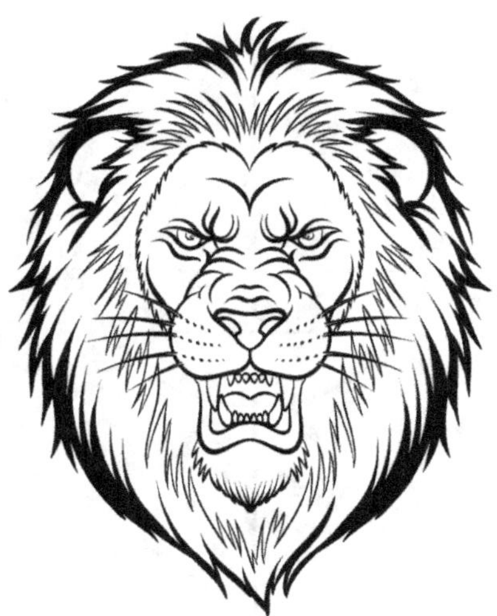

HOW TO DRAW COOL THINGS

ZOMBIE MUMMY

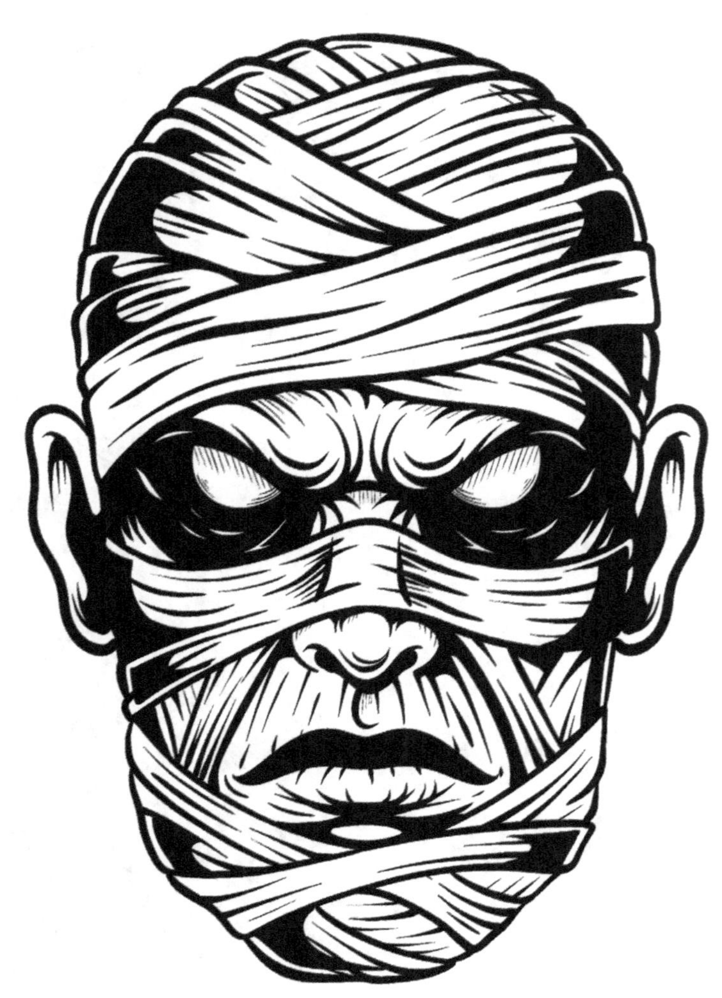

Pro tip:

Start with a head circle, then drop the jaw about half a circle below it and keep the chin width to roughly one third of the circle for a sunken zombie shape.

01   02   03

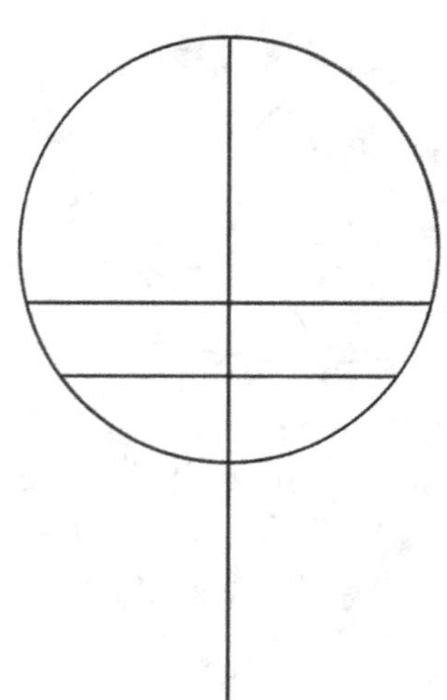
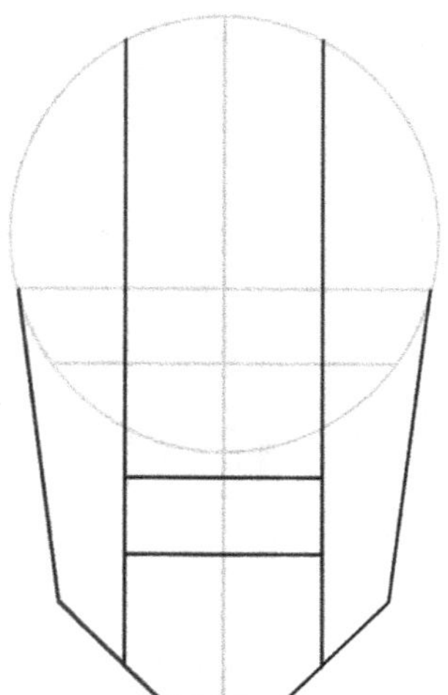
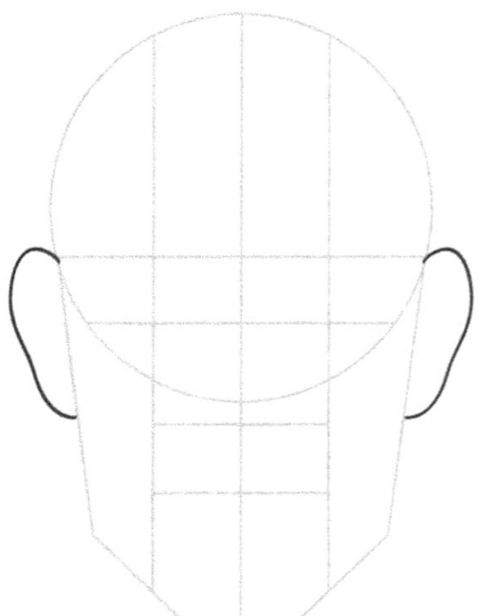

04

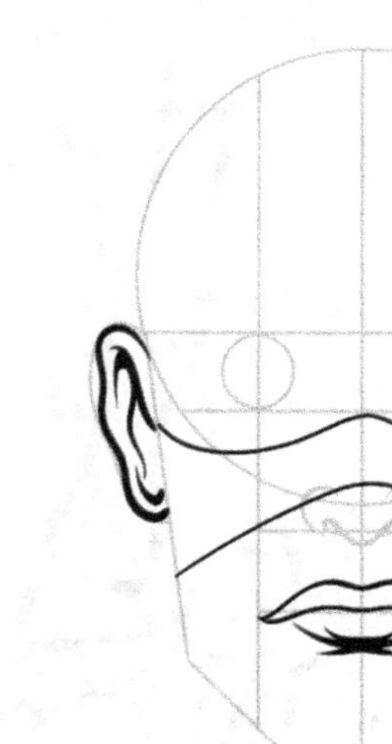

05

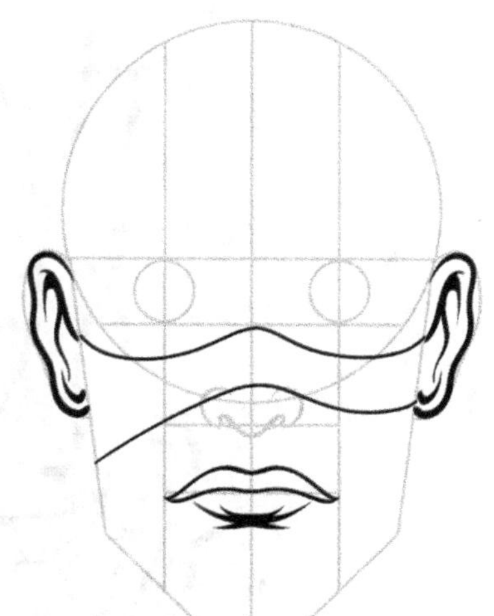

06

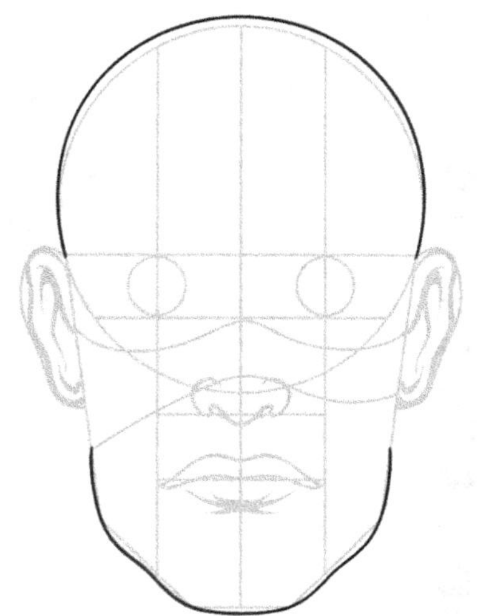

07

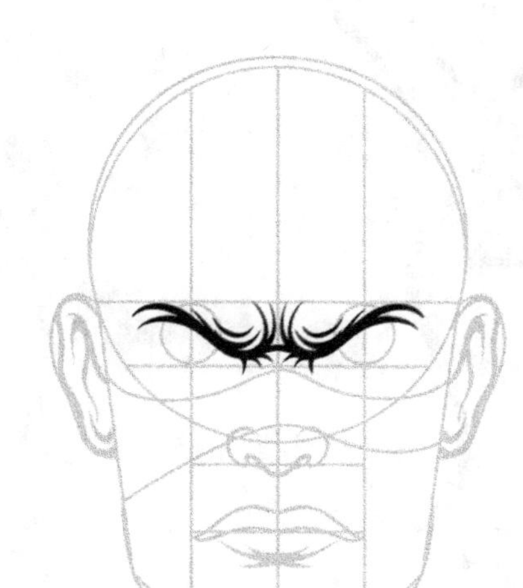

08

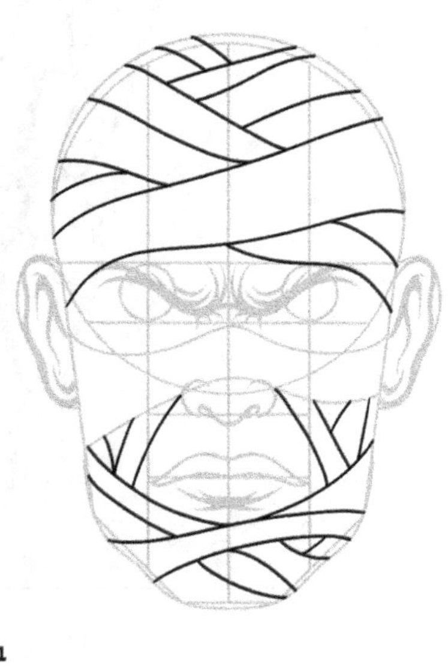

09

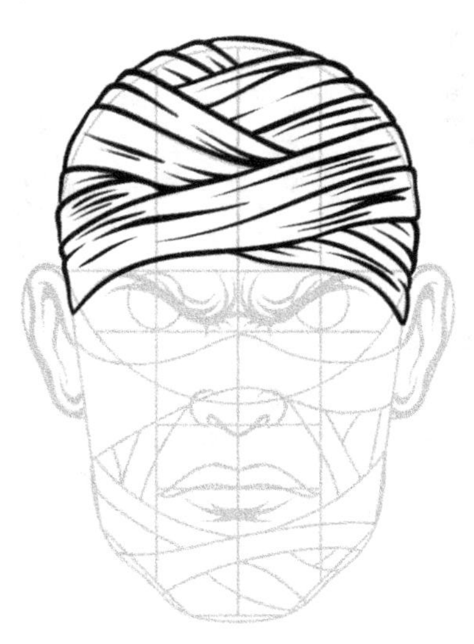

10

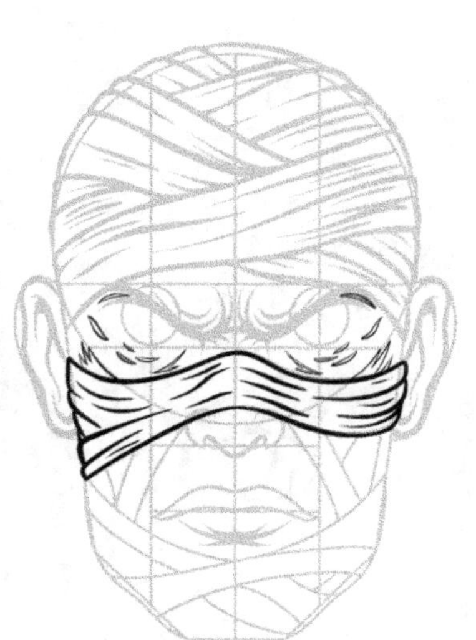

11

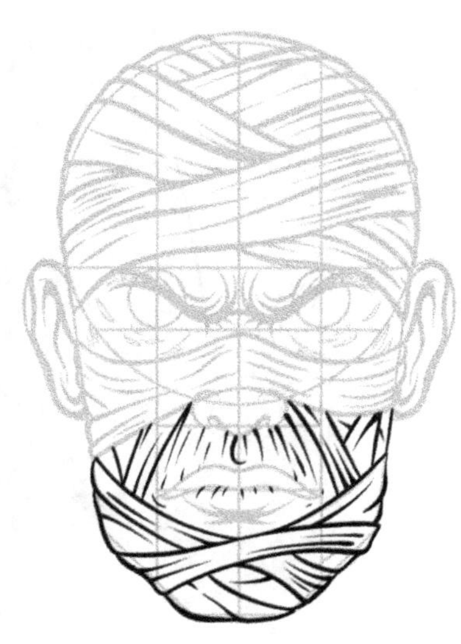

12

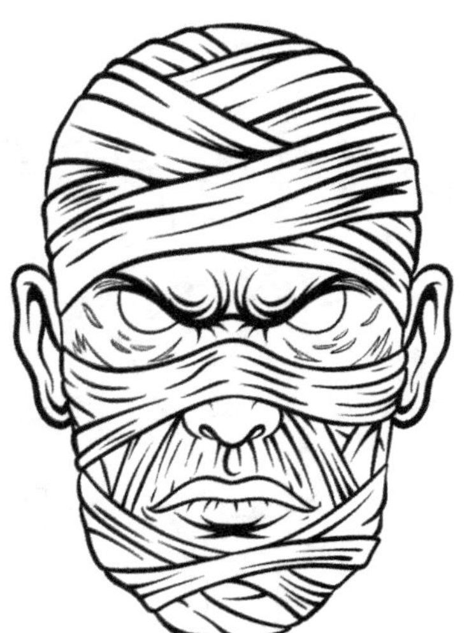

HOW TO DRAW COOL THINGS

SKELETON PEACE SIGN

Pro tip:

Use the fist width as your unit, then make the two raised fingers about 2× that length and keep a gap of roughly one finger-width between them.

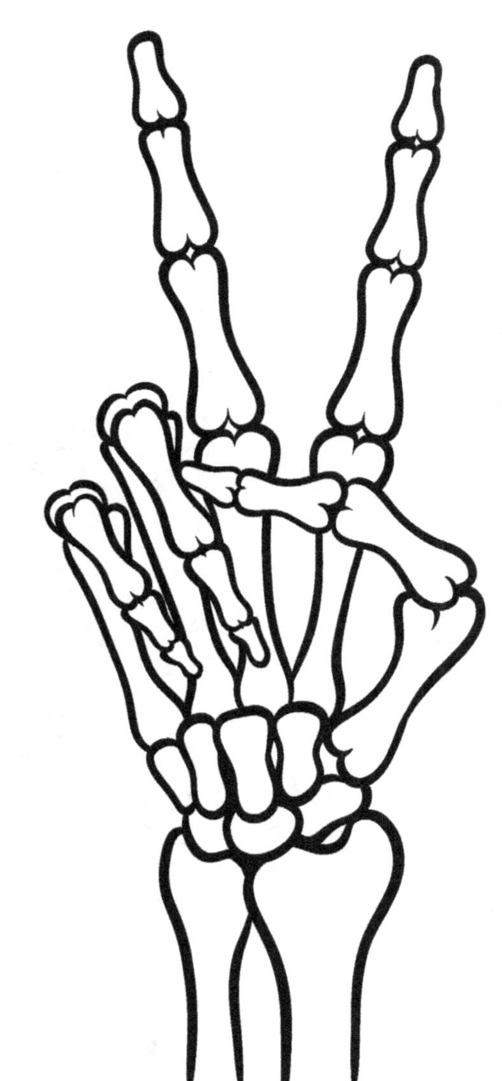

01

02

03

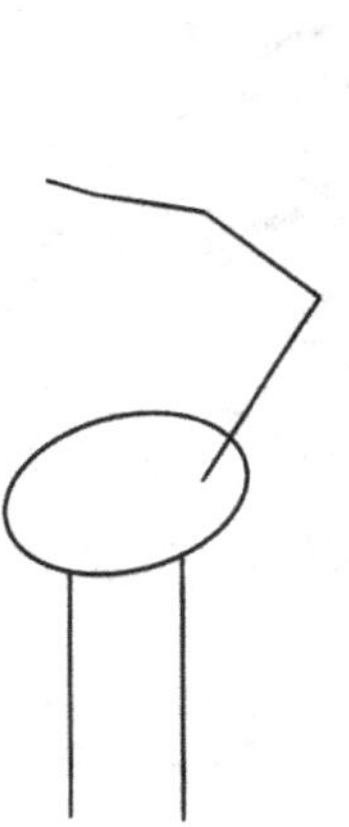

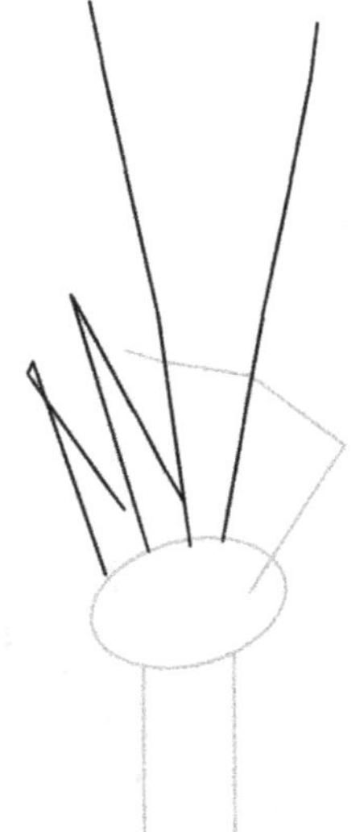

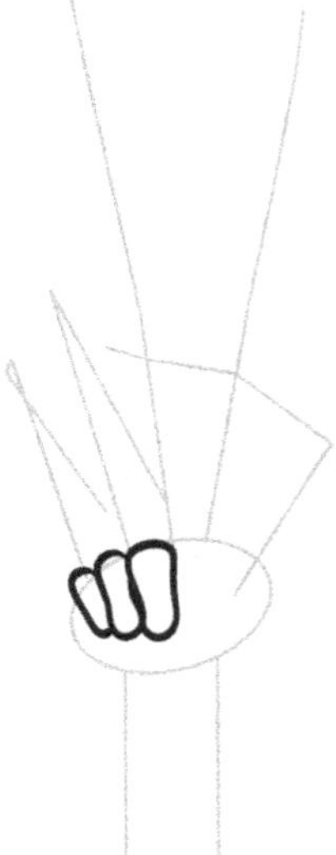

04

05

06

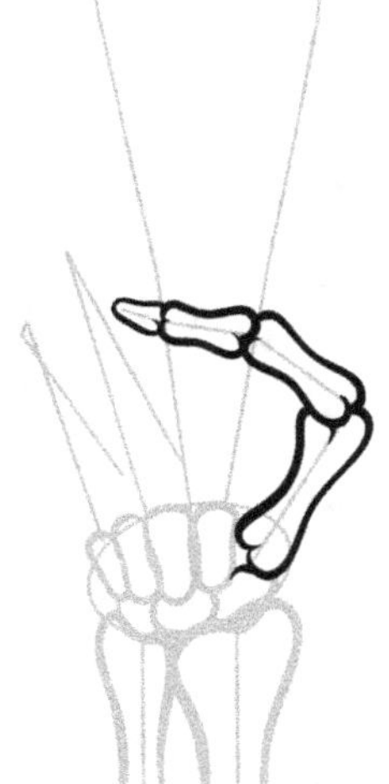

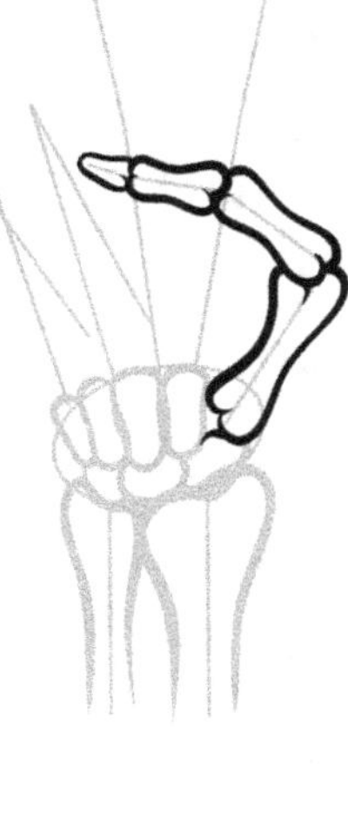

07

08

09

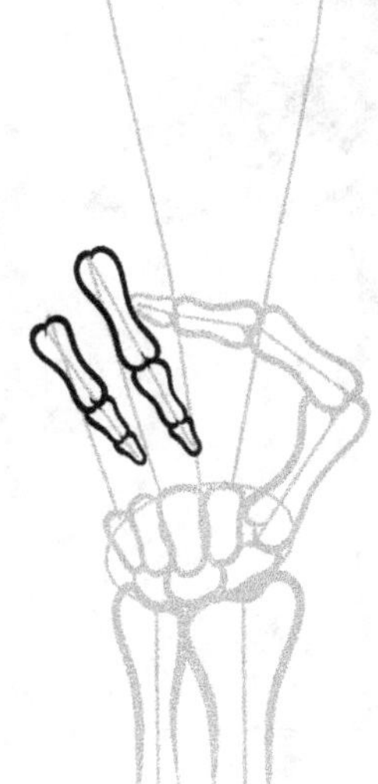

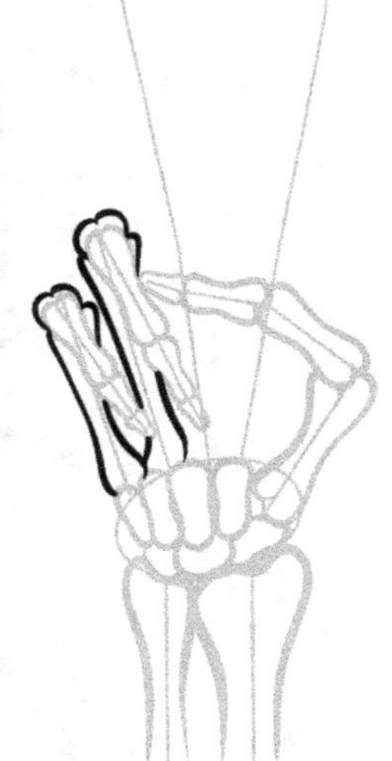

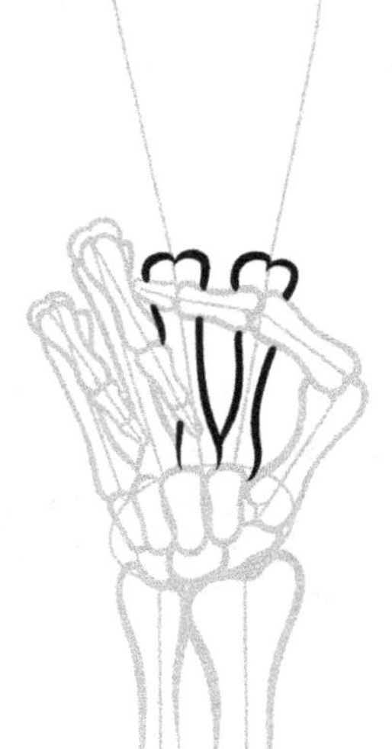

10

11

12

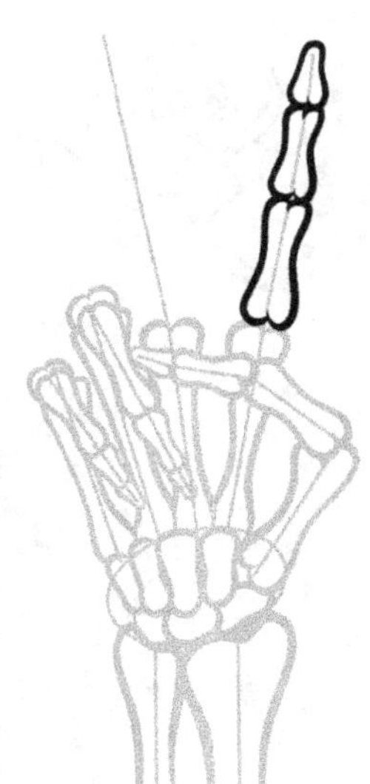

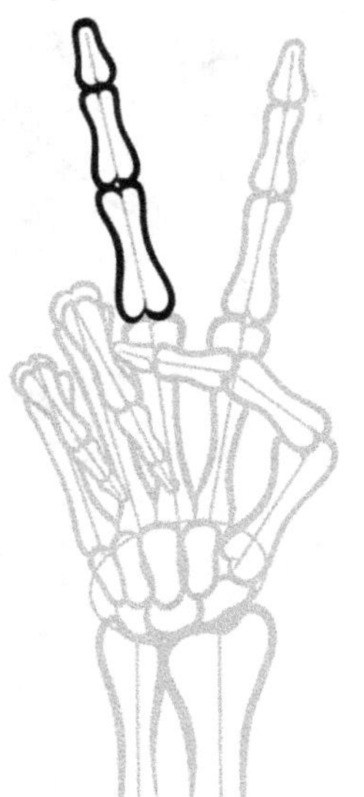

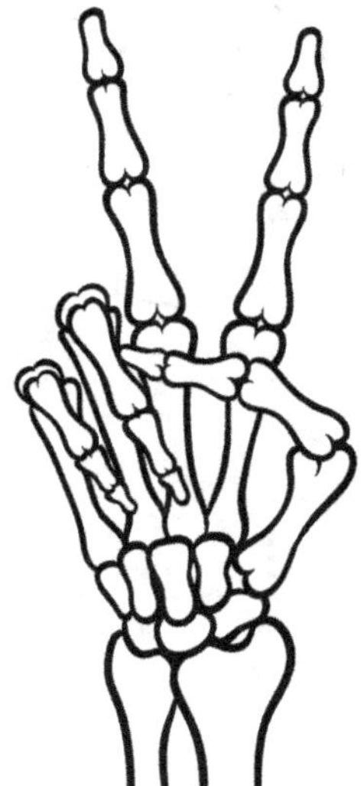

HOW TO DRAW COOL THINGS

ROSE

Pro tip:

Use the outer circle as the bloom
boundary, then keep the first spiral petal
inside the top half and let each new petal
push out by about one sixth of the circle.

01

02

03

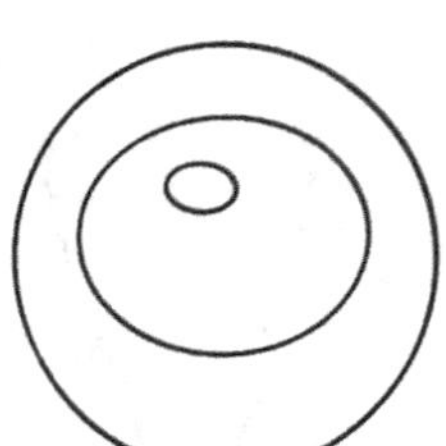

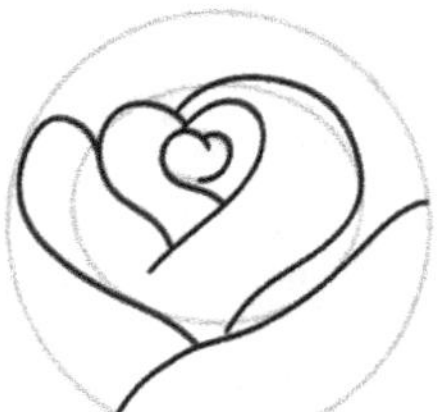

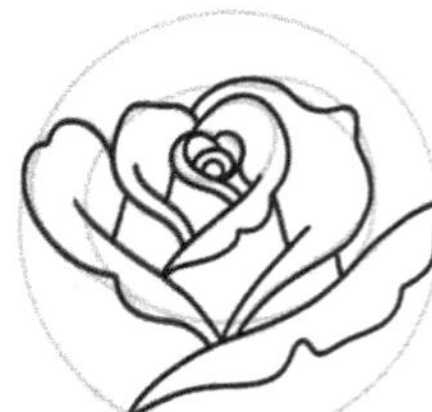

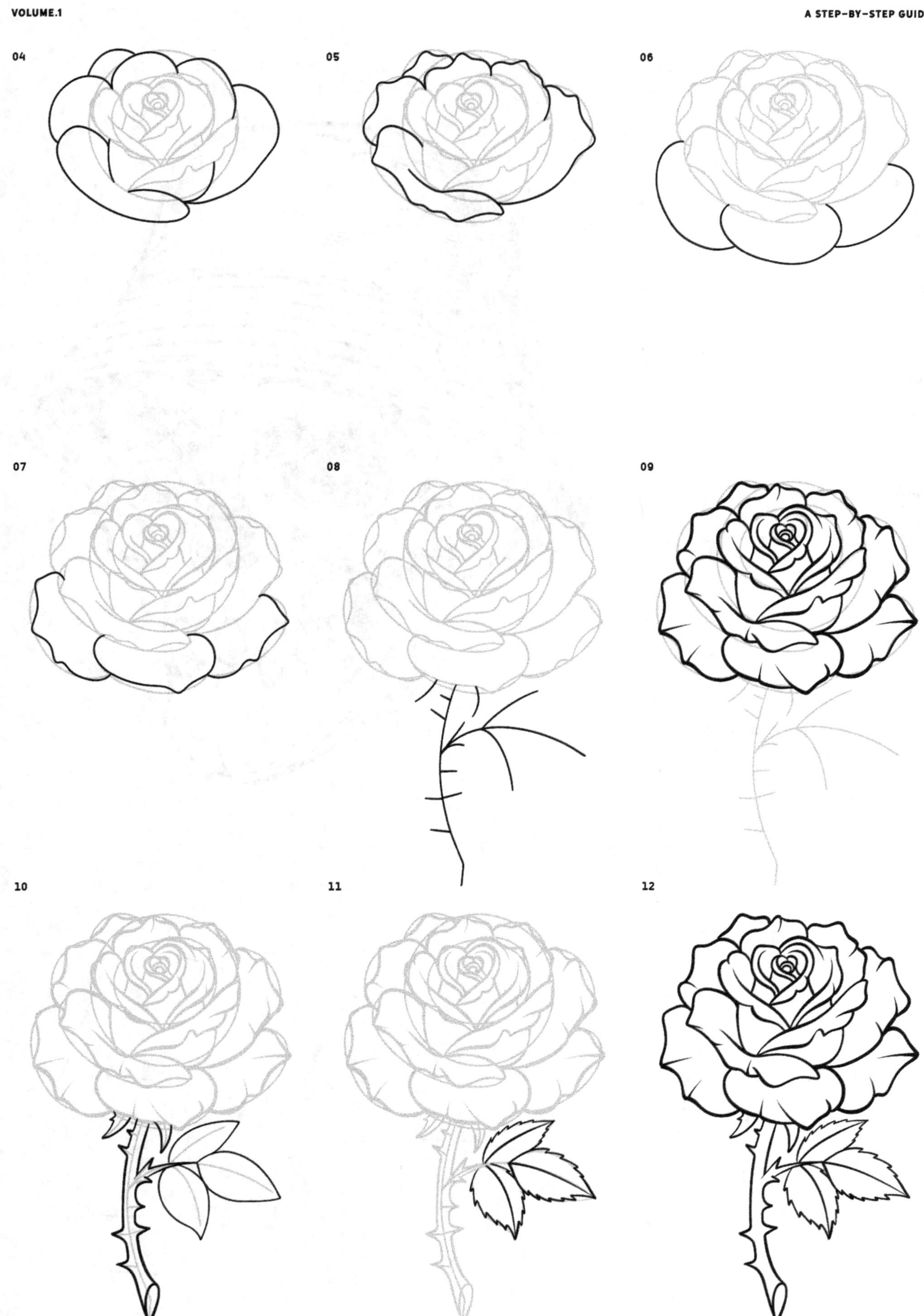

04
05
06
07
08
09
10
11
12
HOW TO DRAW COOL THINGS

SKULL IN BUCKET HAT

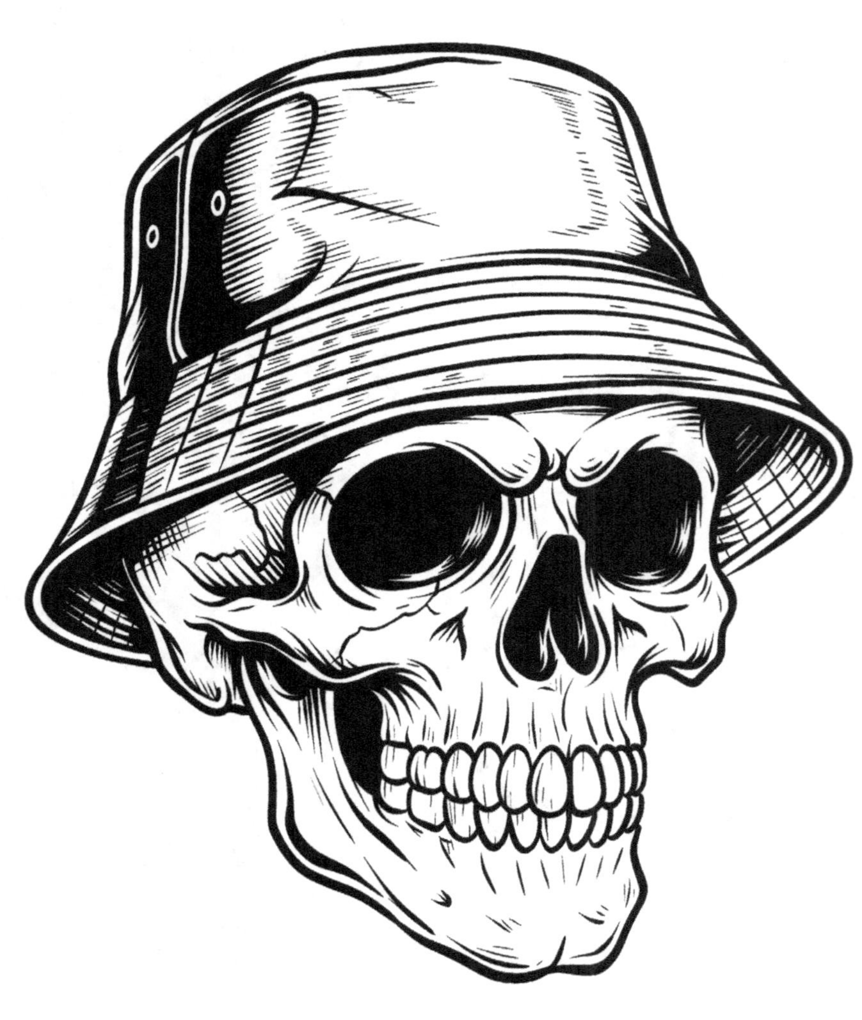

Pro tip:

Treat the head as one circle, then wrap
the brim as an oval about 1.5× the circle's
width, with the crown rising roughly half a
circle above the top.

01

02

03

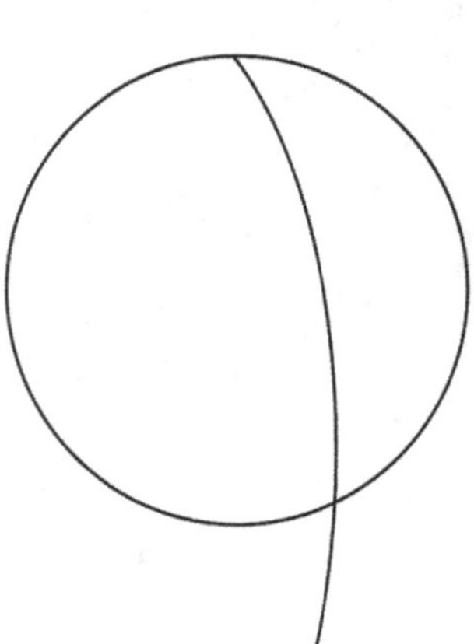

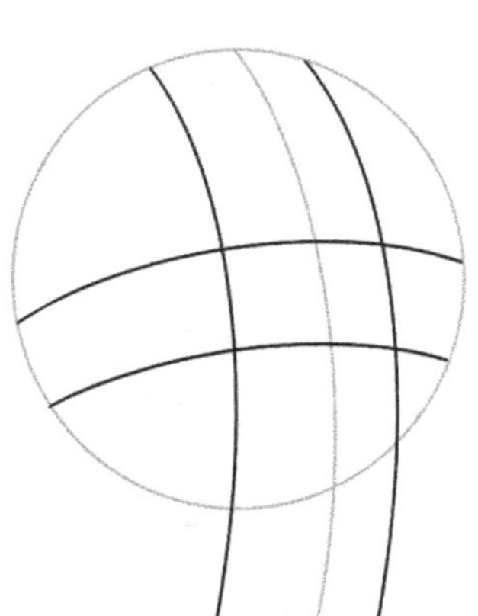

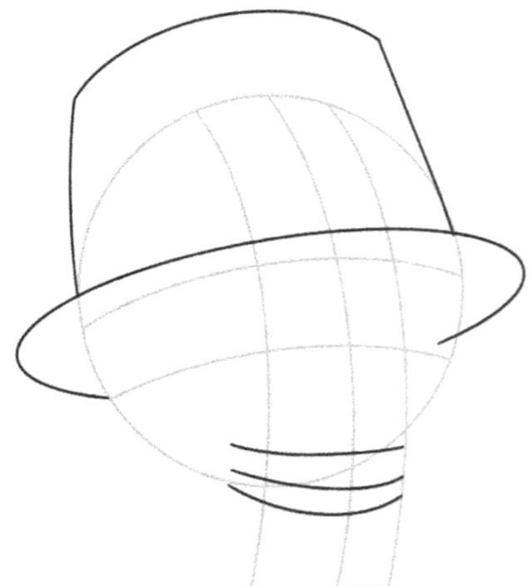

04

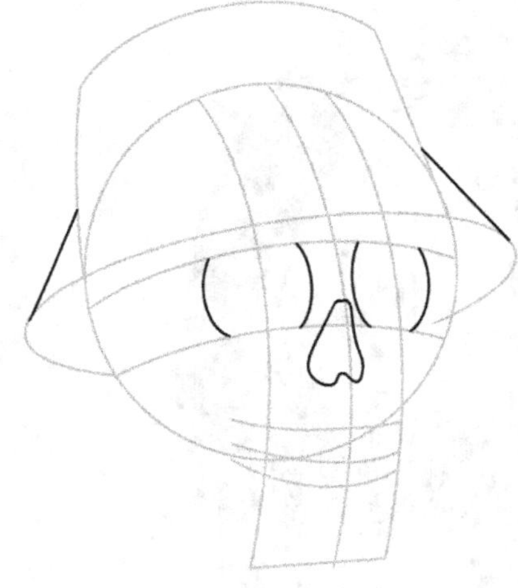

05

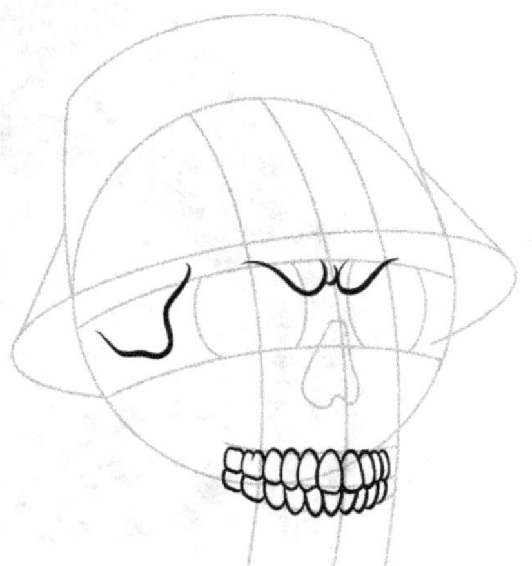

06

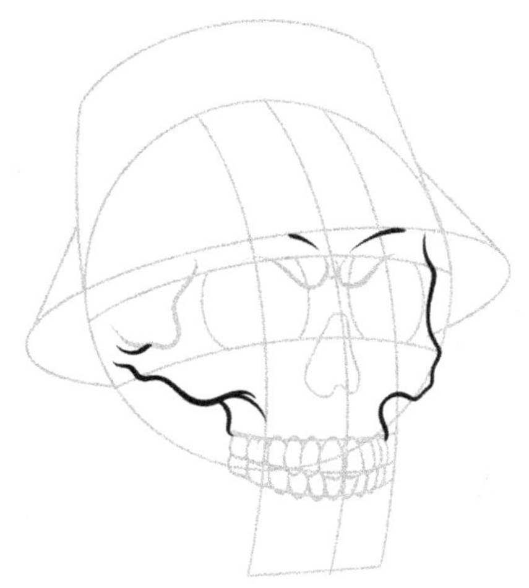

07

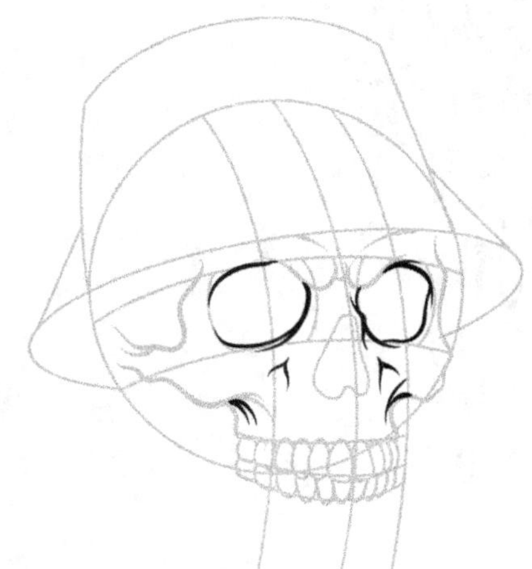

08

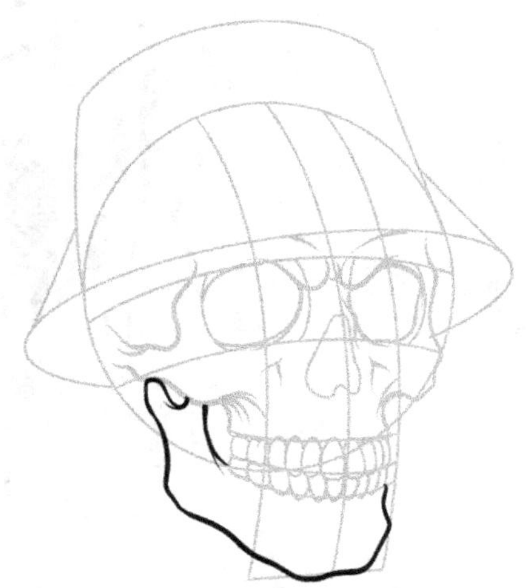

09

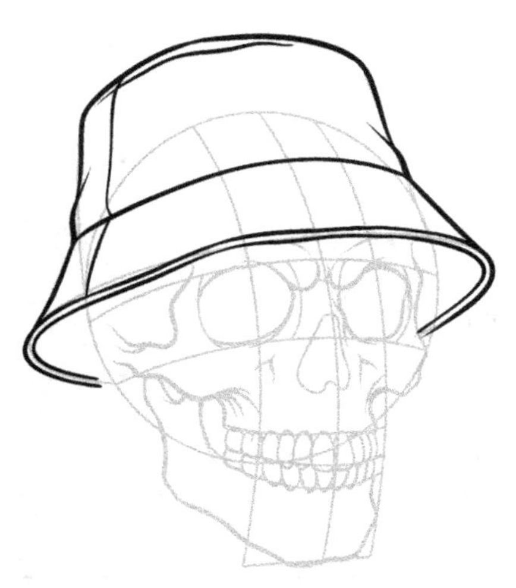

10

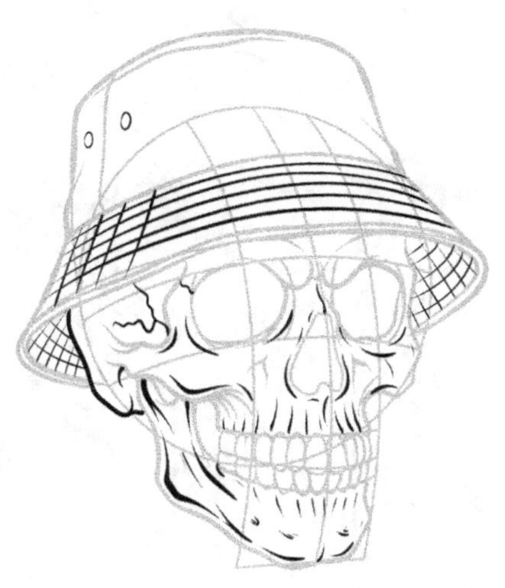

11

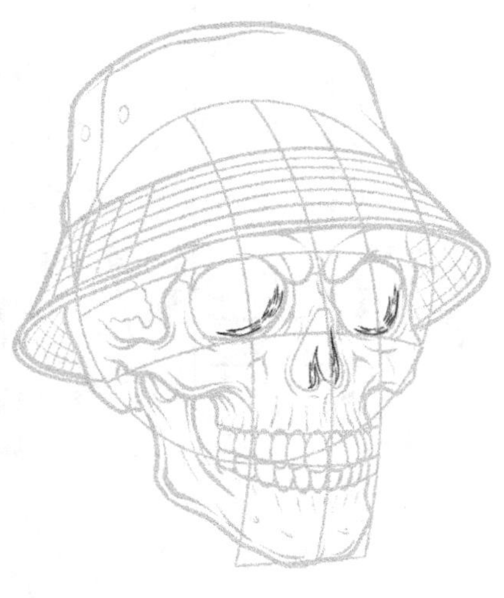

12

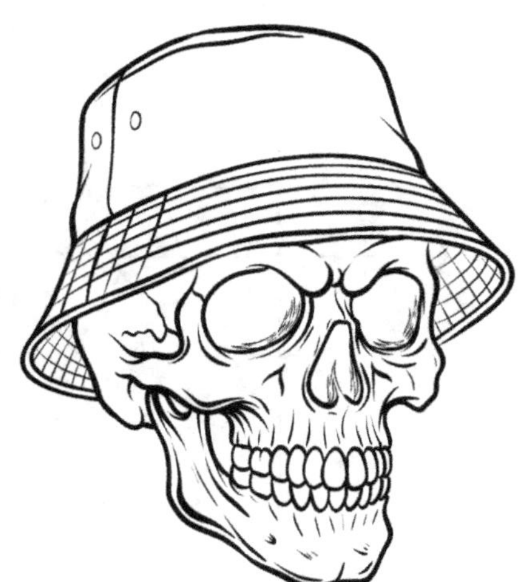

MELTING FACE

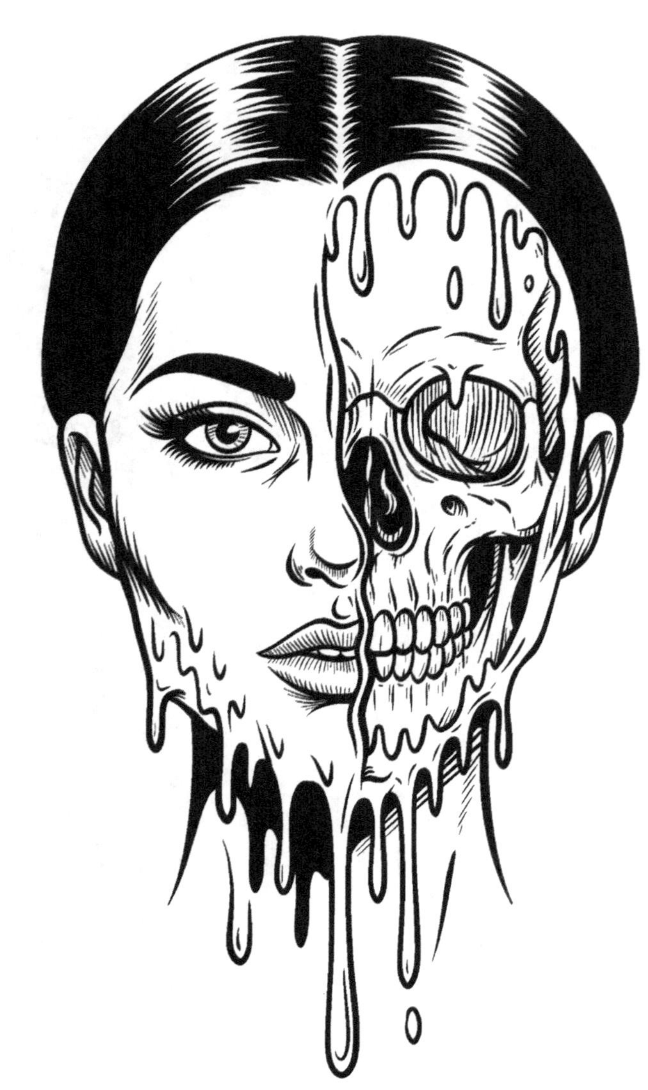

Pro tip:

Start with a circle, then drop the chin
point about half a circle below it and
keep the jaw width to roughly two thirds
of the circle before adding the melt.

01

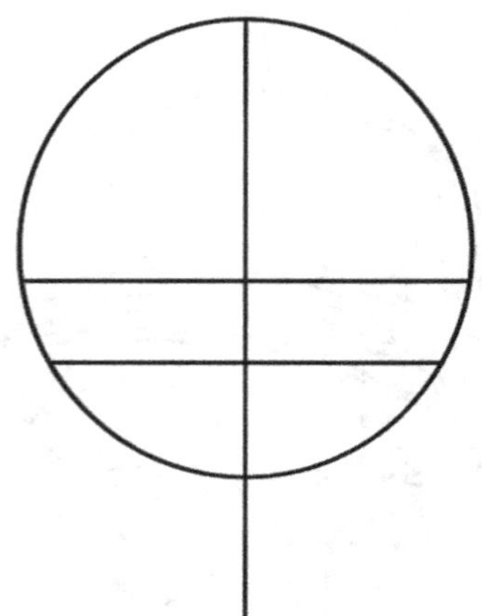

02

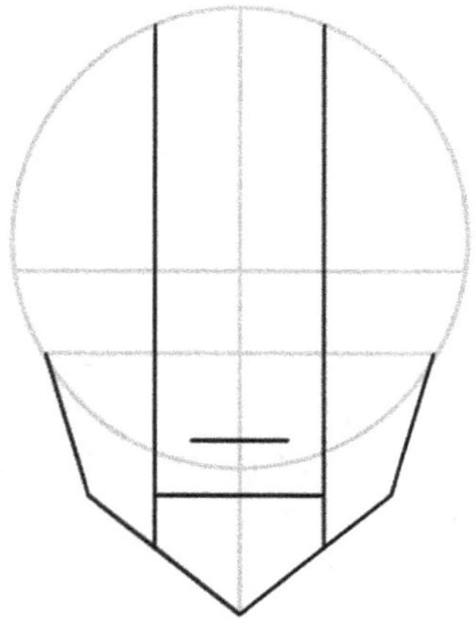

03

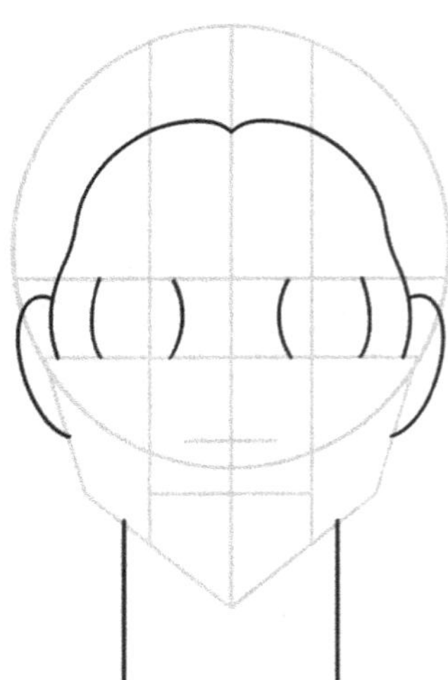

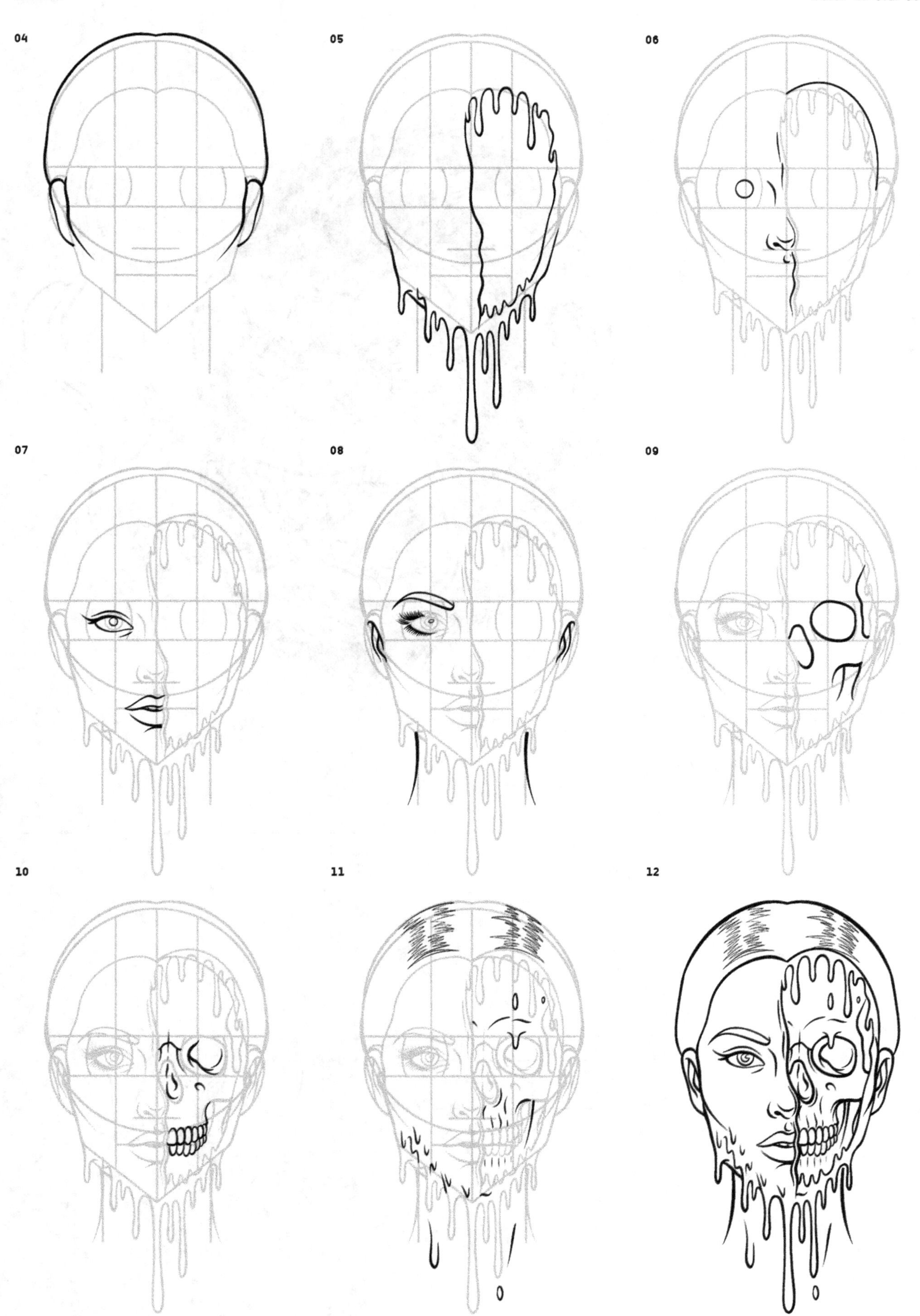

04
05
06
07
08
09
10
11
12

SMOKING APE

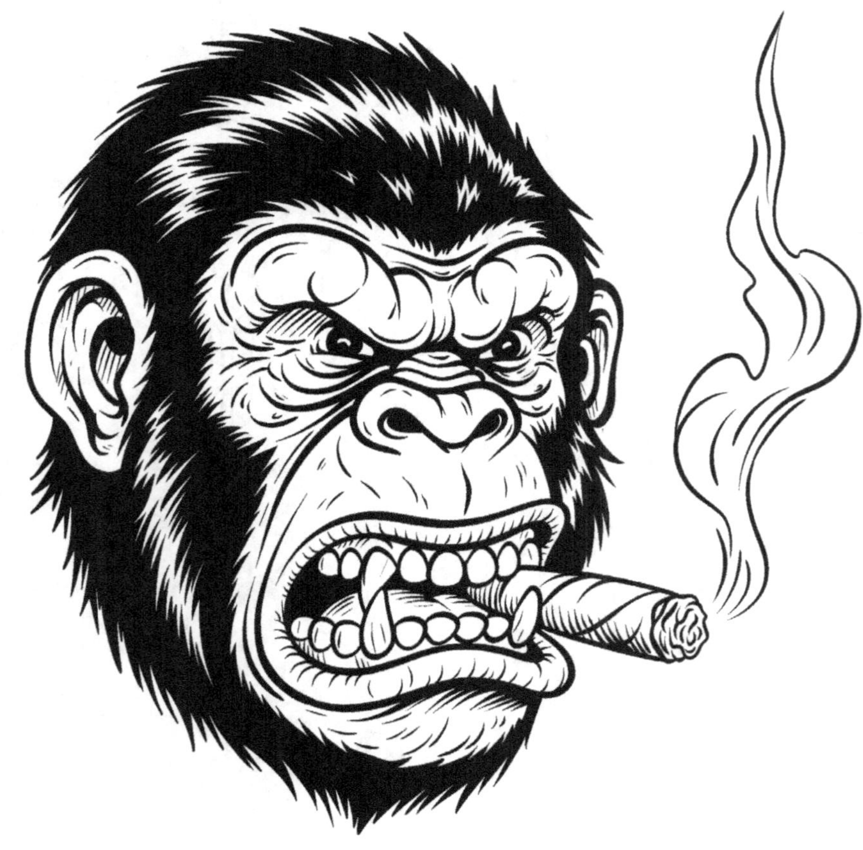

Pro tip:

Use the head circle as your anchor, then make the muzzle mass about half the circle's width and let it hang roughly one third of a circle below the mouth line.

01

02

03

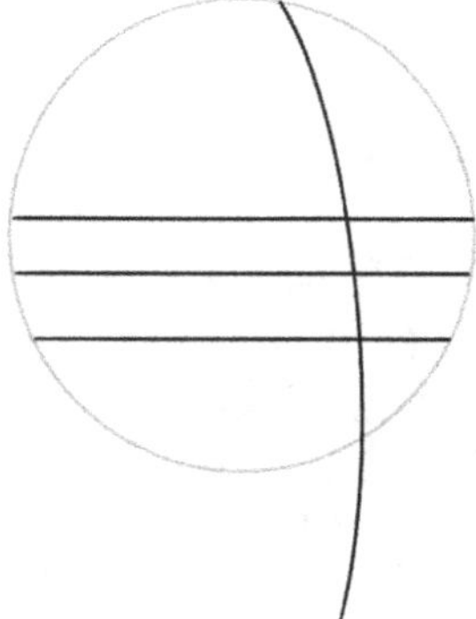

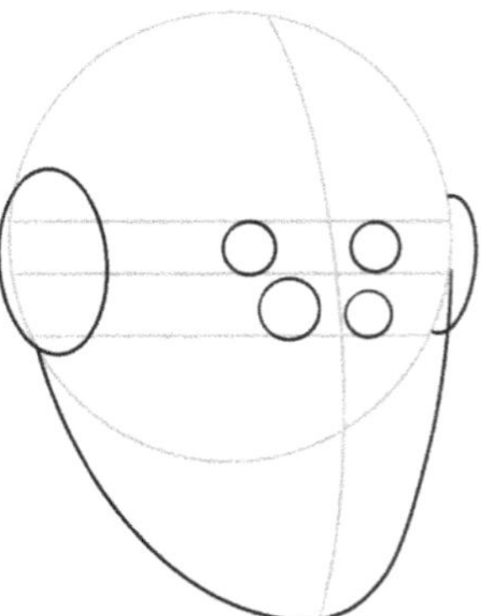

04

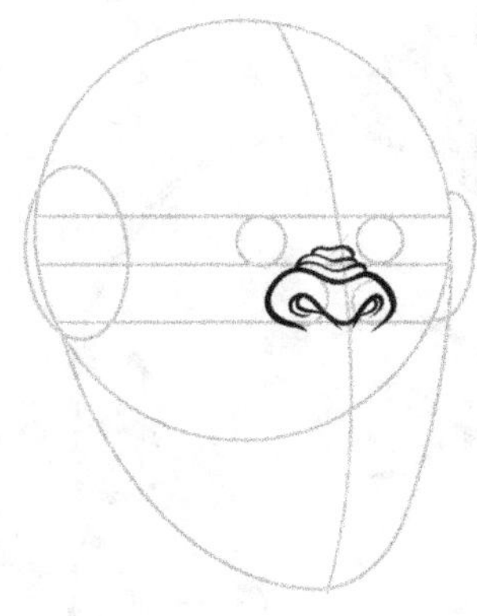

05

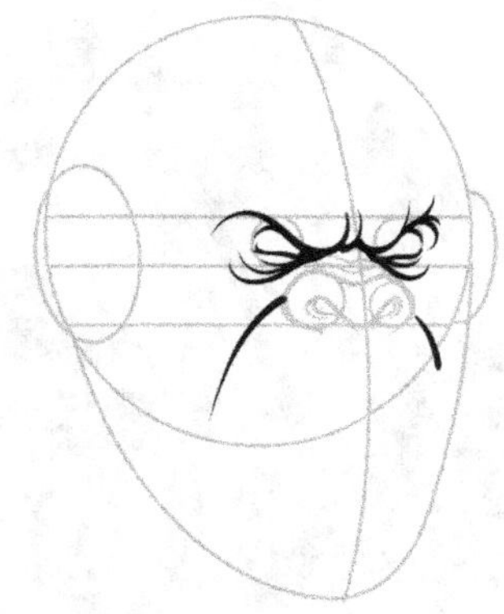

06

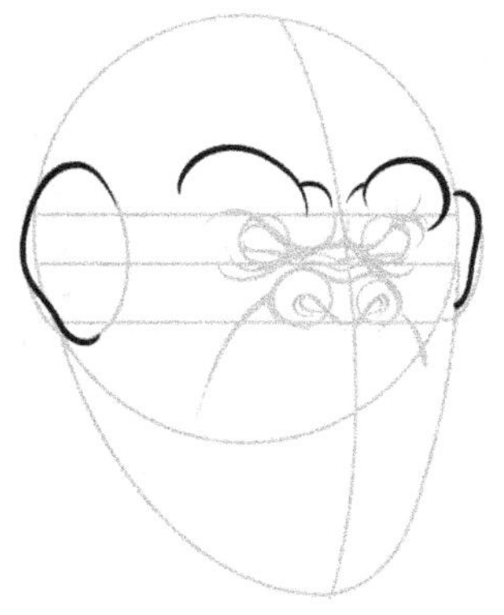

07

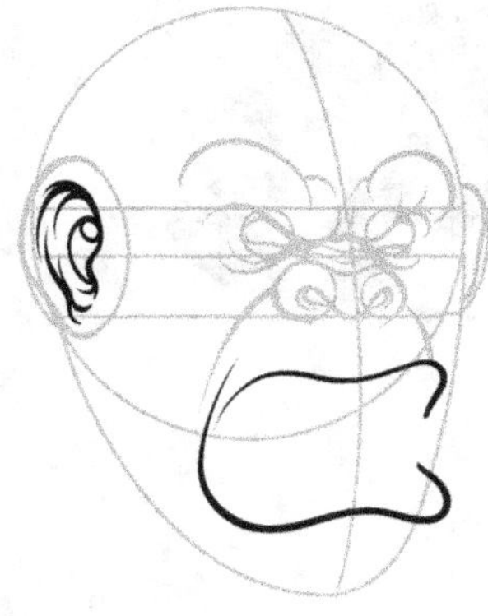

08

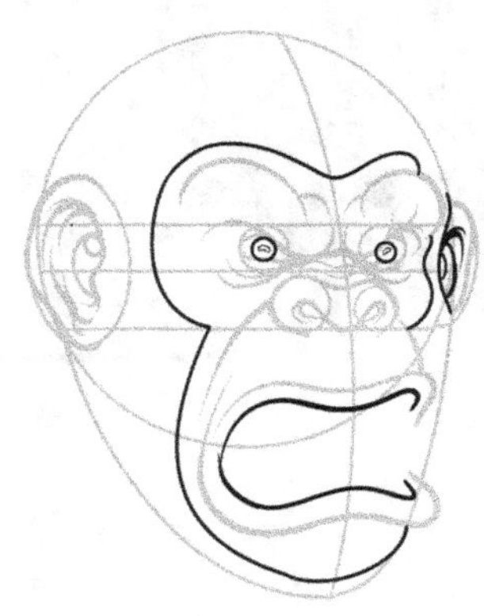

09

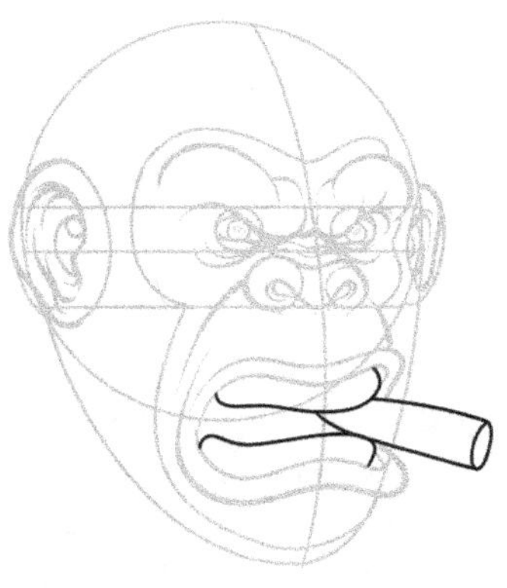

10

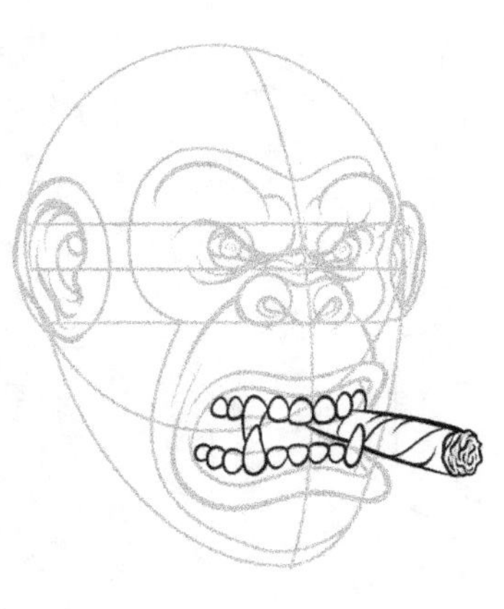

11

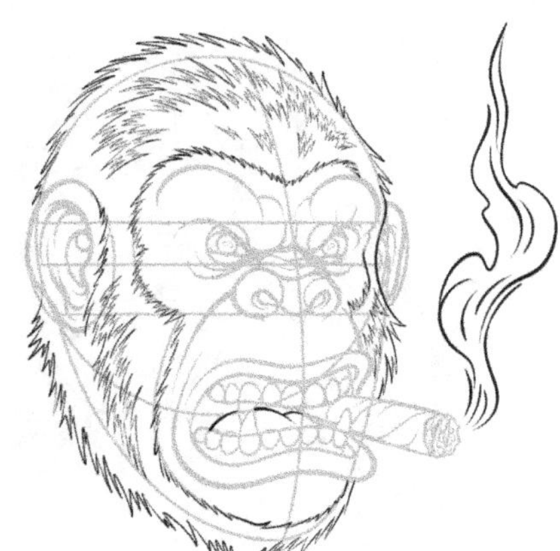

12

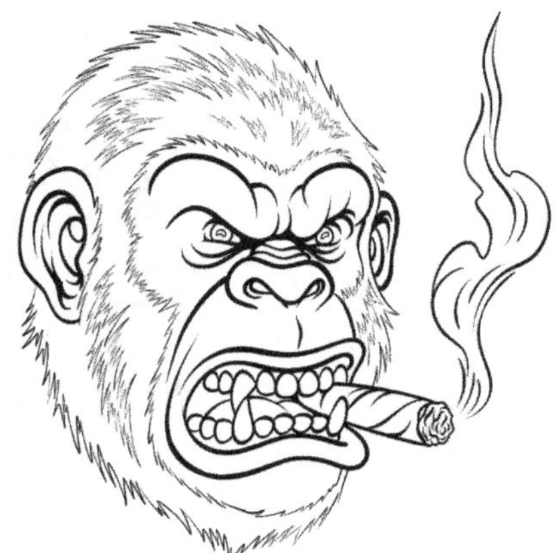

HOW TO DRAW COOL THINGS

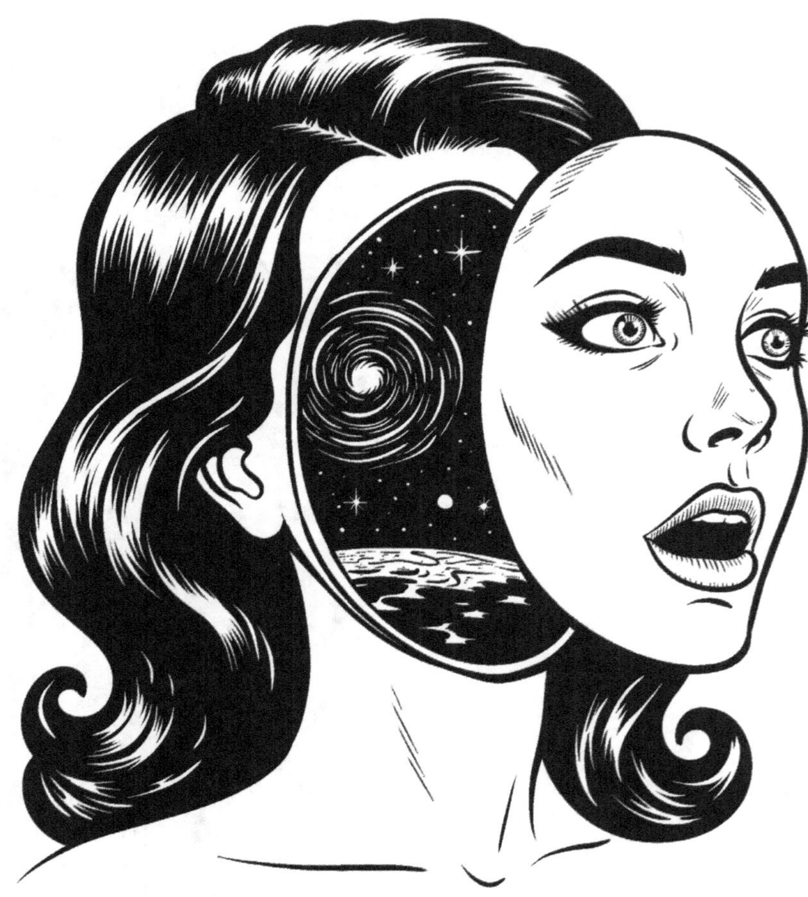

GALAXY GIRL

Pro tip:

Start with a head circle, then place the
front face oval the same height but
slightly narrower, overlapping the circle
by about one quarter of its width.

01   02   03

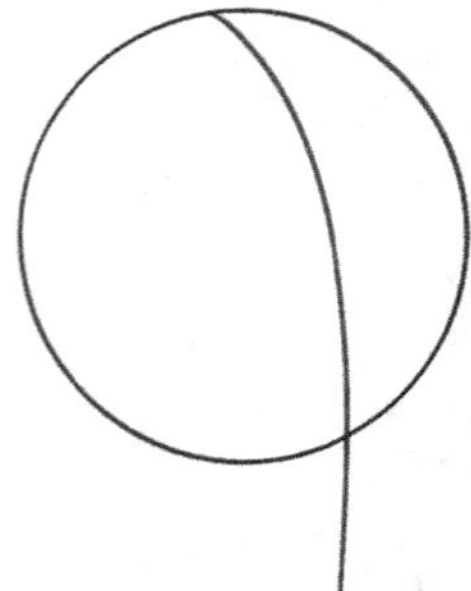

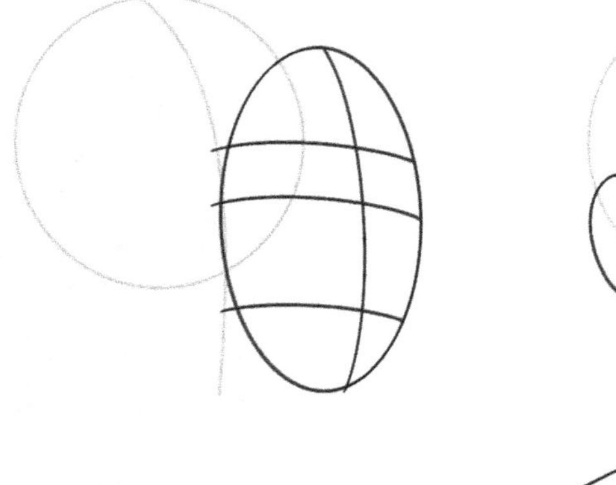

04

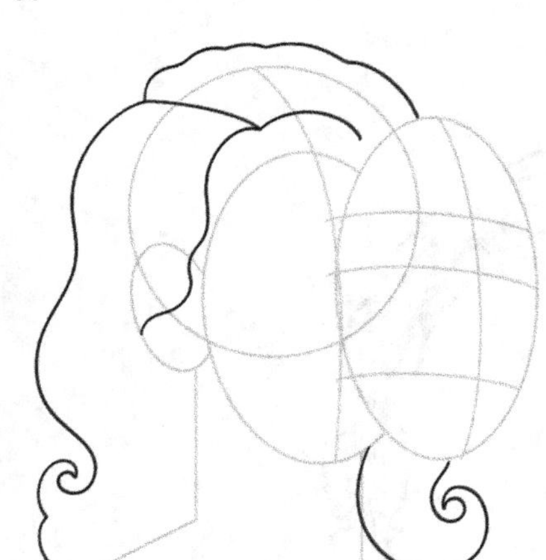

05

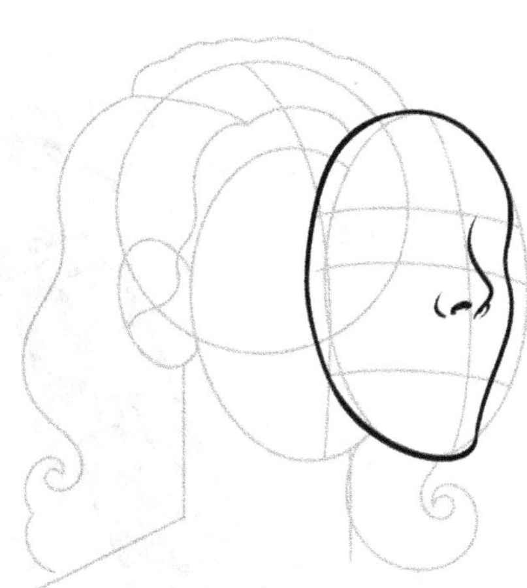

06

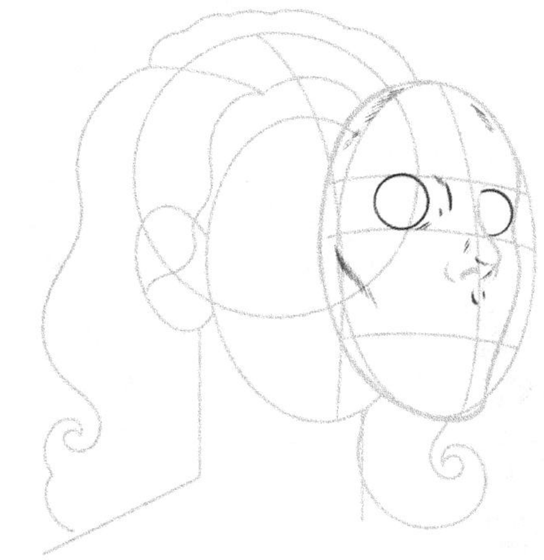

07

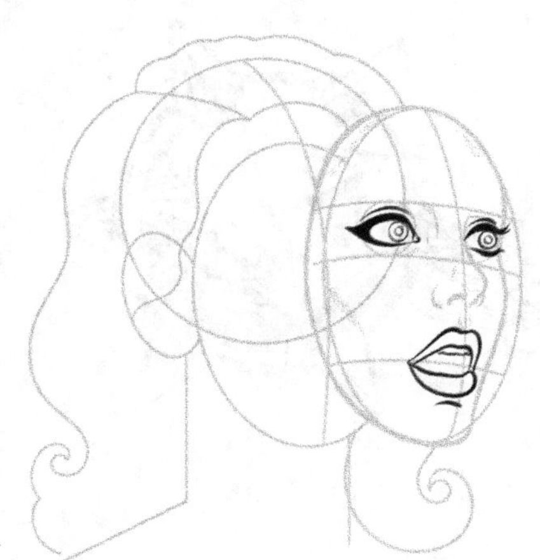

08

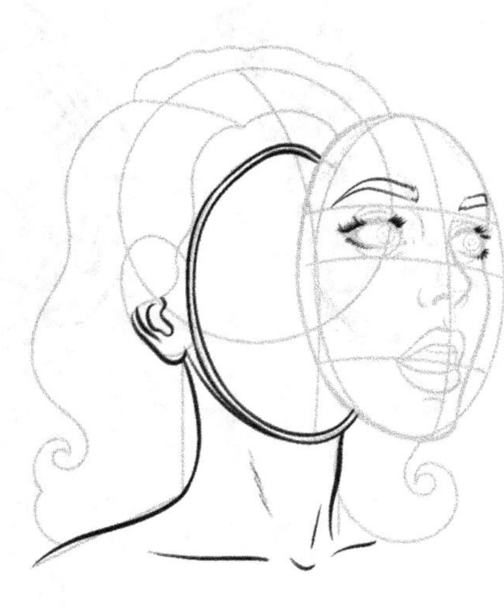

09

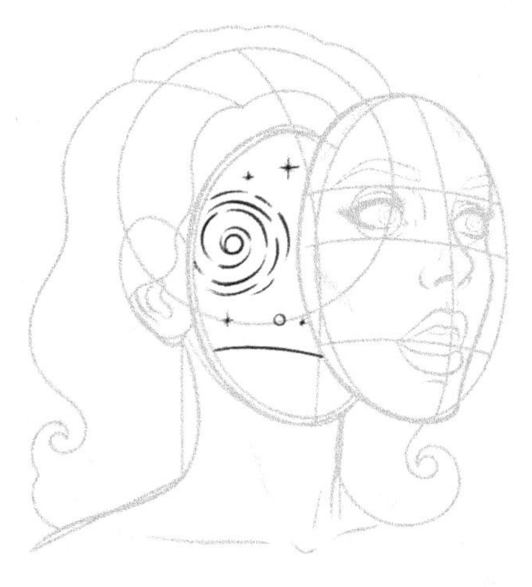

10

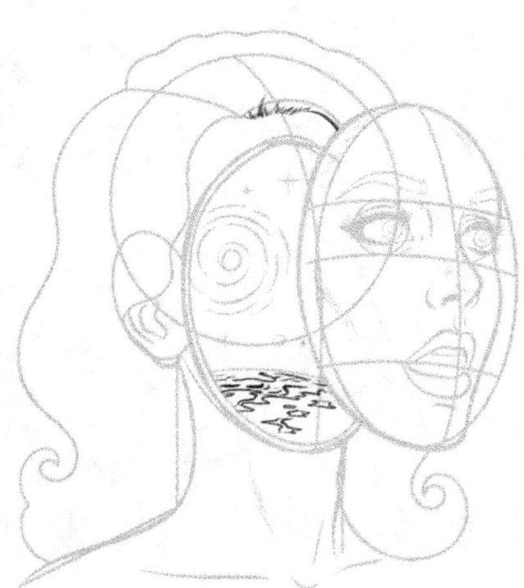

11

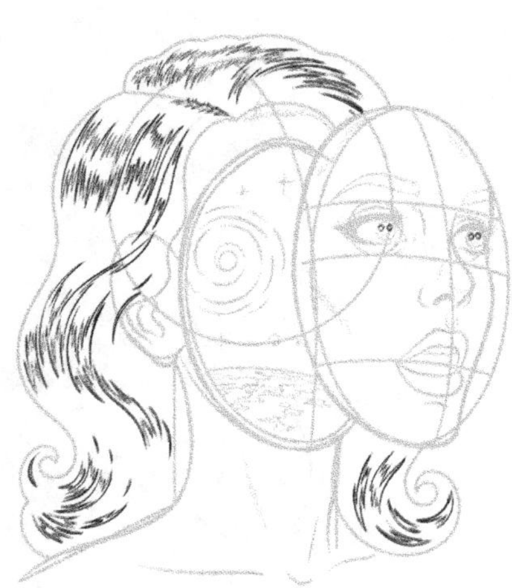

12

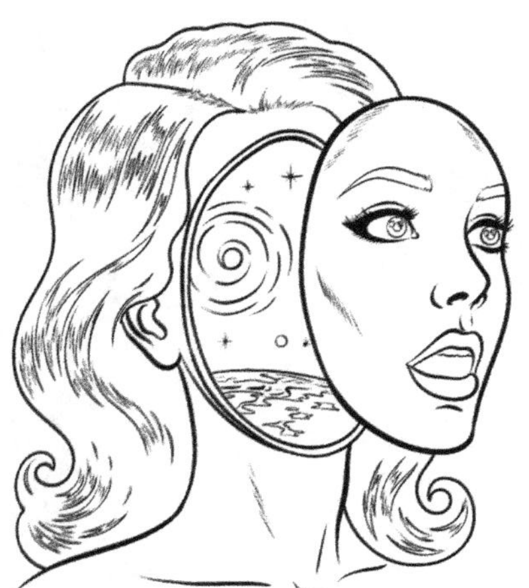

SPIKED FLAIL

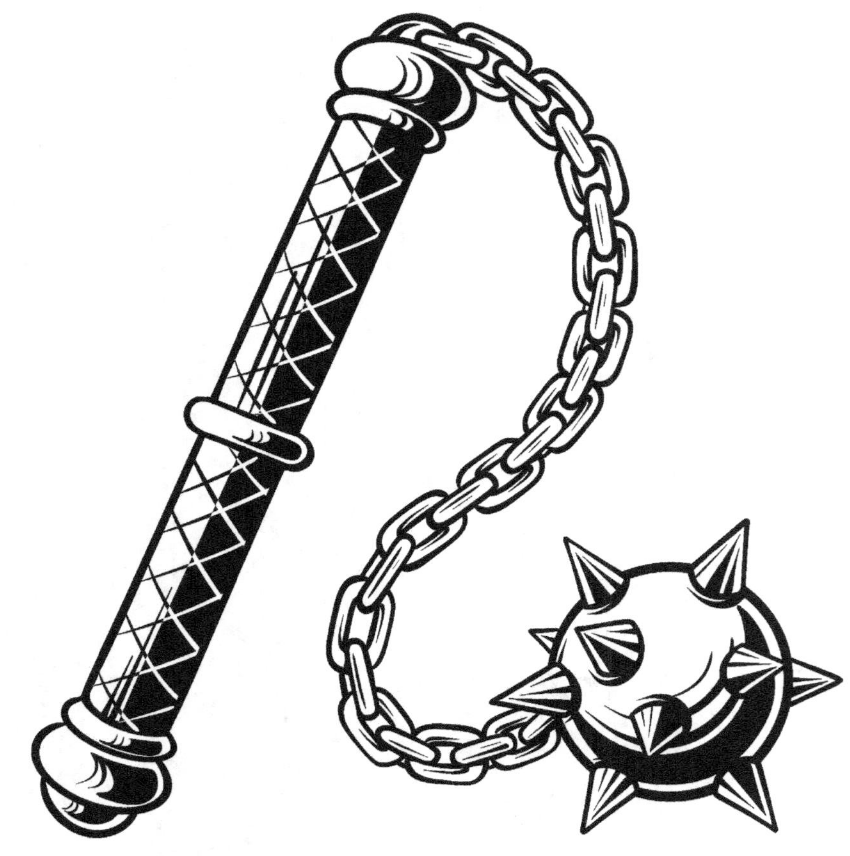

Pro tip:

Use the ball circle as your unit, then make
the handle about 5× that diameter and
run the chain in a loose S that swings
about 2× the ball's diameter away before
attaching the ball.

01   02   03

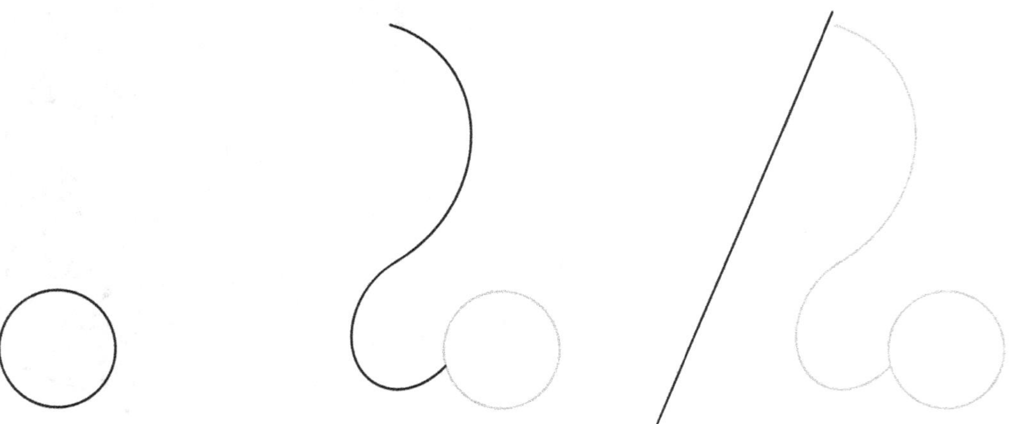

04

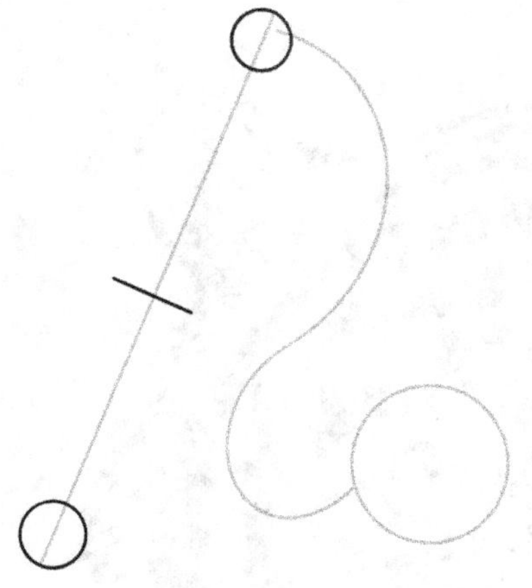

05

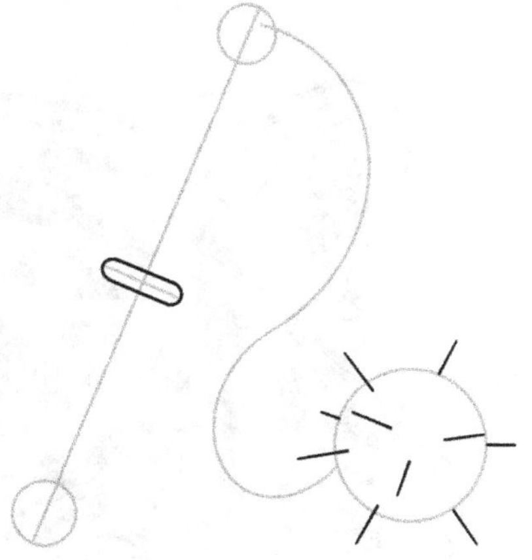

06

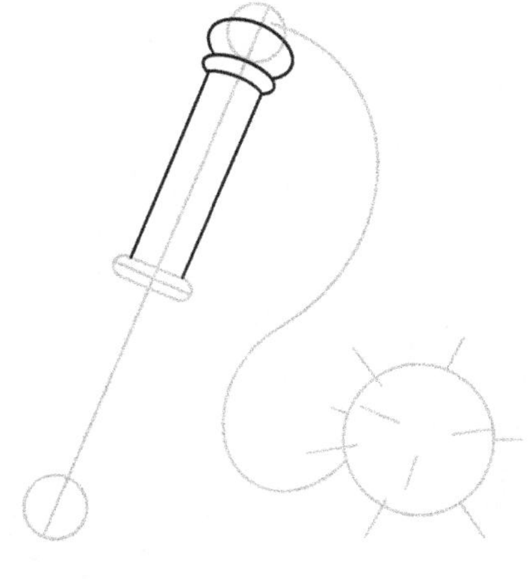

07

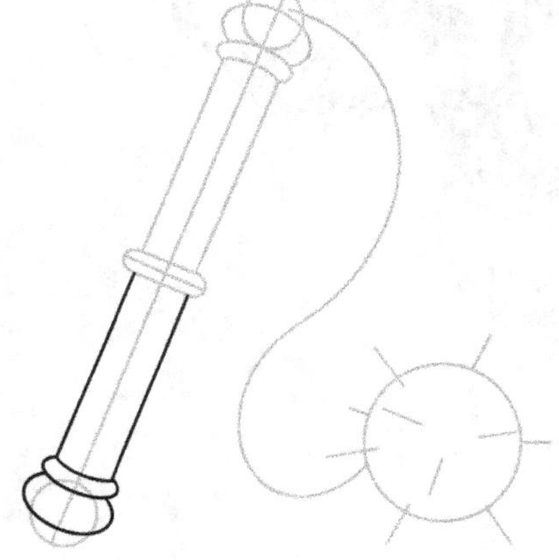

08

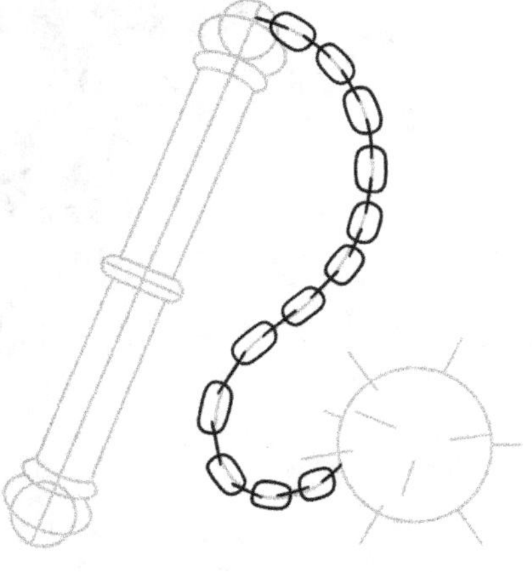

09

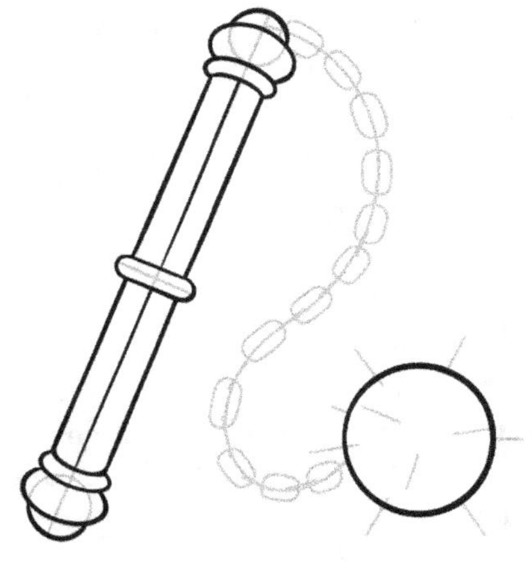

10

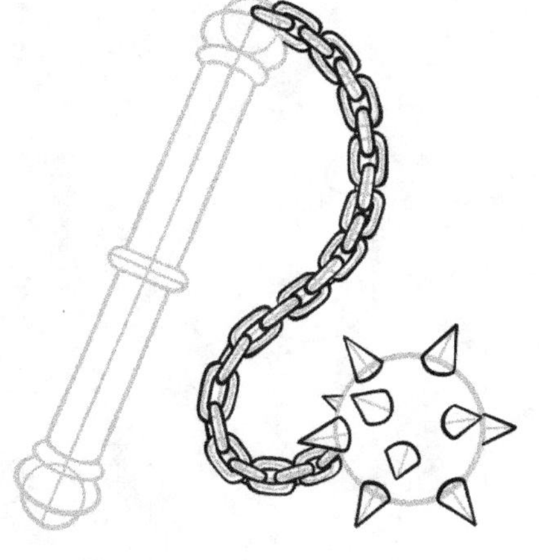

11

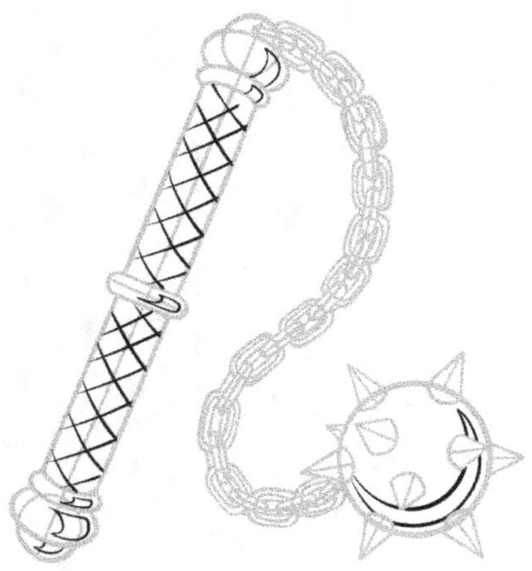

12

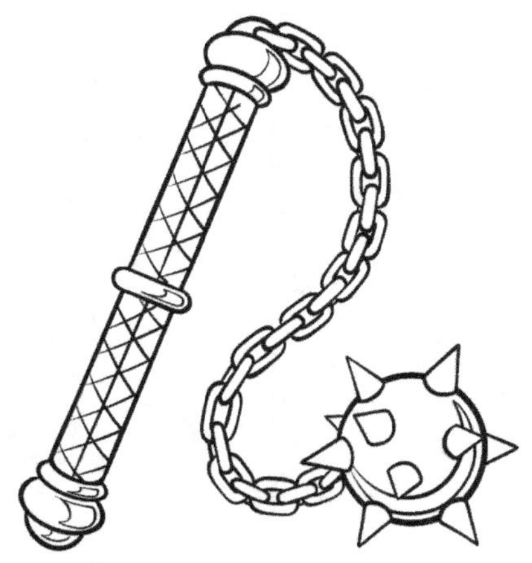

TIGER

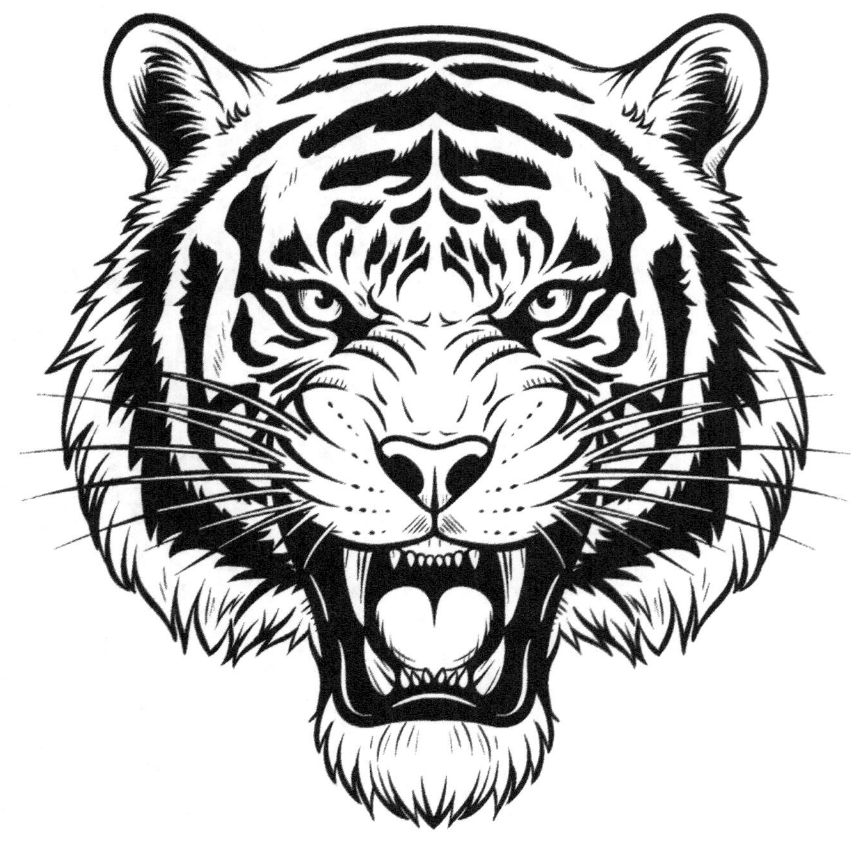

Pro tip:

Place the nose on the centre line, about halfway between the eye line and the bottom of the head circle, then build the muzzle as two cheek ovals each about one third of the circle's width.

01

02

03

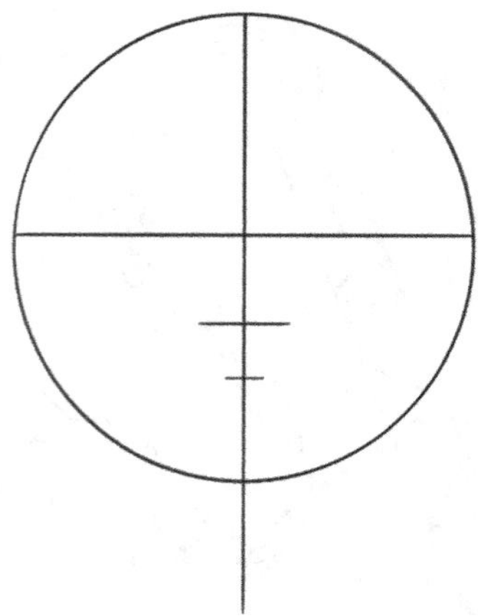

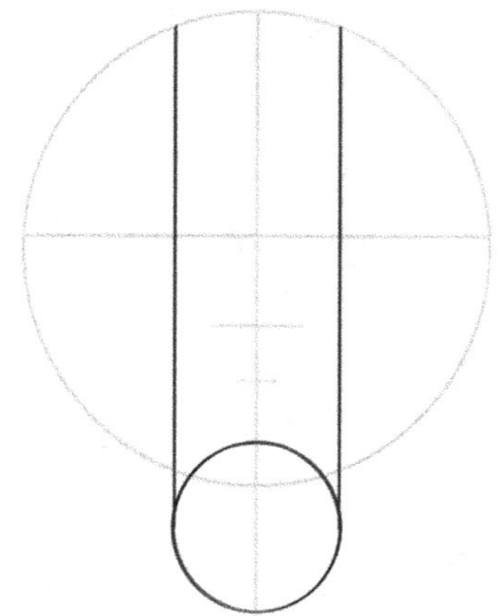

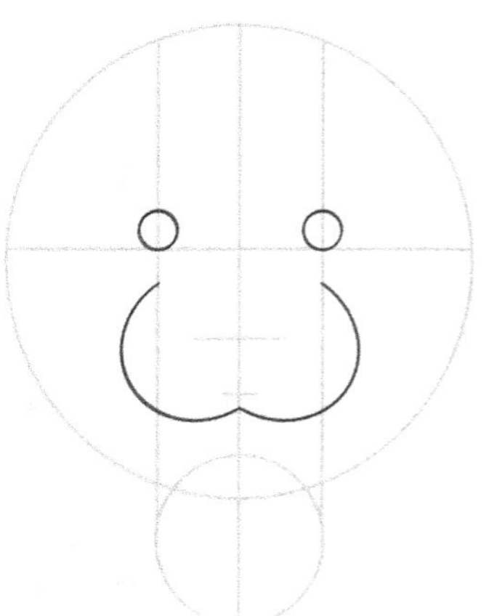

04

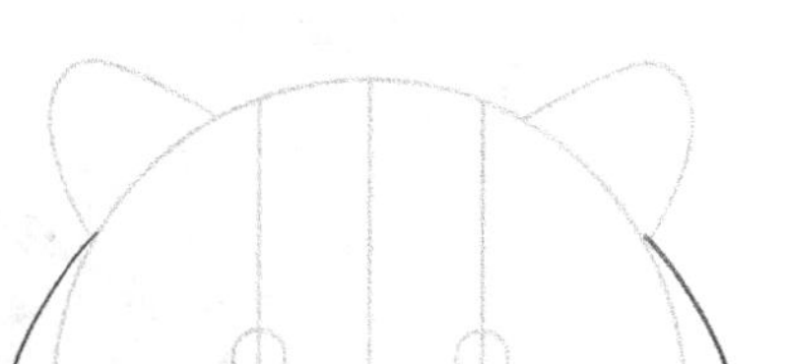

05

06

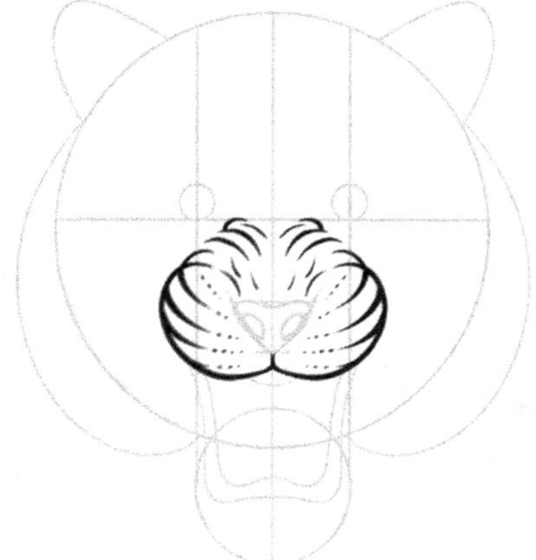

07

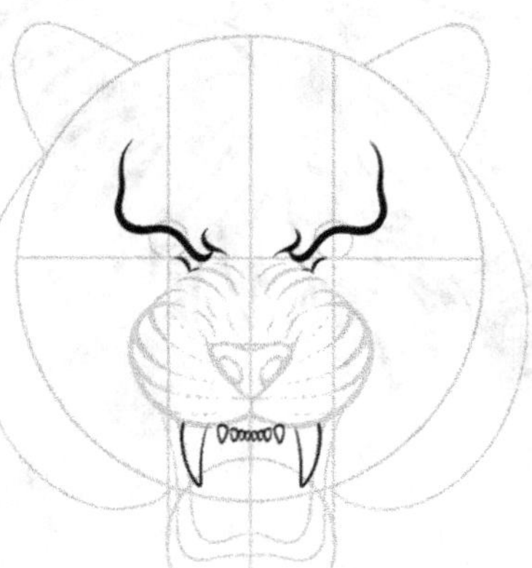

08

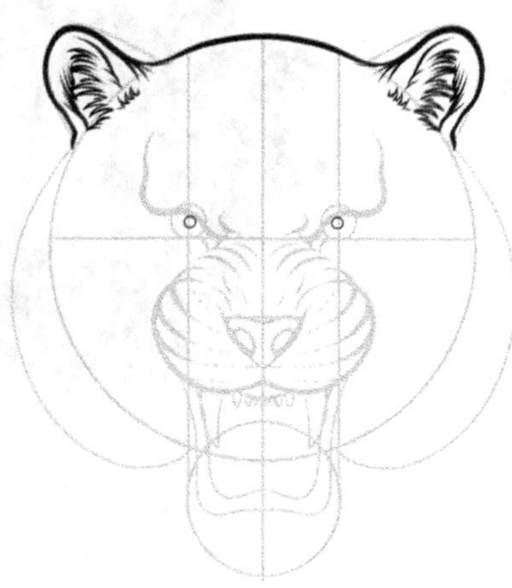

09

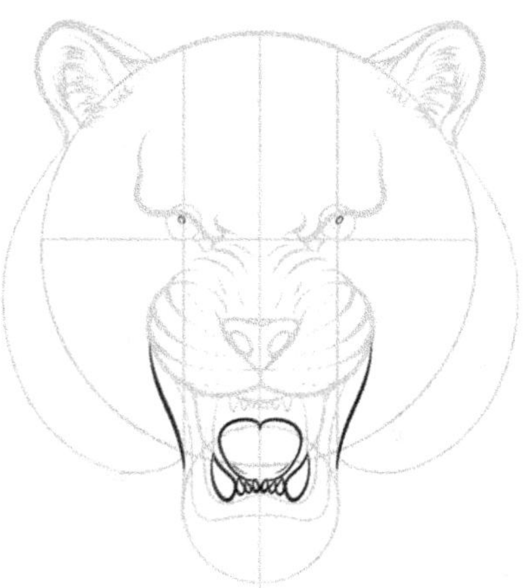

10

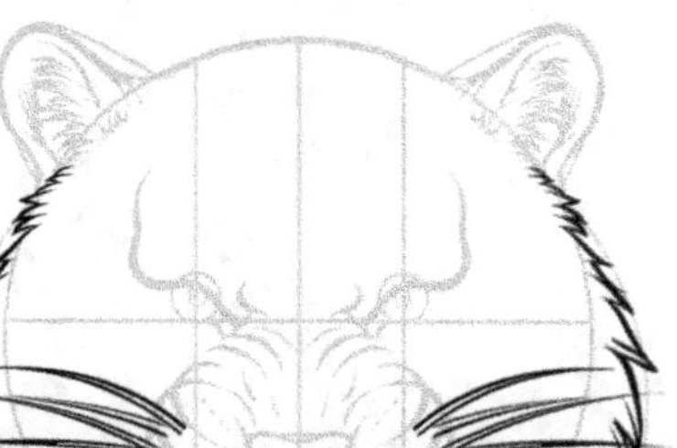

11

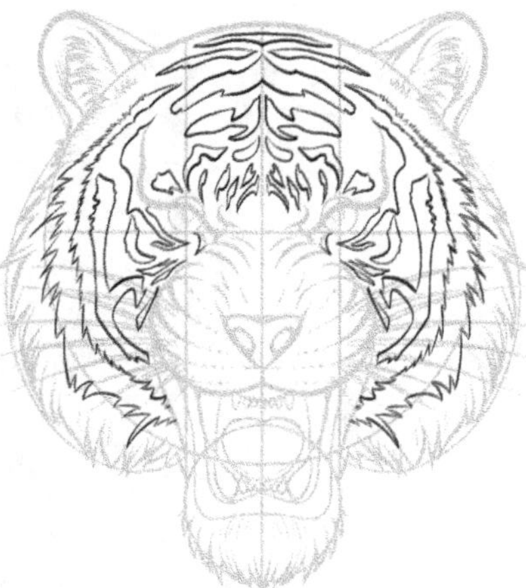

12

VULTURE

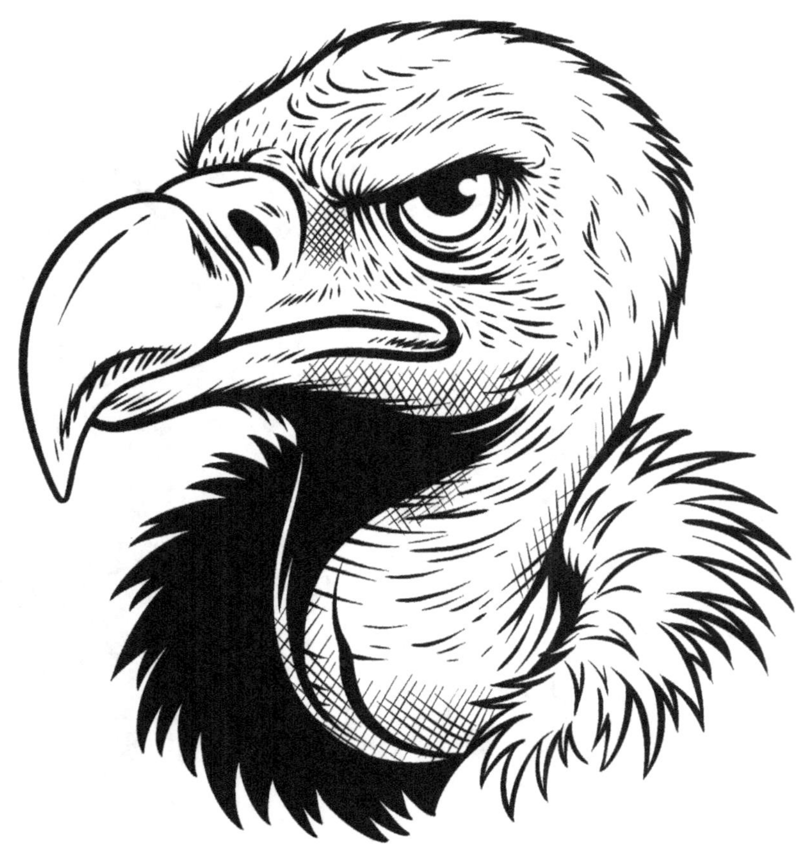

Pro tip:

Use the head circle as your unit, then draw the ruff as two side lobes each about one circle wide, starting around the circle's lower third and meeting under the neck.

01

02

03

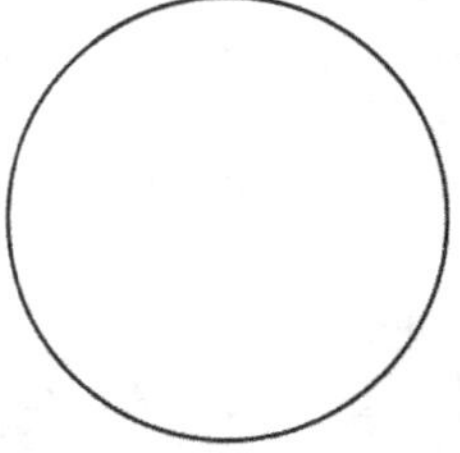

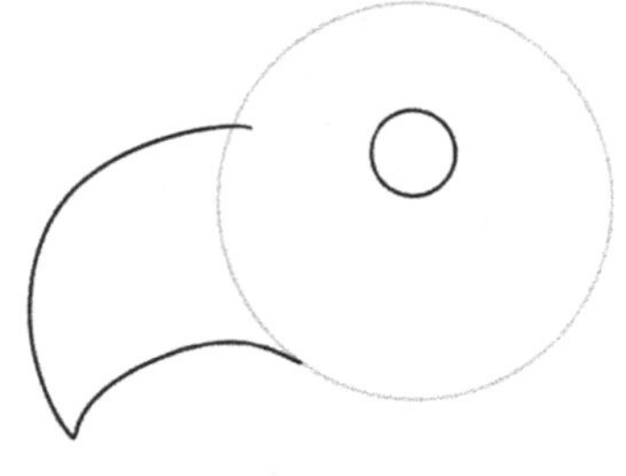

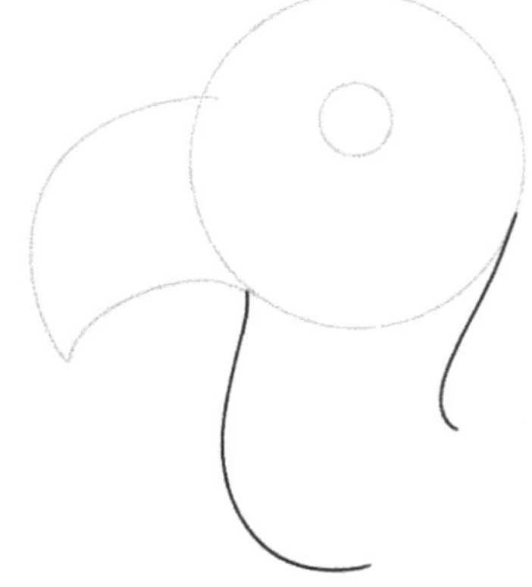

04

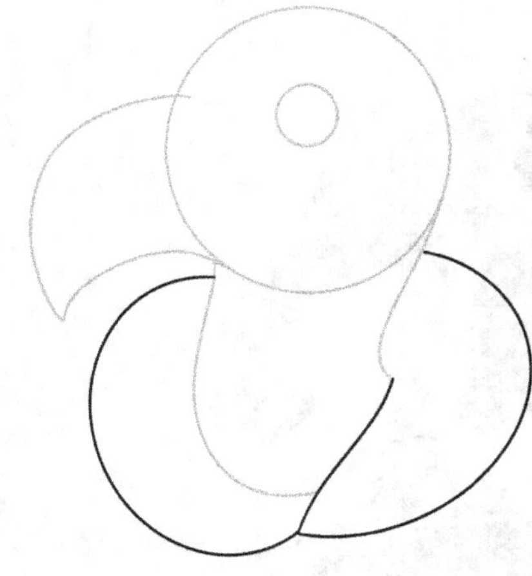

05

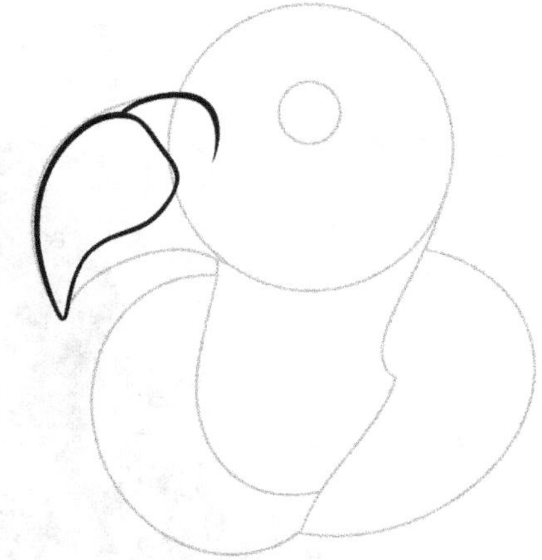

06

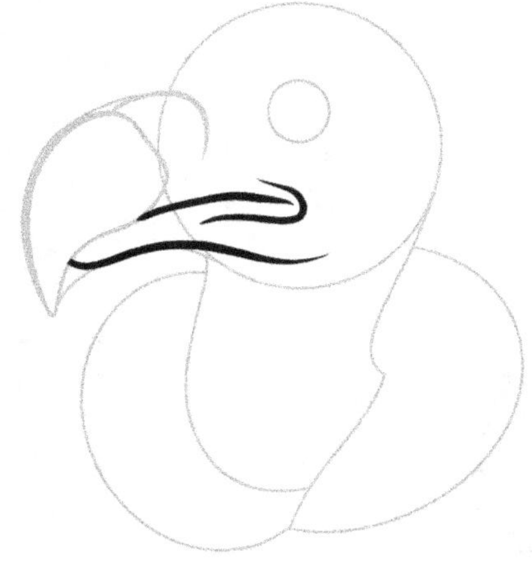

07

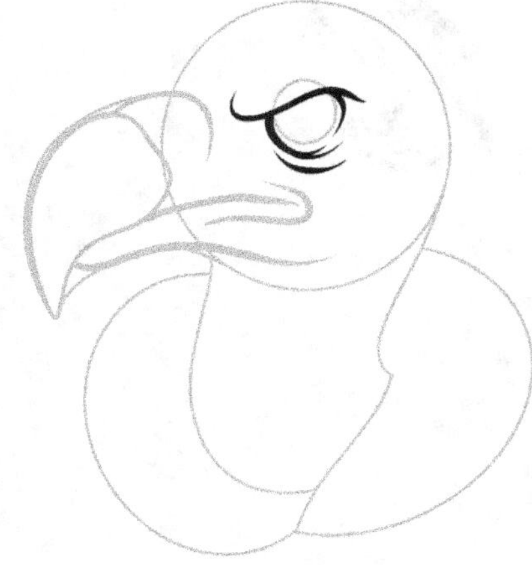

08

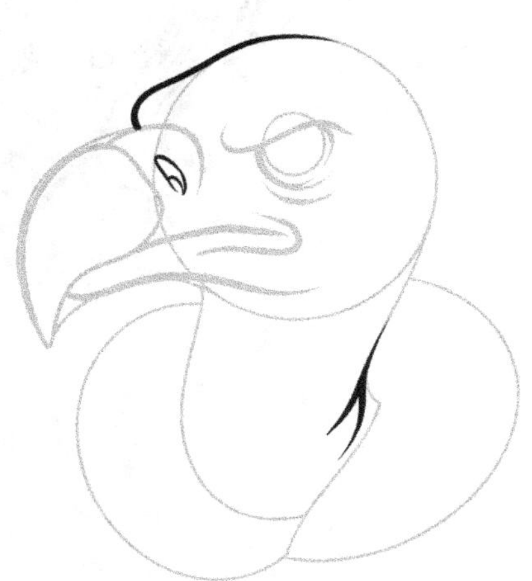

09

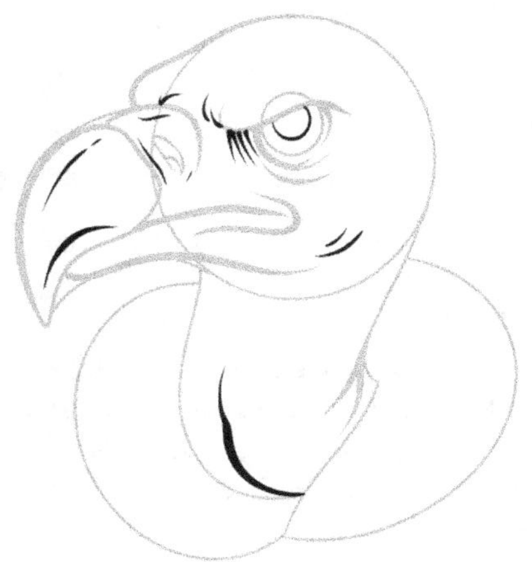

10

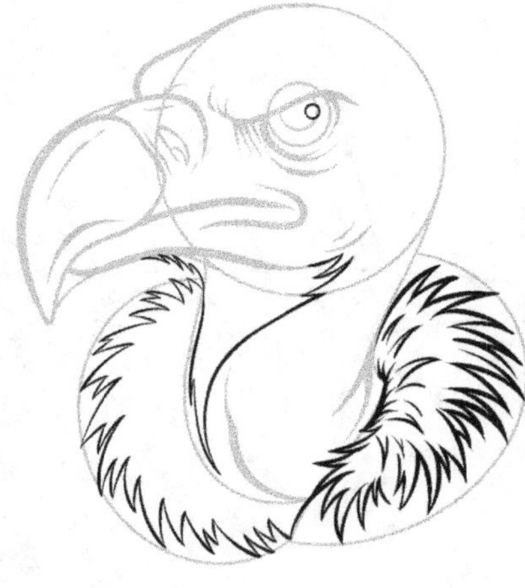

11

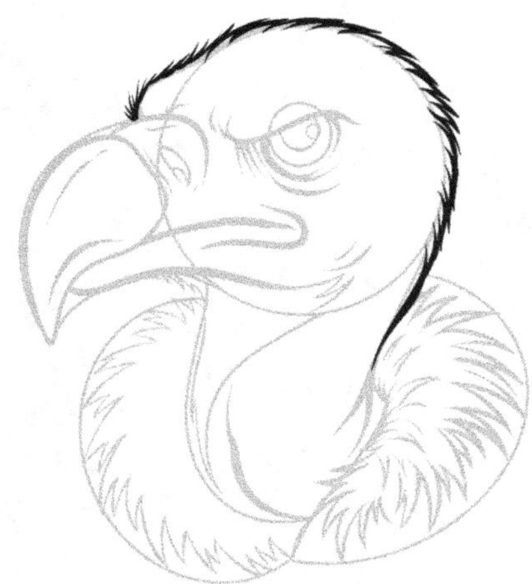

12

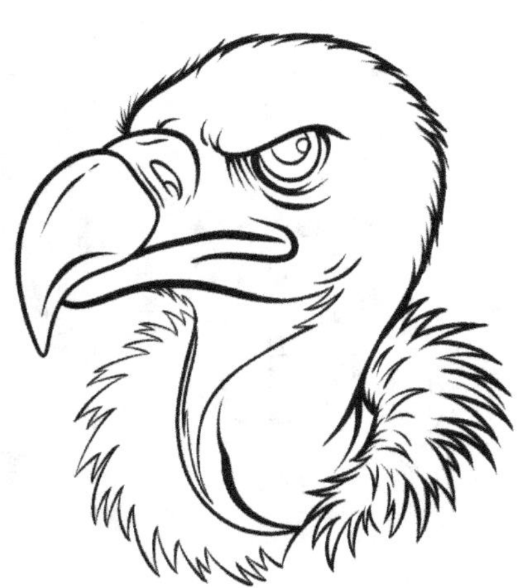

WITCH

Pro tip:

Use the head circle as your unit, then
make the hat brim about 3× the circle's
width and place it across the eye line,
with the crown rising about 1.5× above
the circle.

---

01   **02**   **03**

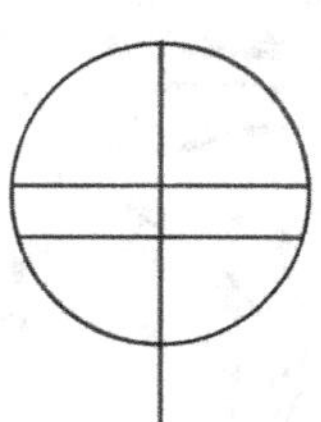

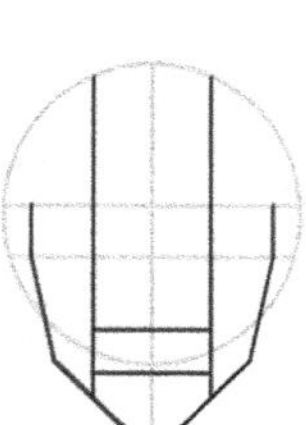

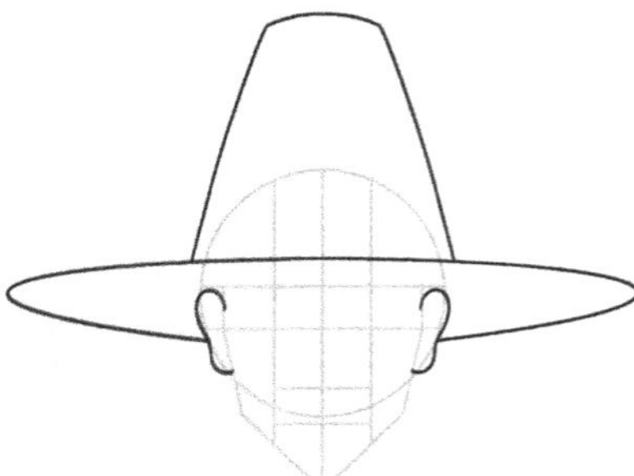

04

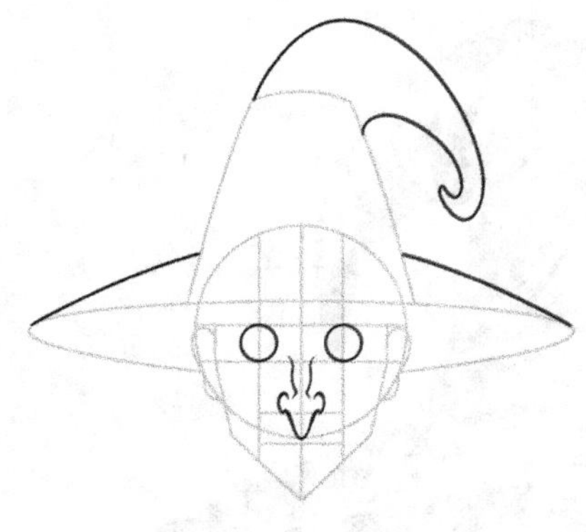

05

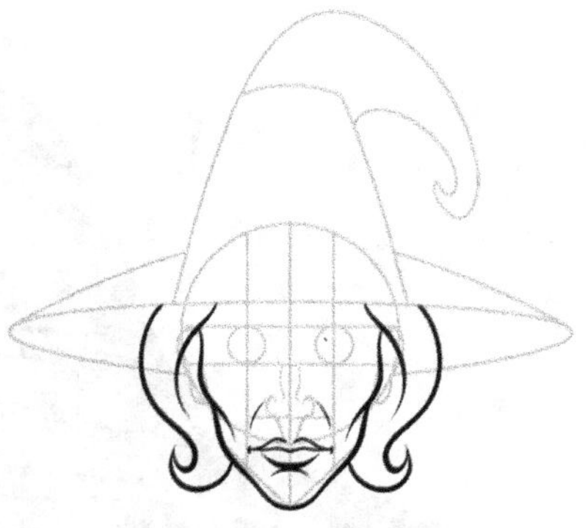

06

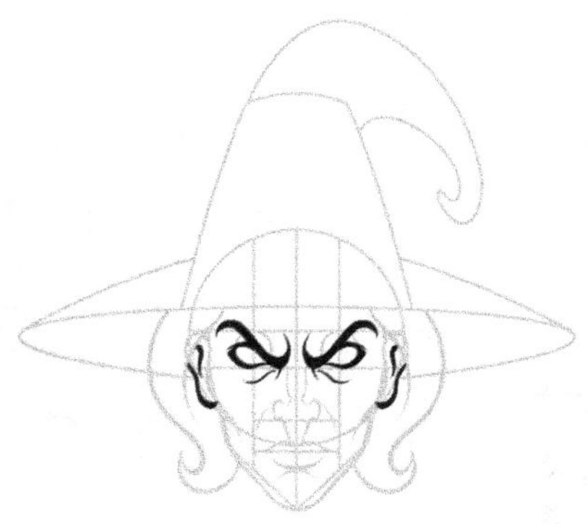

07

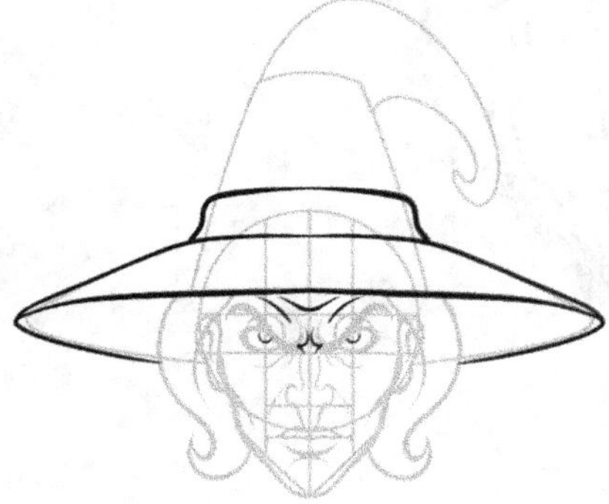

08

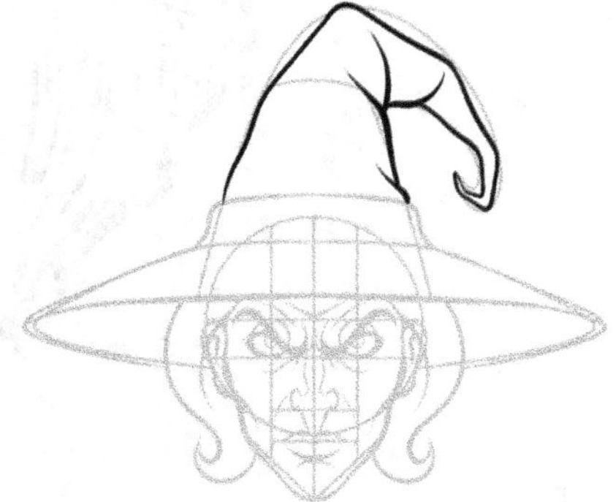

09

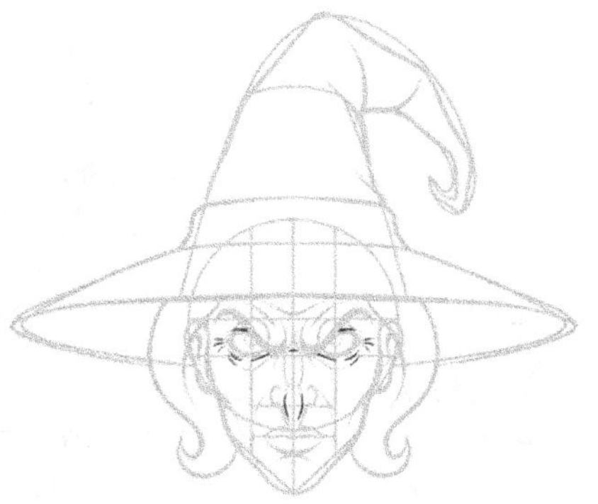

10

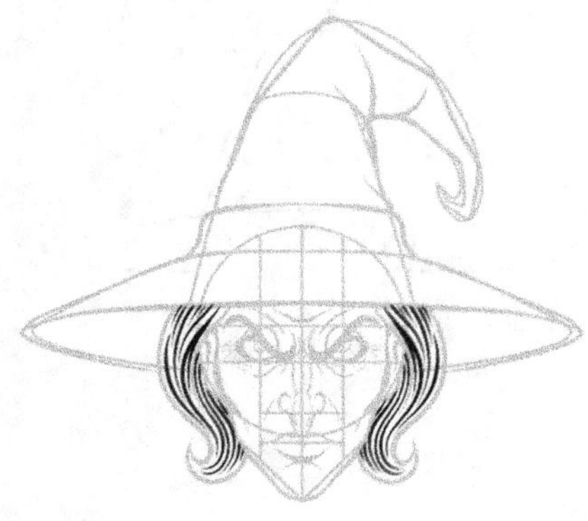

11

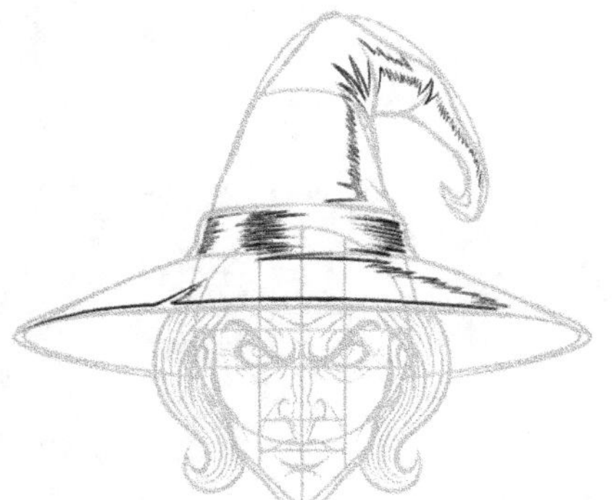

12

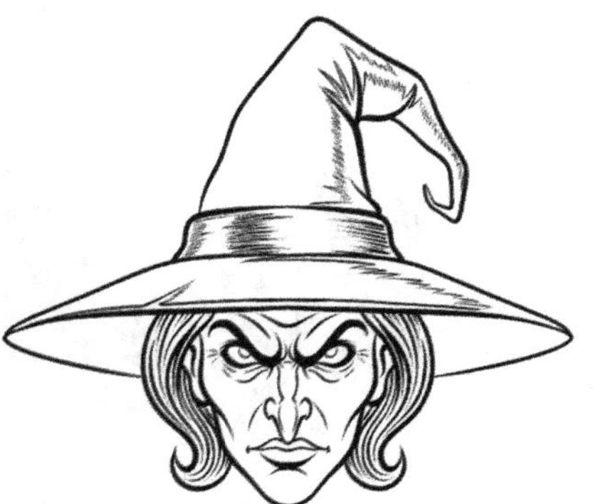

WIZARD

Pro tip:

Use the head circle as your unit, then
make the brim about 3× the circle's width
and lift the crown to about 1.5× the circle
above the top.

01   02   03

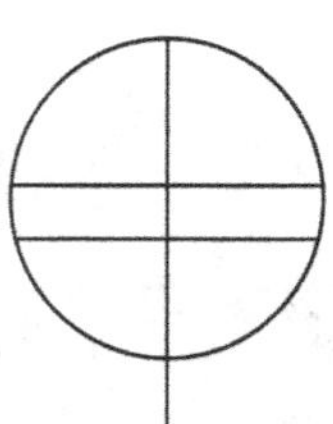

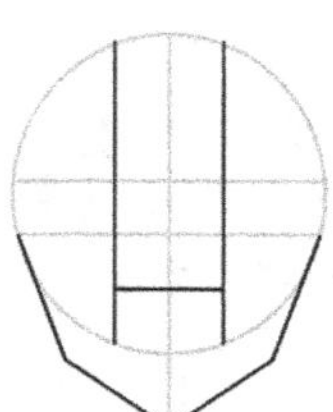

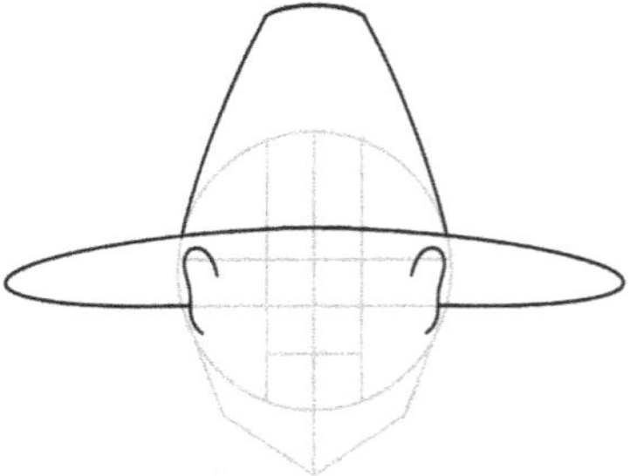

04

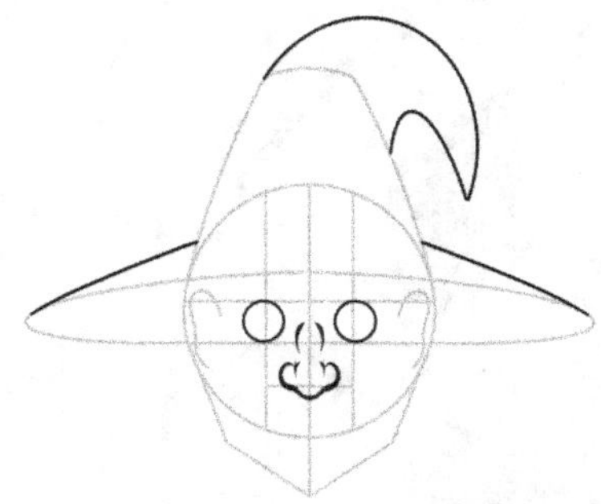

05

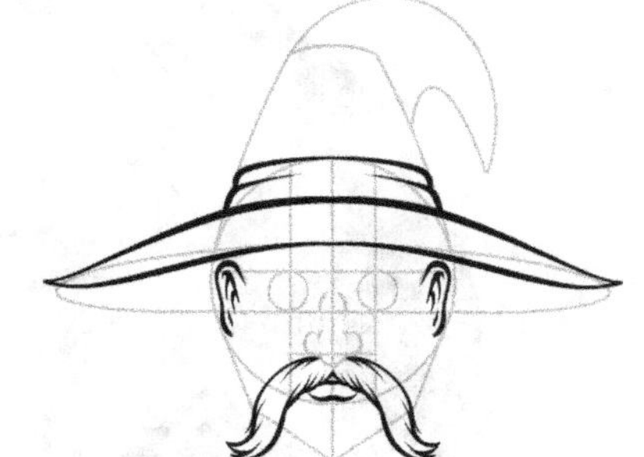

06

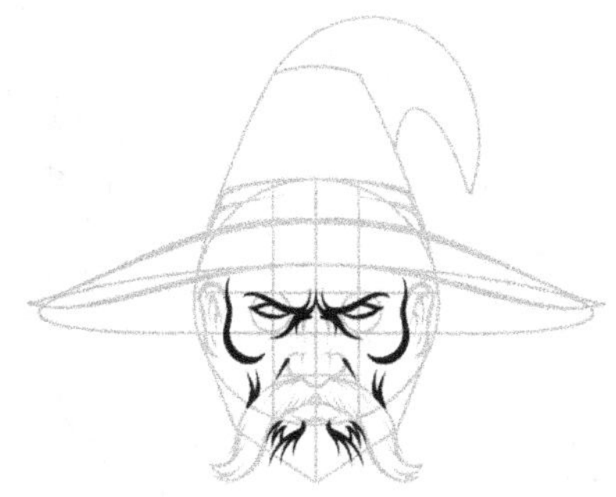

07

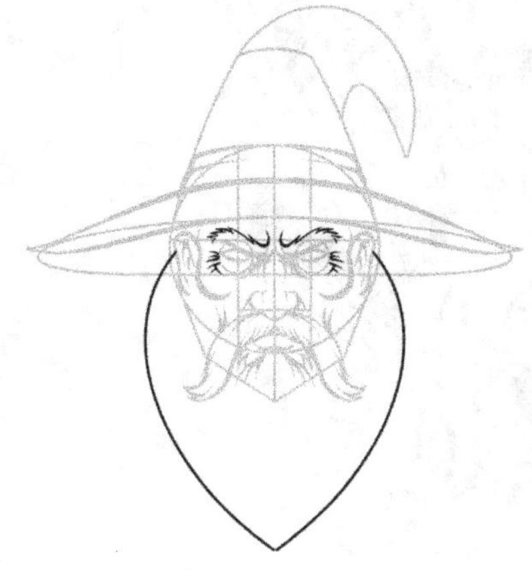

08

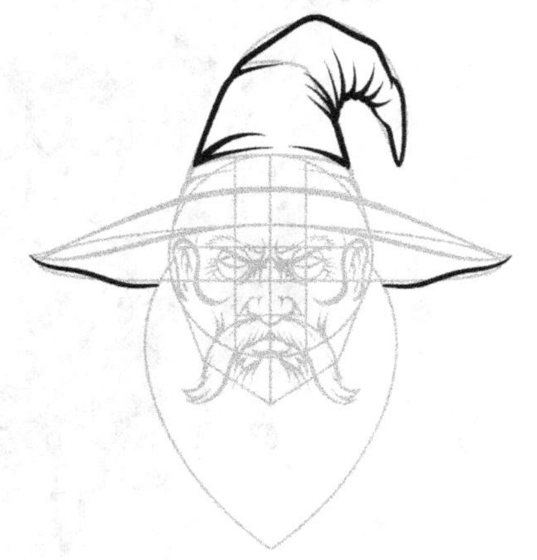

09

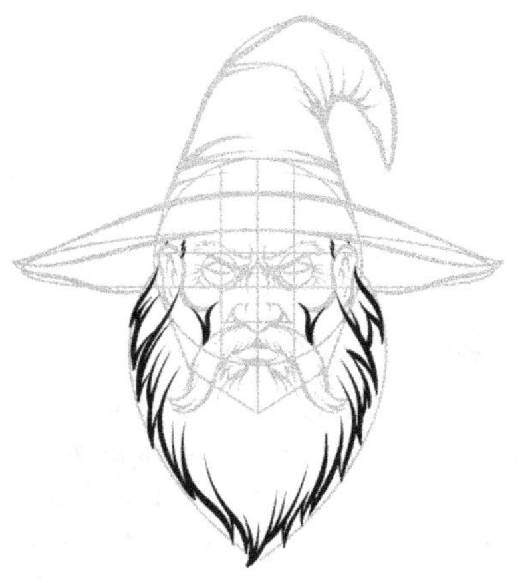

10

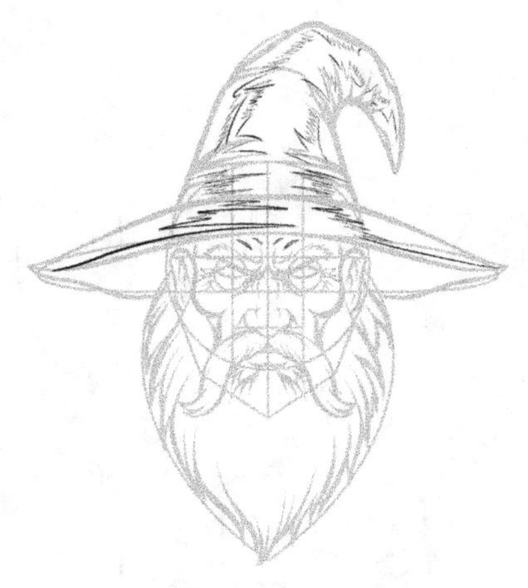

11

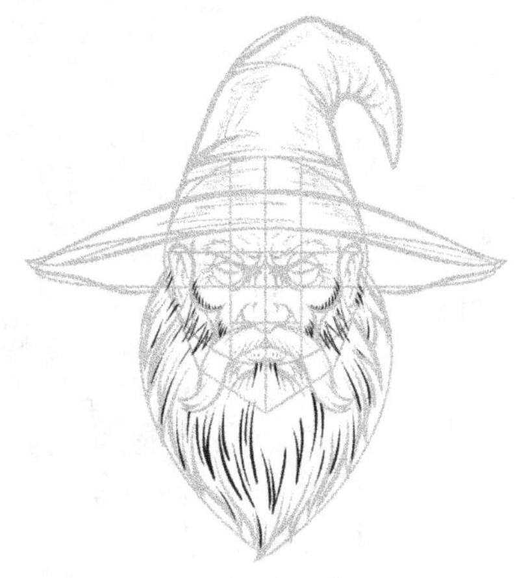

12

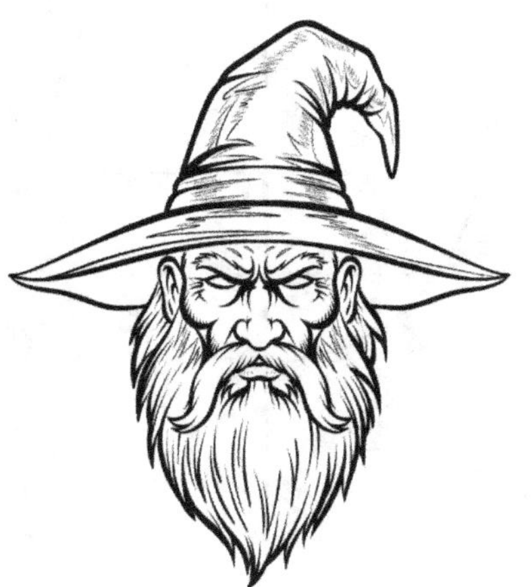

ZOMBIE

Pro tip:

Start with a head circle, then drop the jaw
to about half a circle below it and keep
the chin block roughly one third of the
circle's width for a gaunt zombie shape.

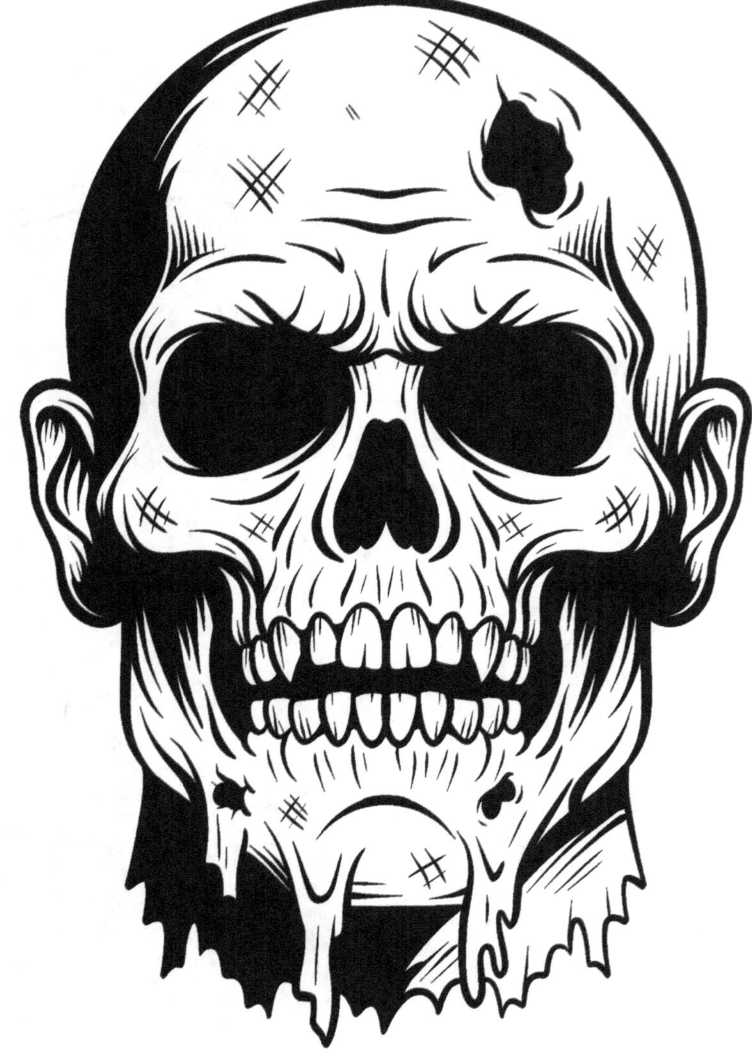

01

02

03

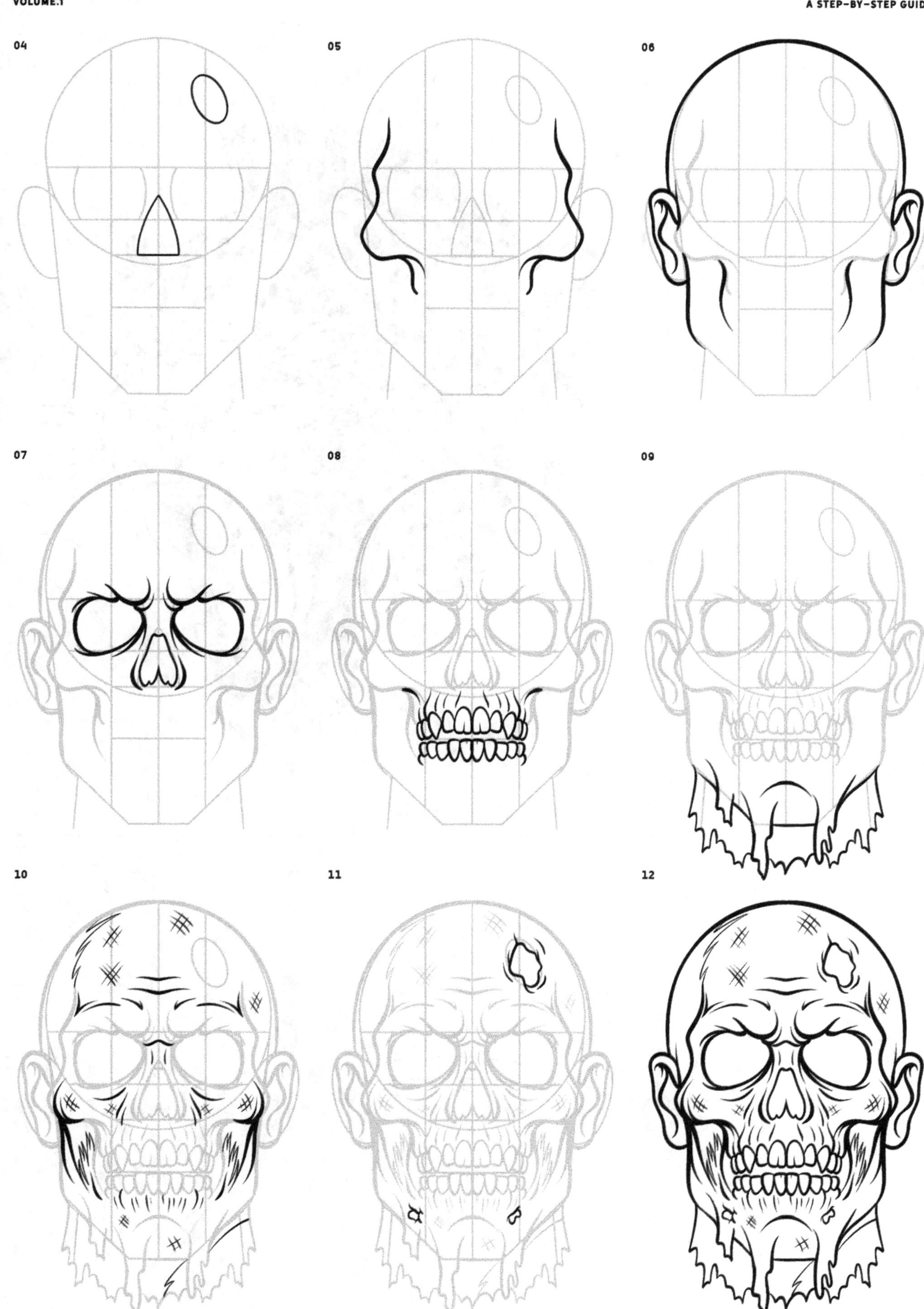
04
05
06
07
08
09
10
11
12
HOW TO DRAW COOL THINGS

PUNK CHEETAH

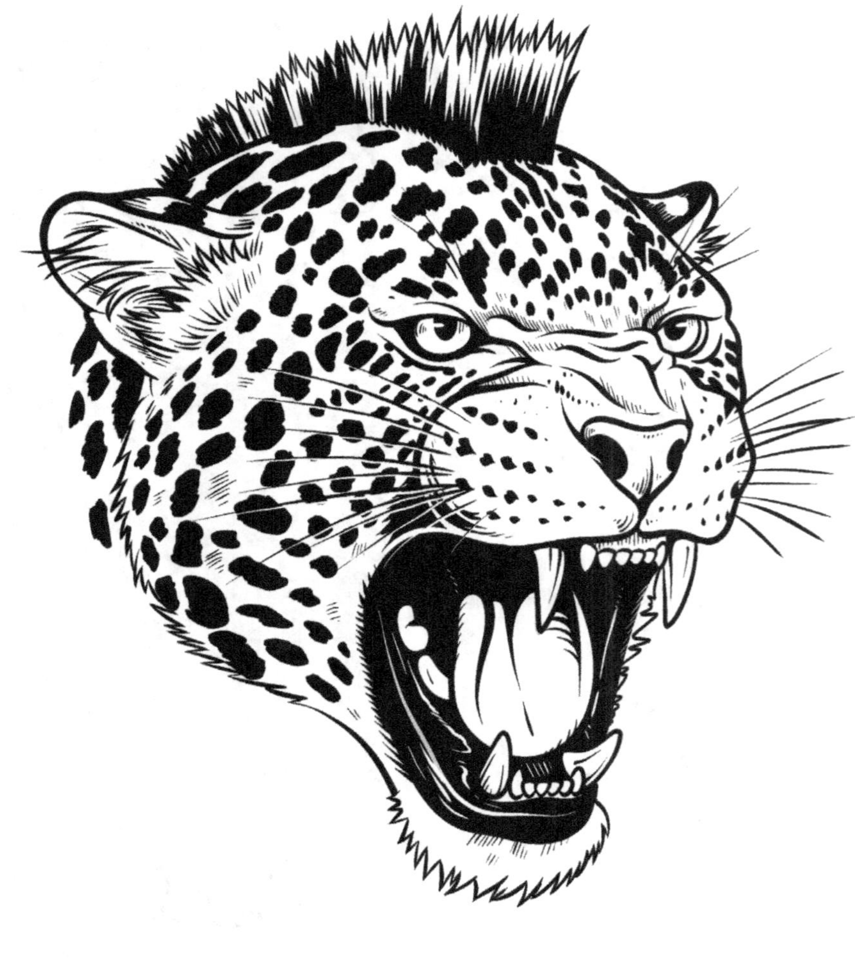

Pro tip:

Use the head circle as your unit, then place the muzzle oval about half a circle wide, pushed to the front edge with its tip reaching roughly one quarter of a circle past the outline.

01

02

03

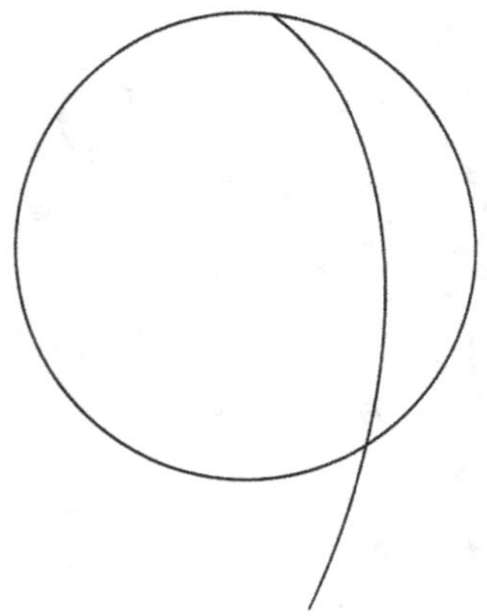

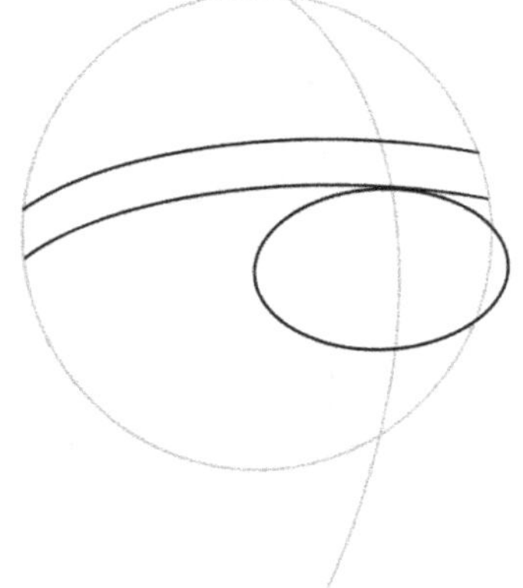

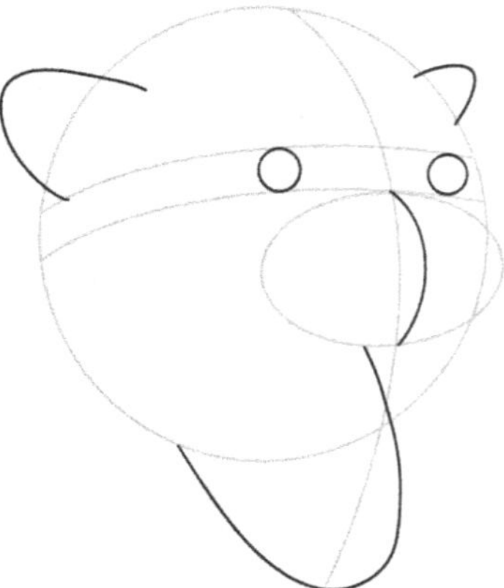

04

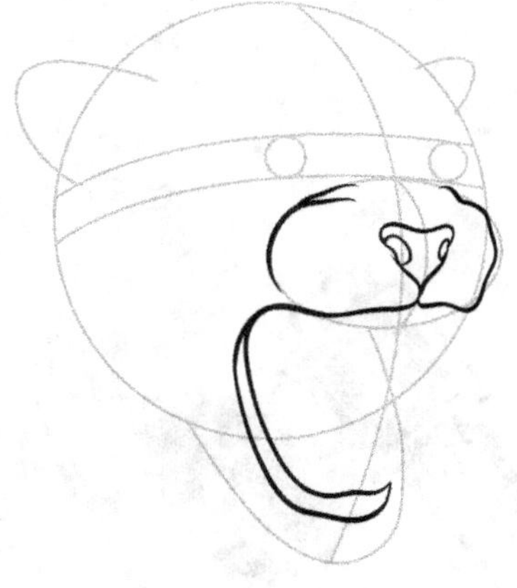

05

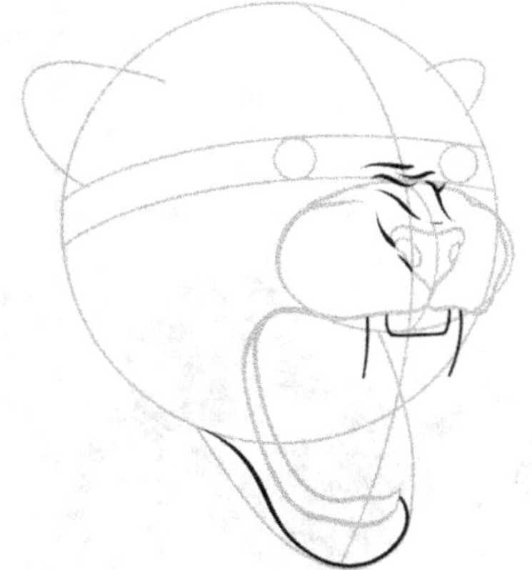

06

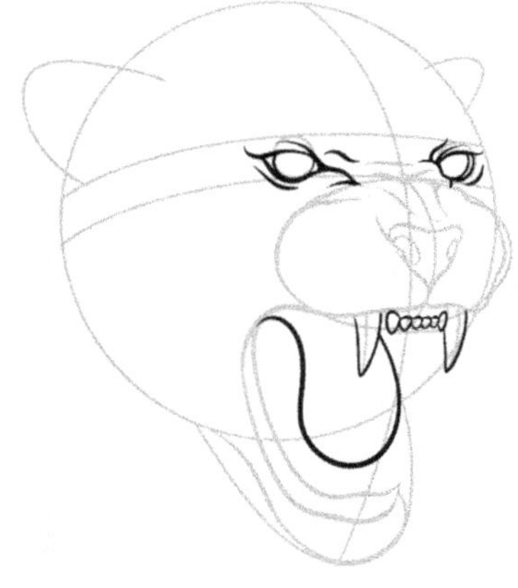

07

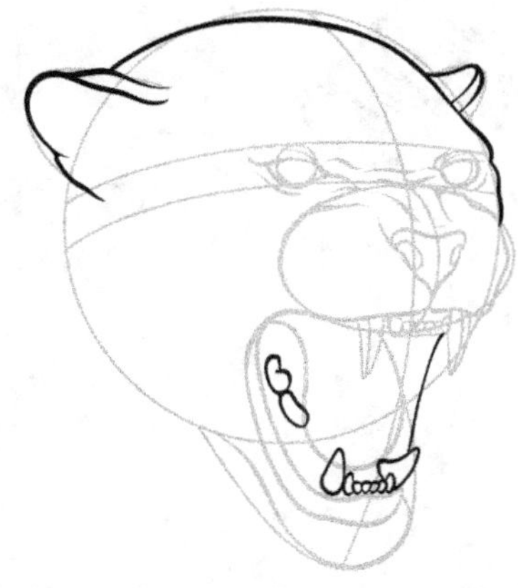

08

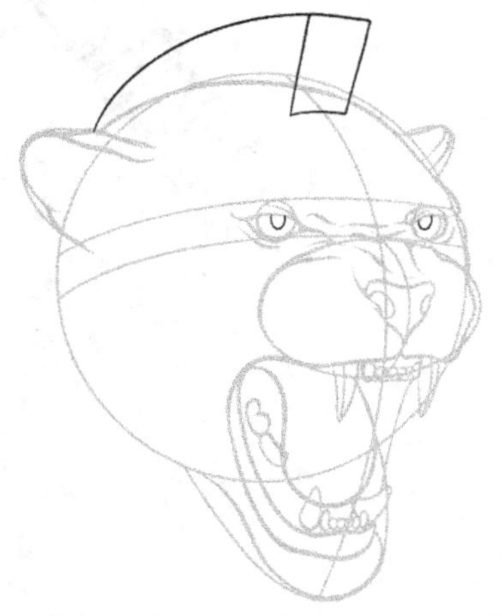

09

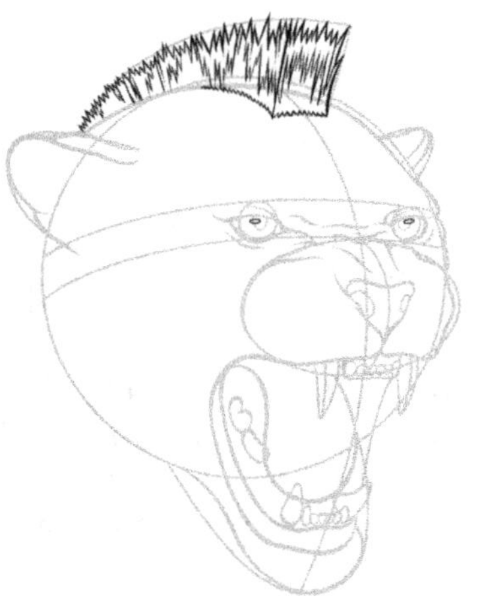

10

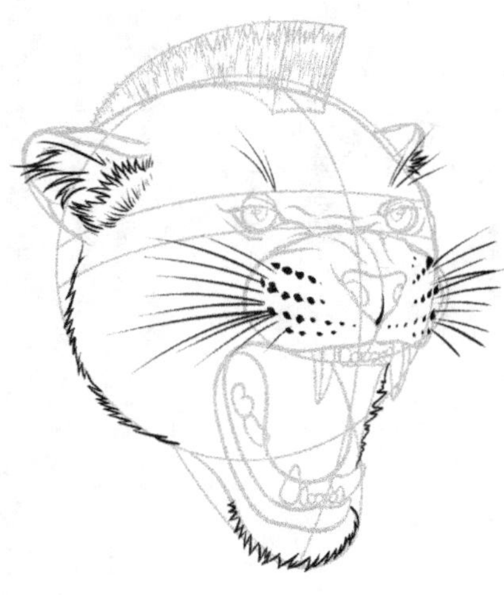

11

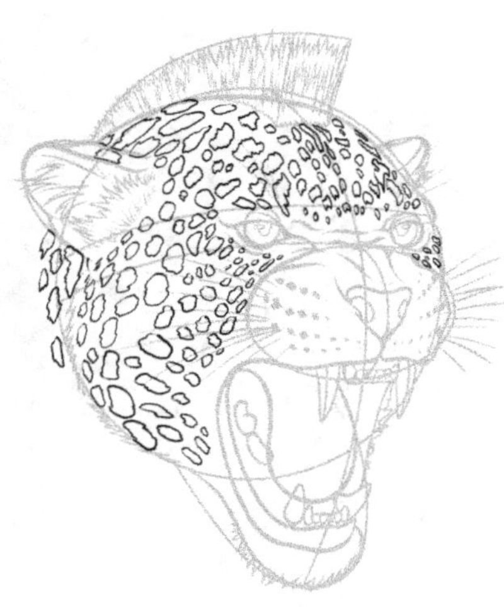

12

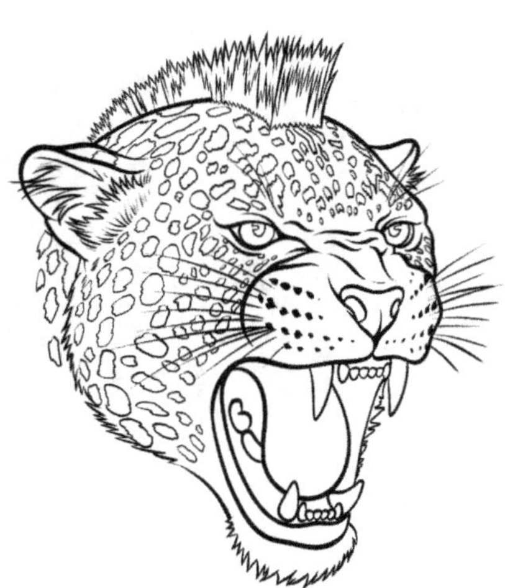

CROSSED AXES

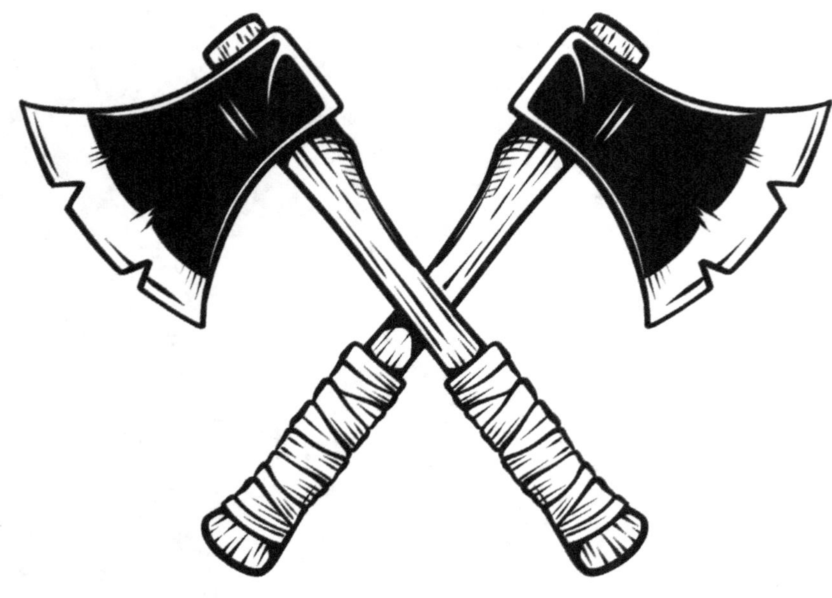

Pro tip:

Draw a clean X first, then build both
axe handles to the same length and
thickness, keeping the crossing point
centred so the heads sit evenly on top.

01

02

03

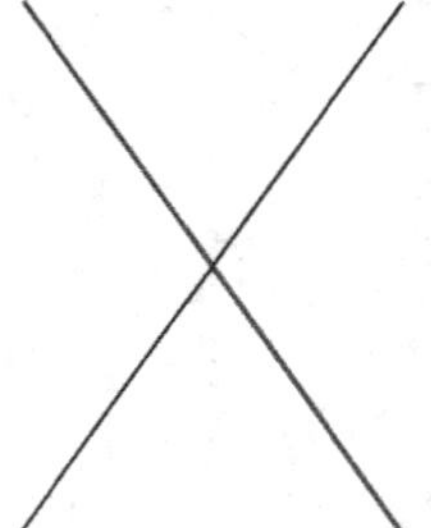

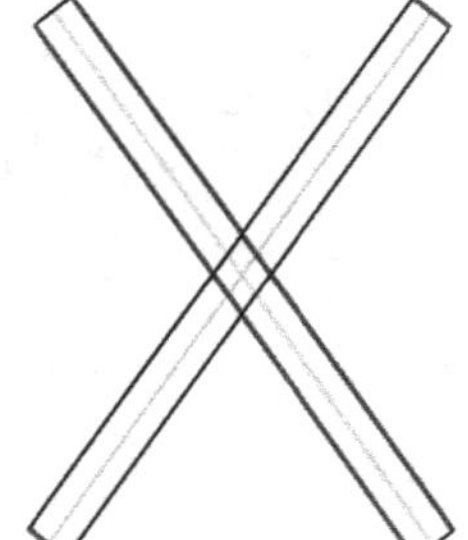

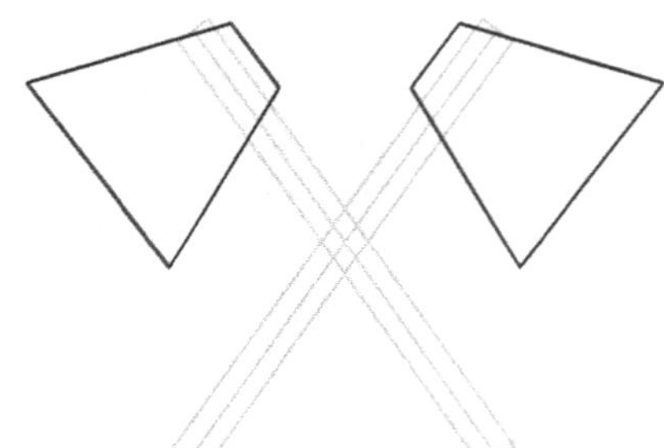

04   05   06

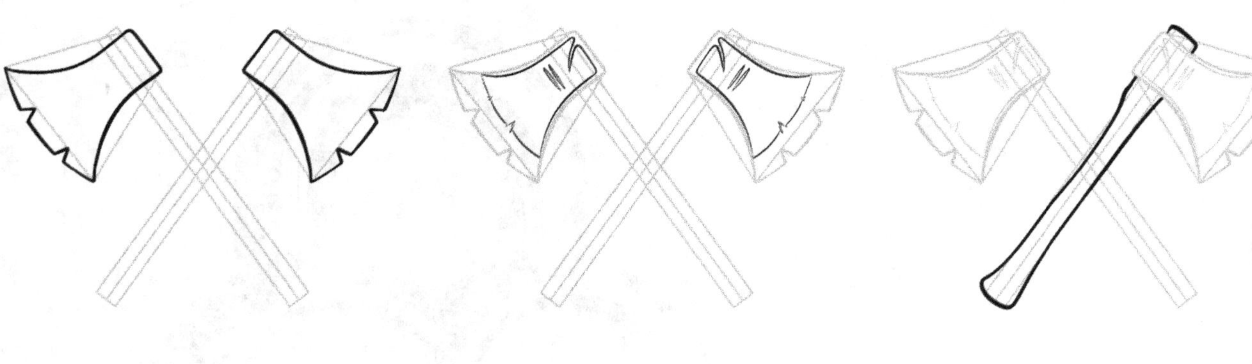

07   08   09

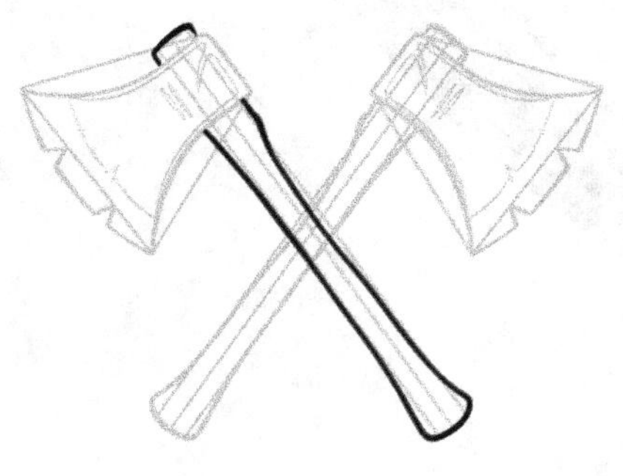
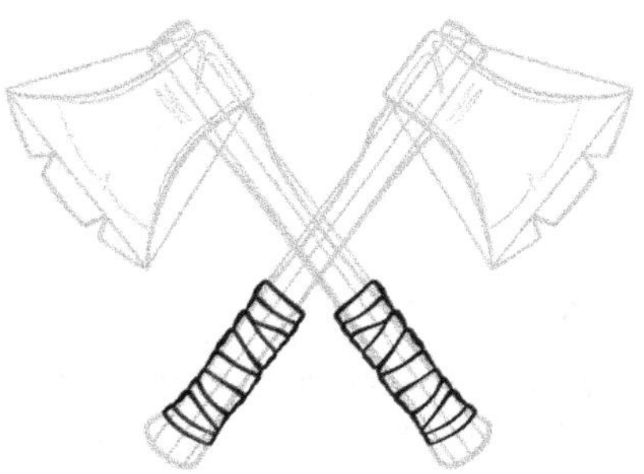

10   11   12

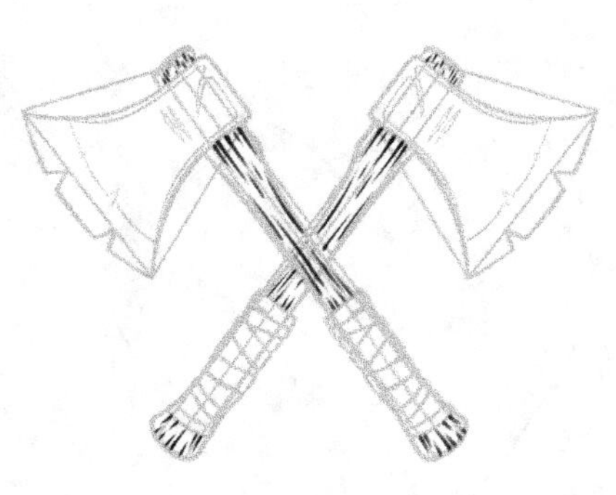
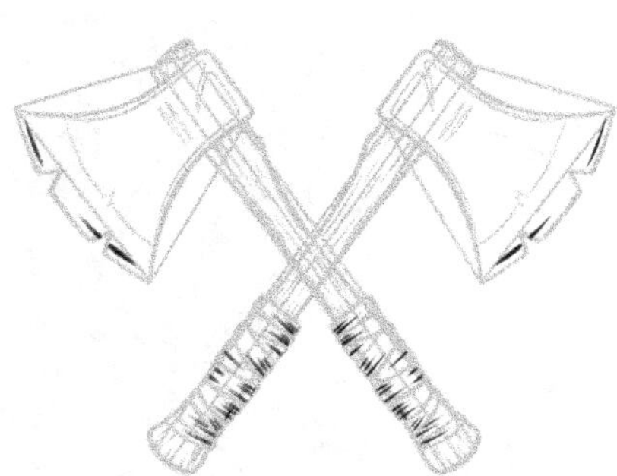
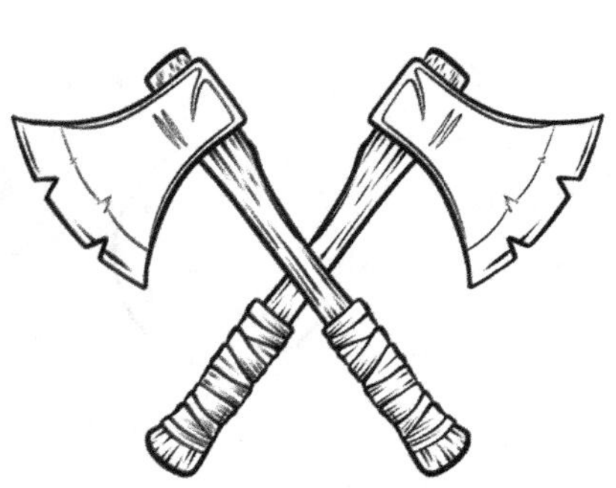

HEAERT LOCKET

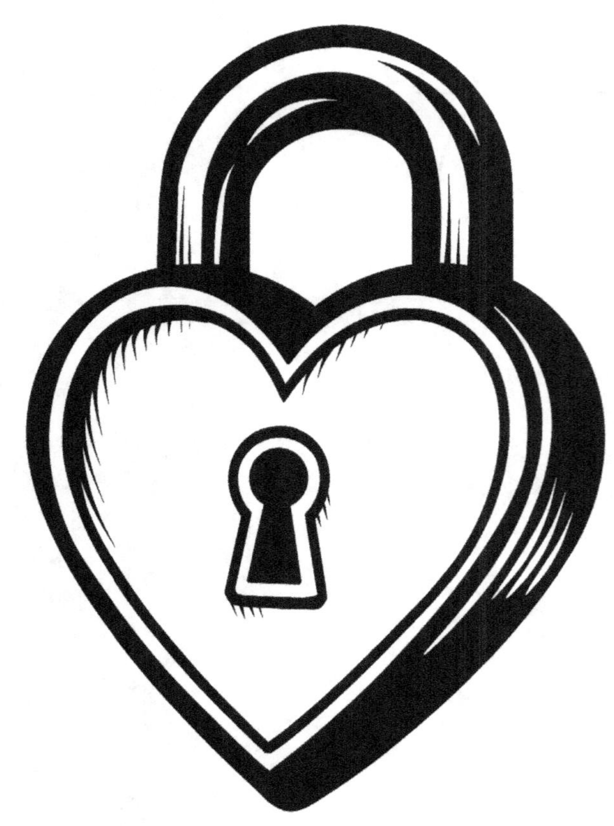

Pro tip:

Start with two equal circles side-by-side, then pull the sides down to a point about one circle height below, keeping the heart symmetrical on the join.

01

02

03

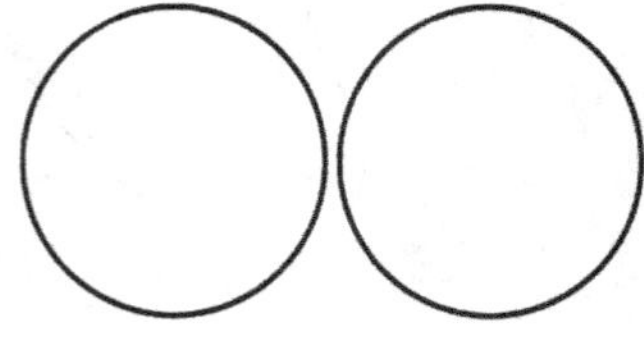

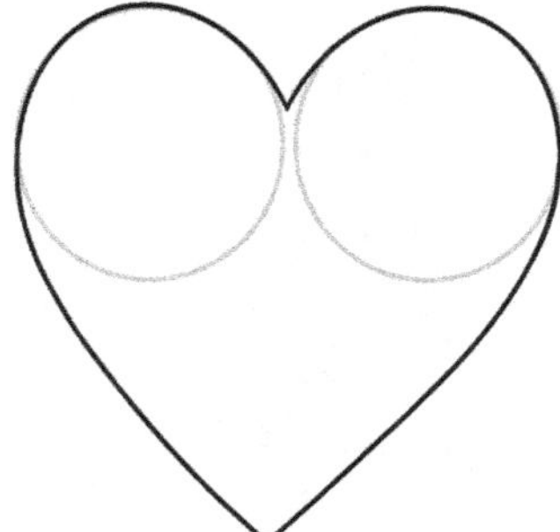

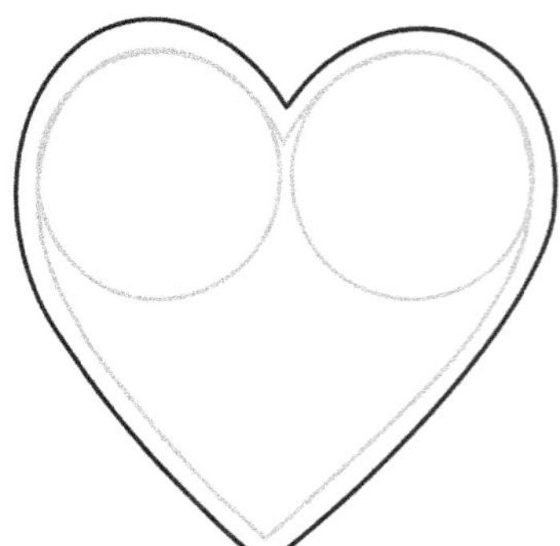

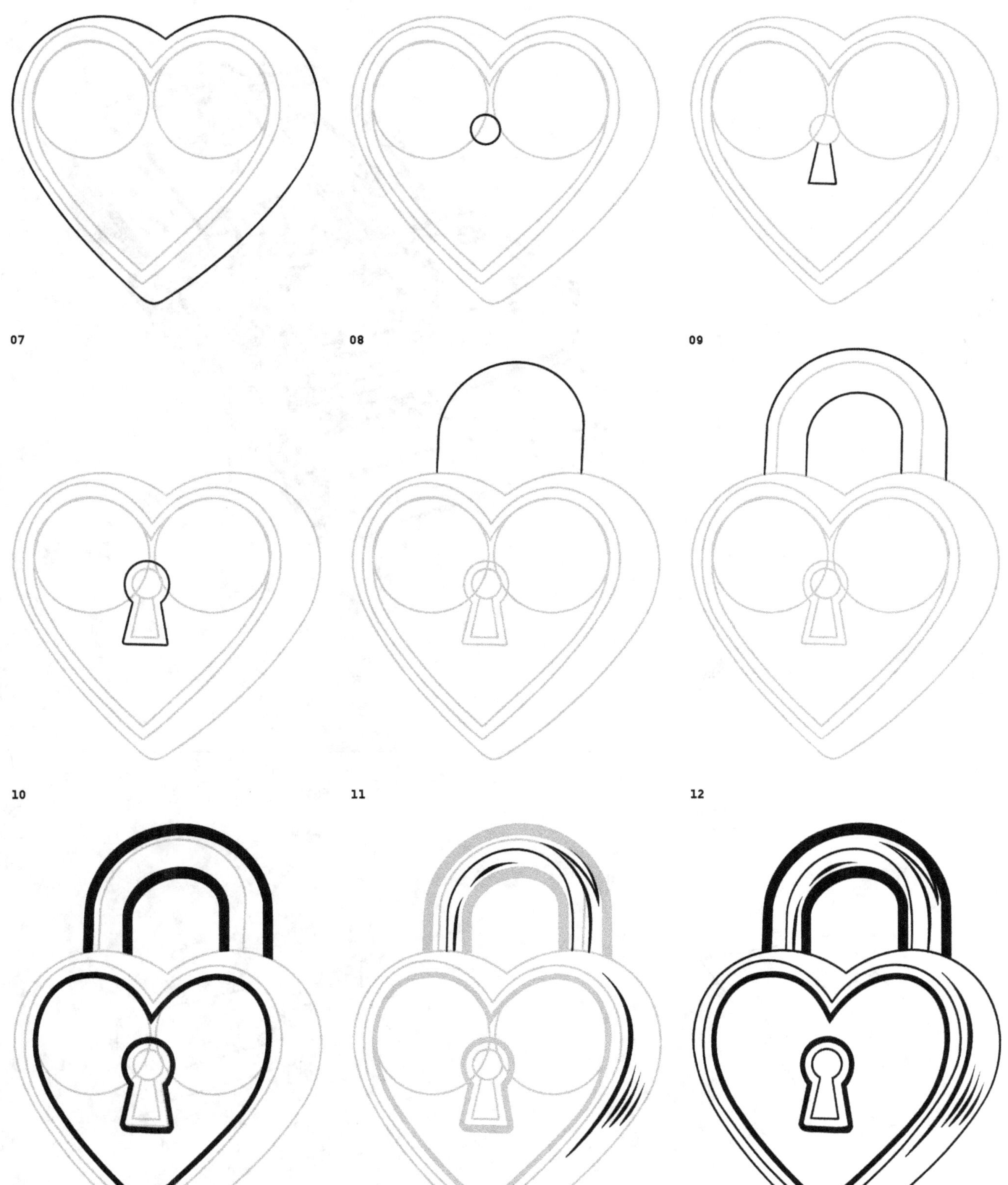

04
05
06
07
08
09
10
11
12
HOW TO DRAW COOL THINGS

MONEY TRAP

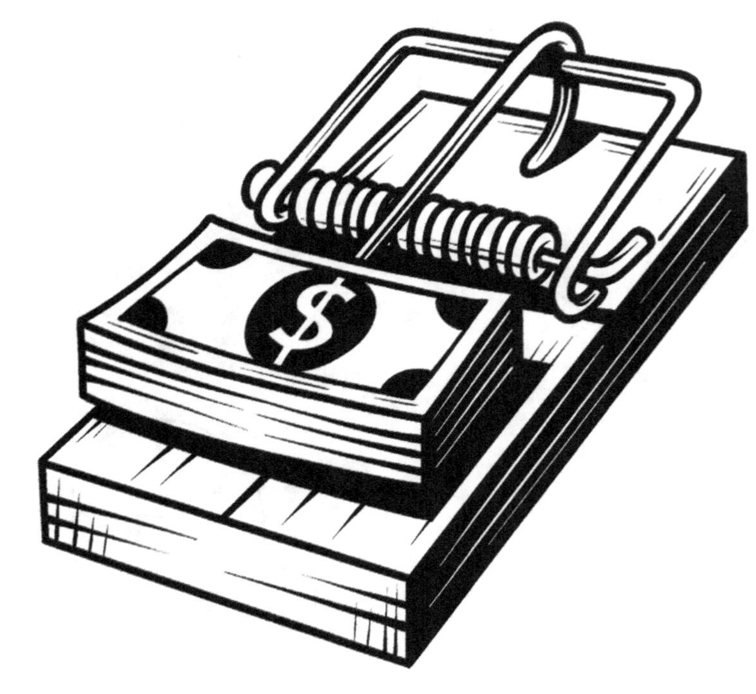

Pro tip:

Make the bait platform about half the
base's width, then centre the bill oval
inside it, keeping the oval about one third
of the platform's length.

01   02   03

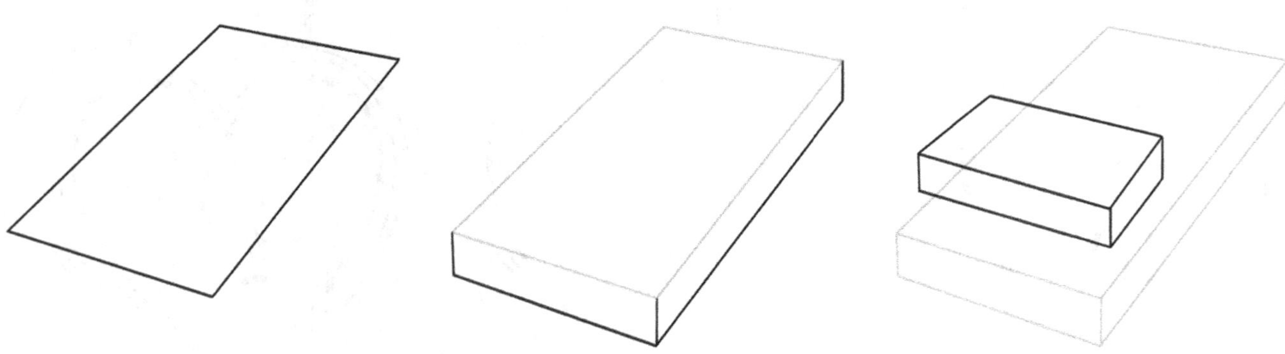

04

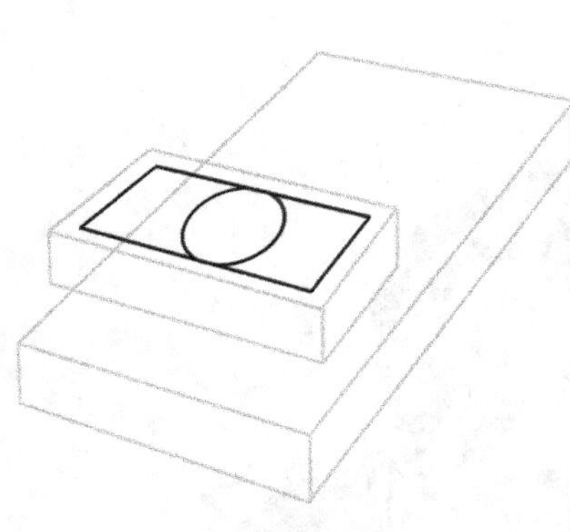

05

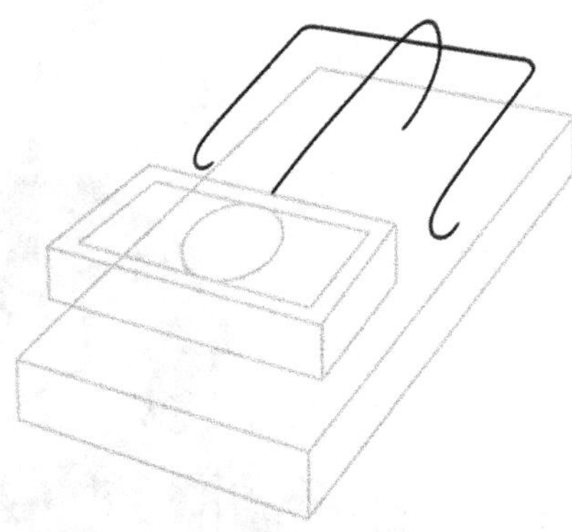

06

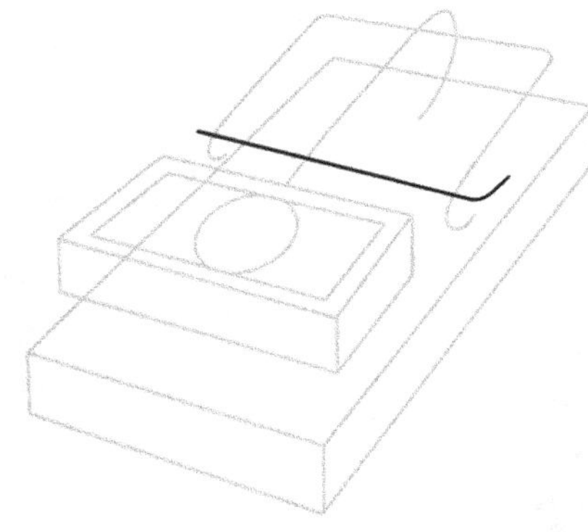

07

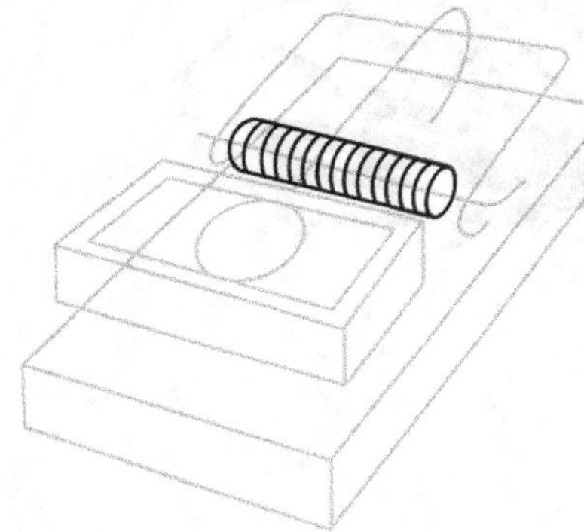

08

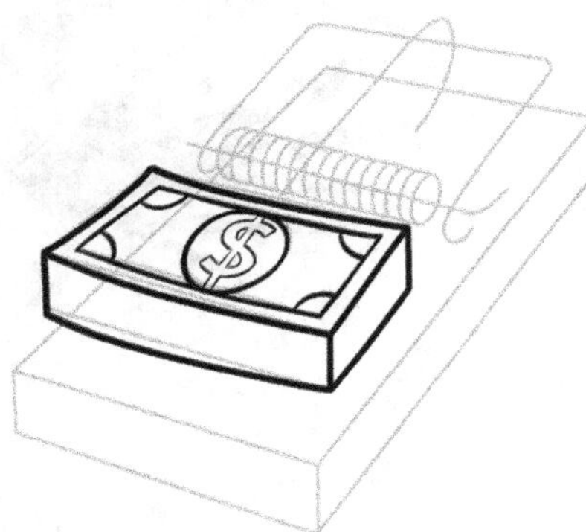

09

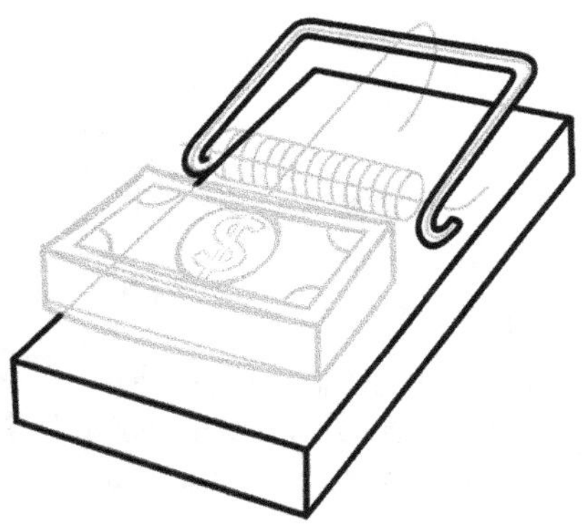

10

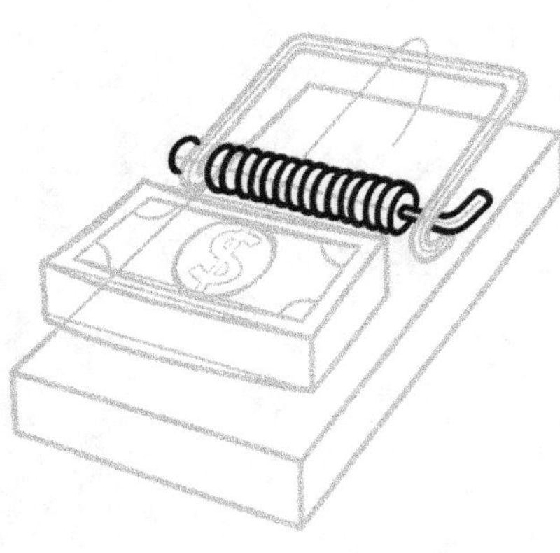

11

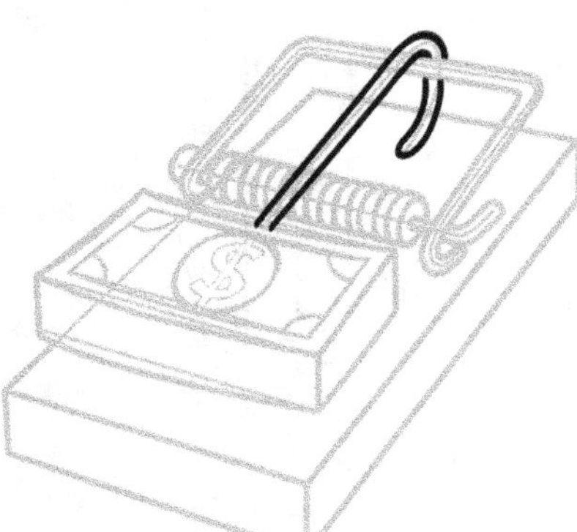

12

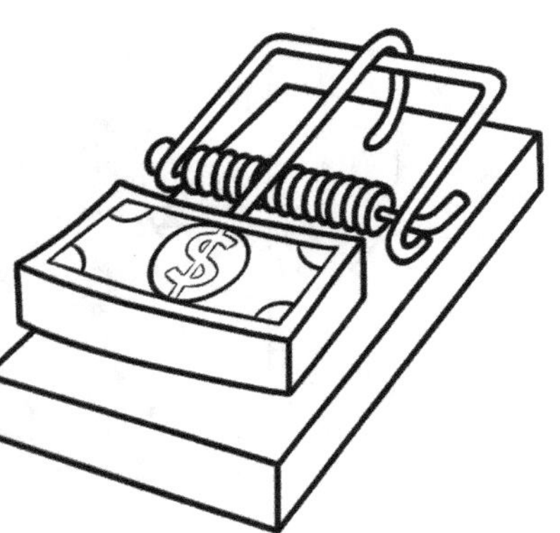

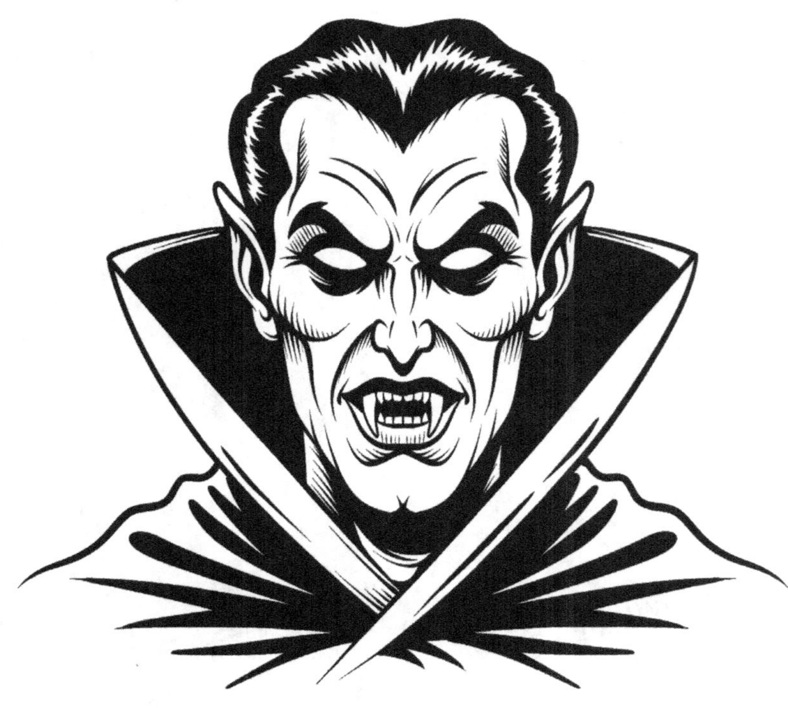

VAMPIRE

Pro tip:

Start with a head circle, then pull the chin down about half a circle and taper the jaw so the chin width lands around one third of the circle.

01

02

03

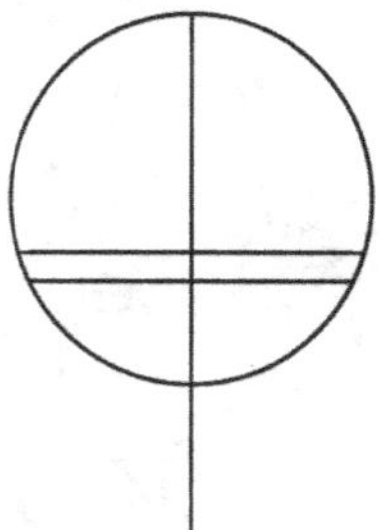

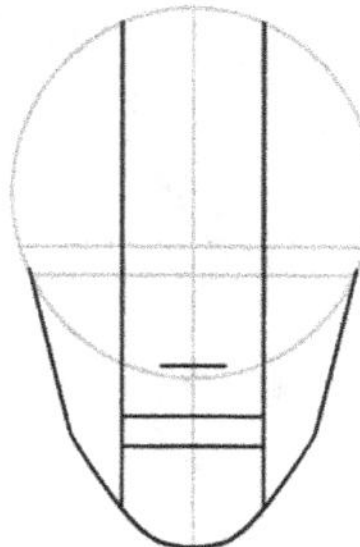

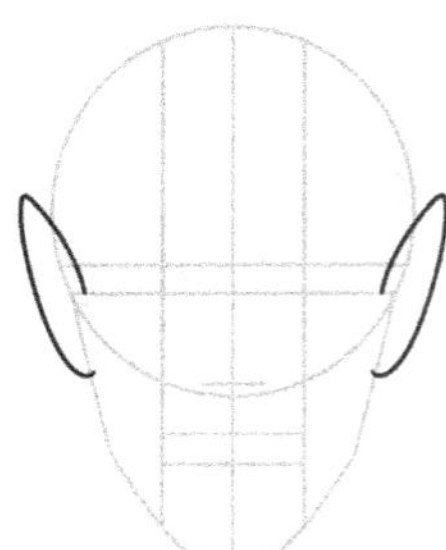

04

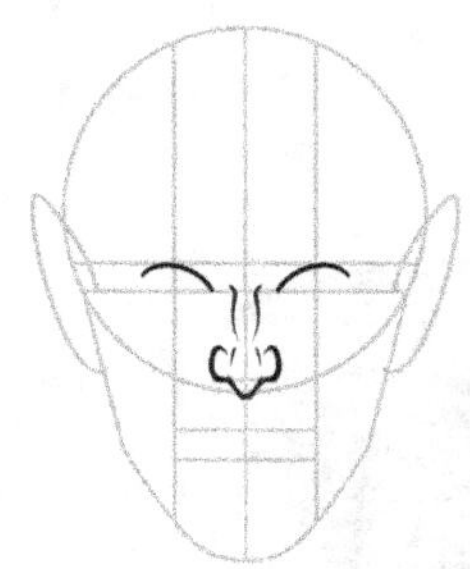

05

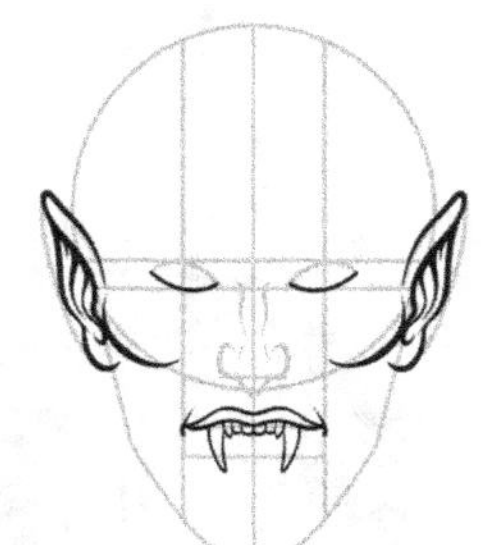

06

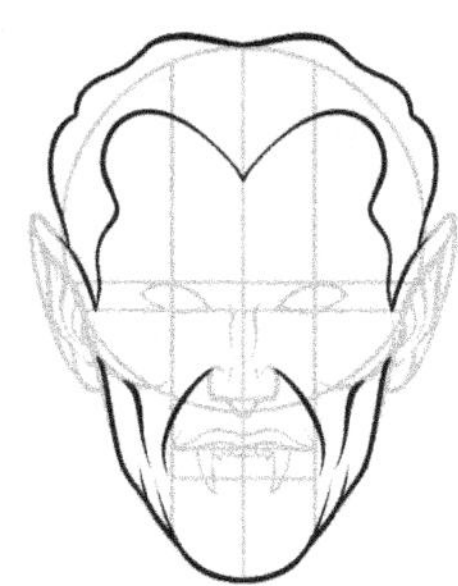

07

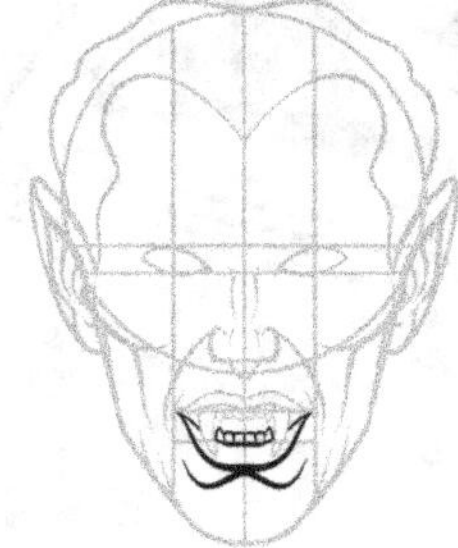

08

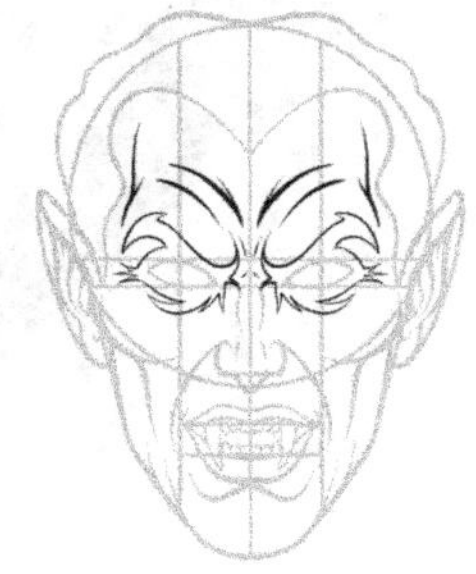

09

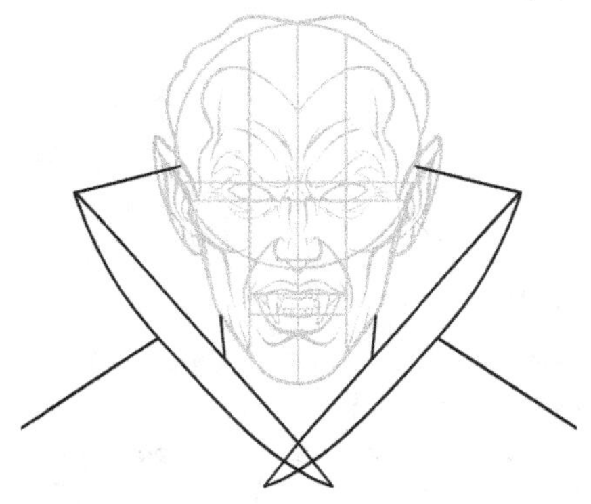

10

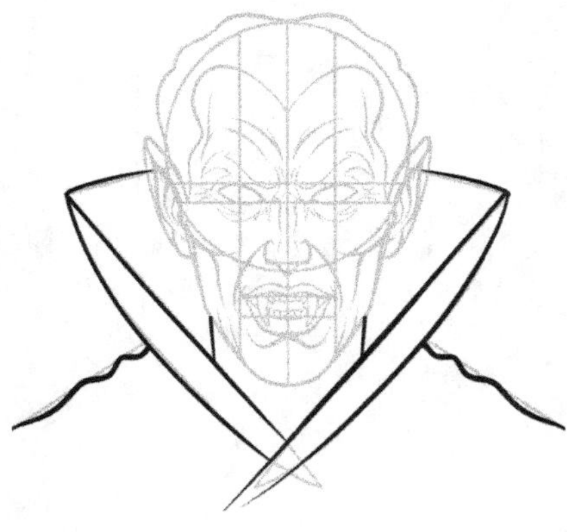

11

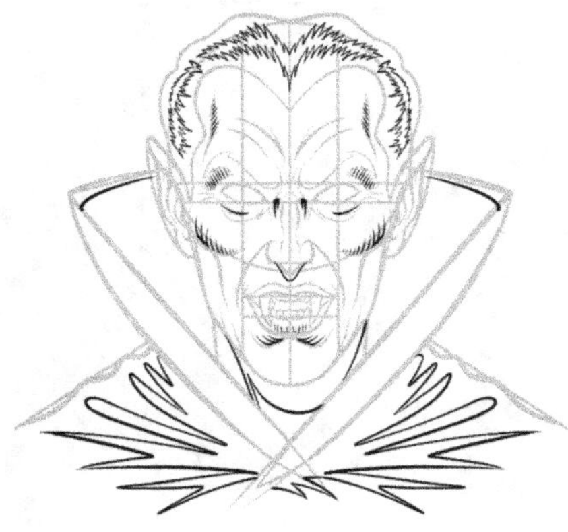

12

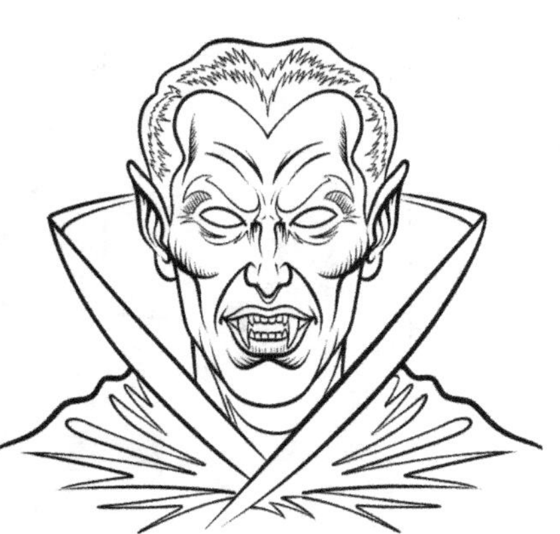

RETRO COMPUTER

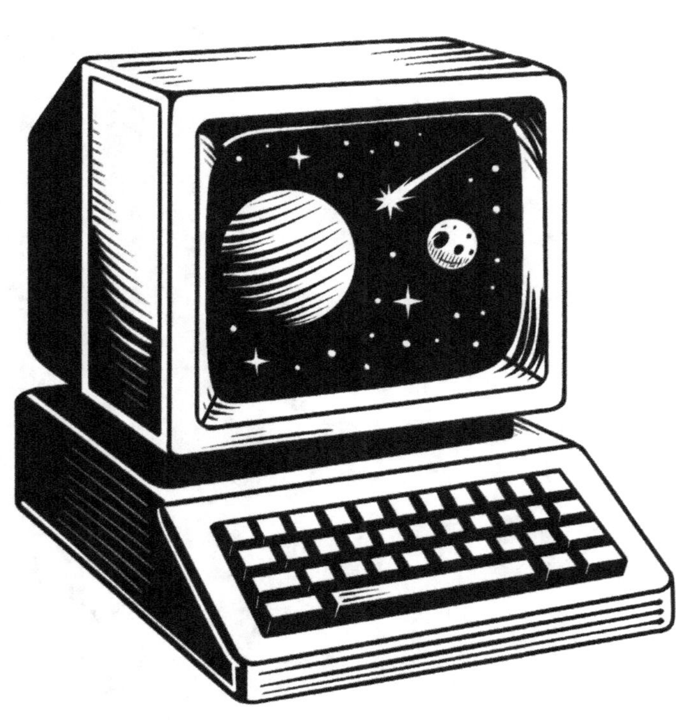

Pro tip:

Draw the front face as a rectangle, then
extend the depth back by about one third
of that width and inset the screen border
by roughly one tenth all round.

01

02

03

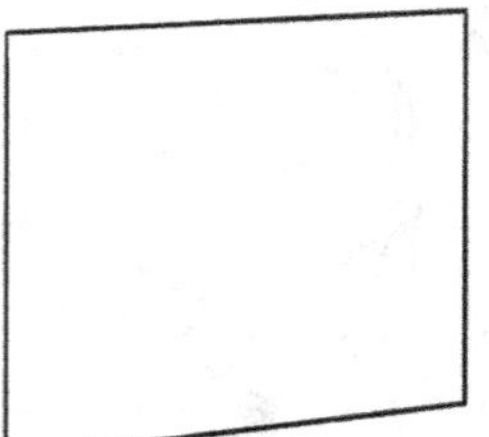

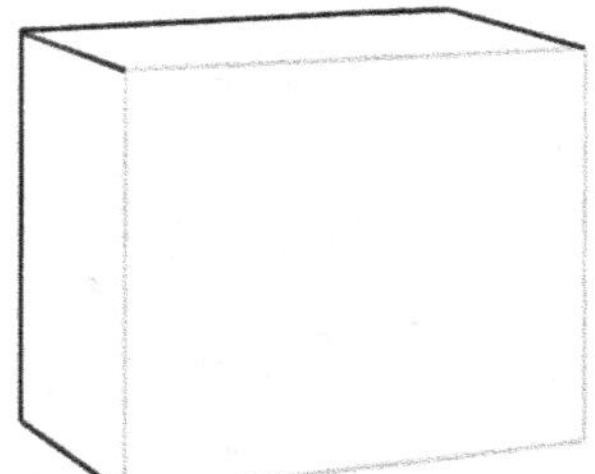

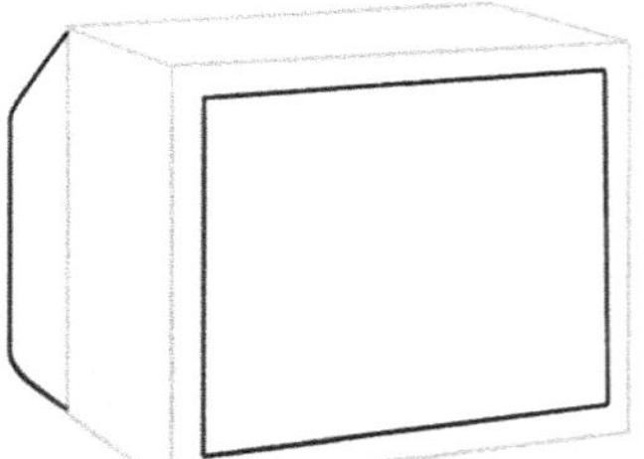

04

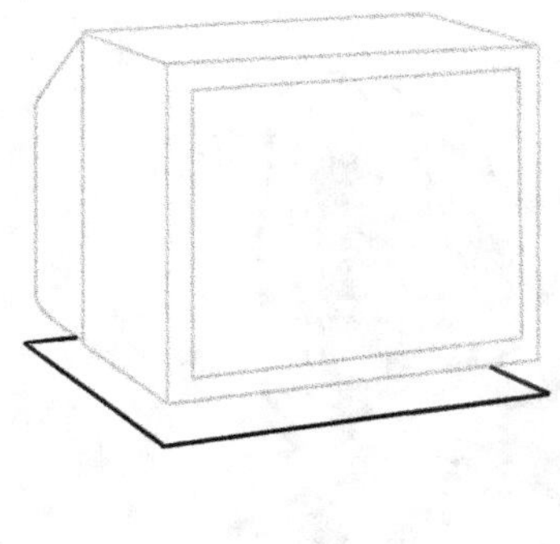

05

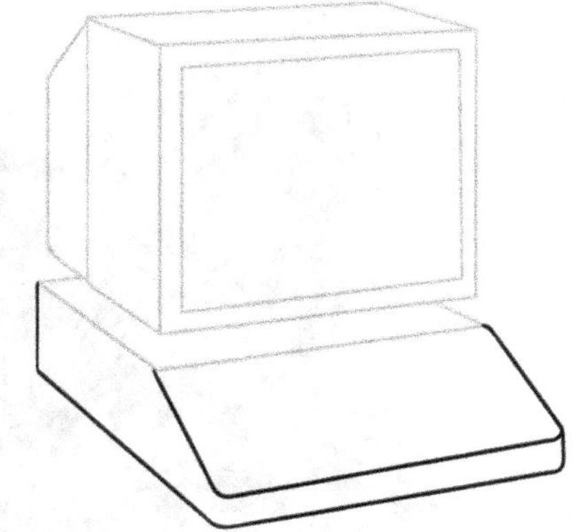

06

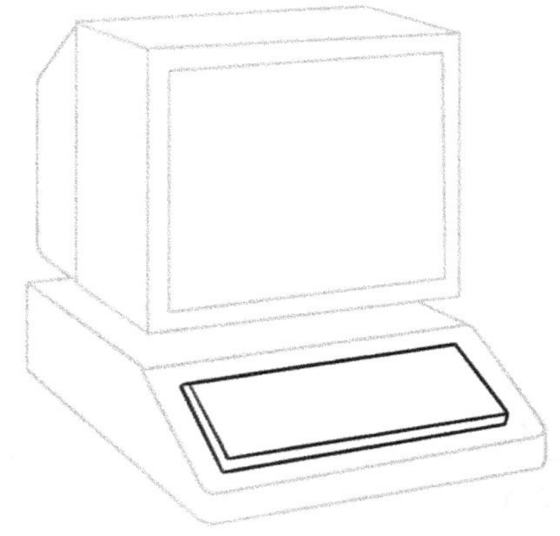

07

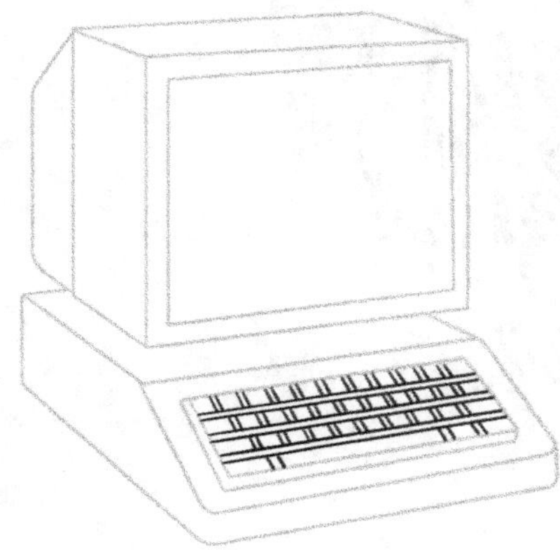

08

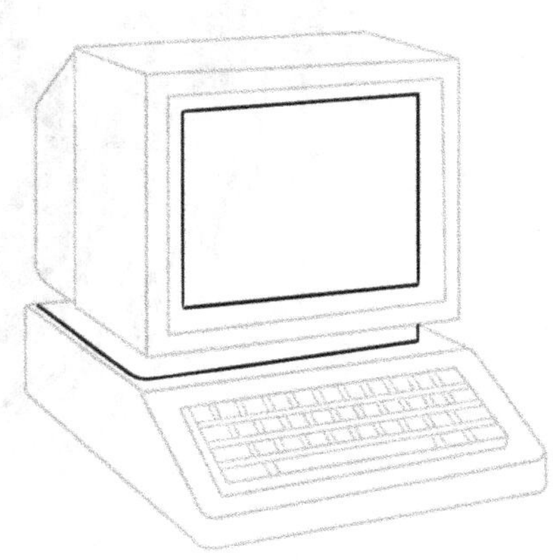

09

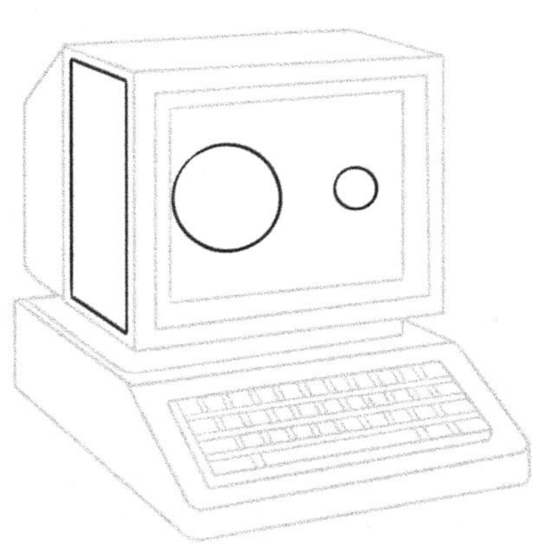

10

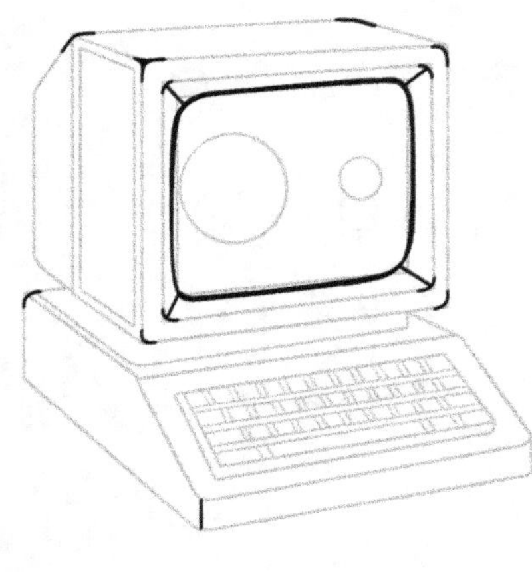

11

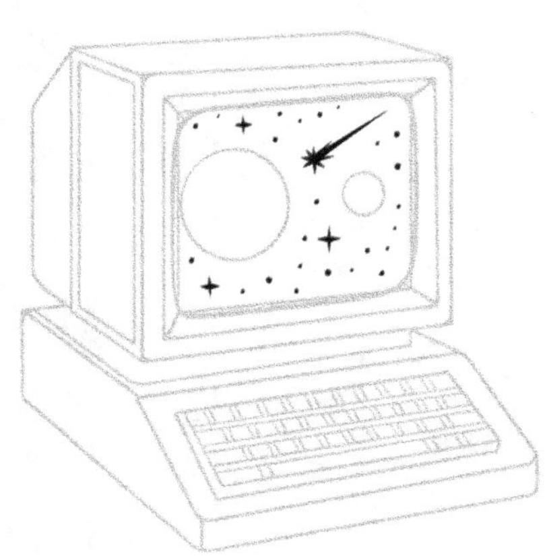

12

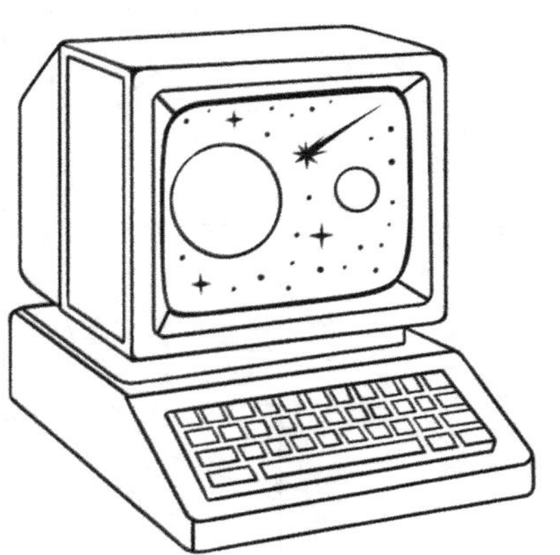

WOLF

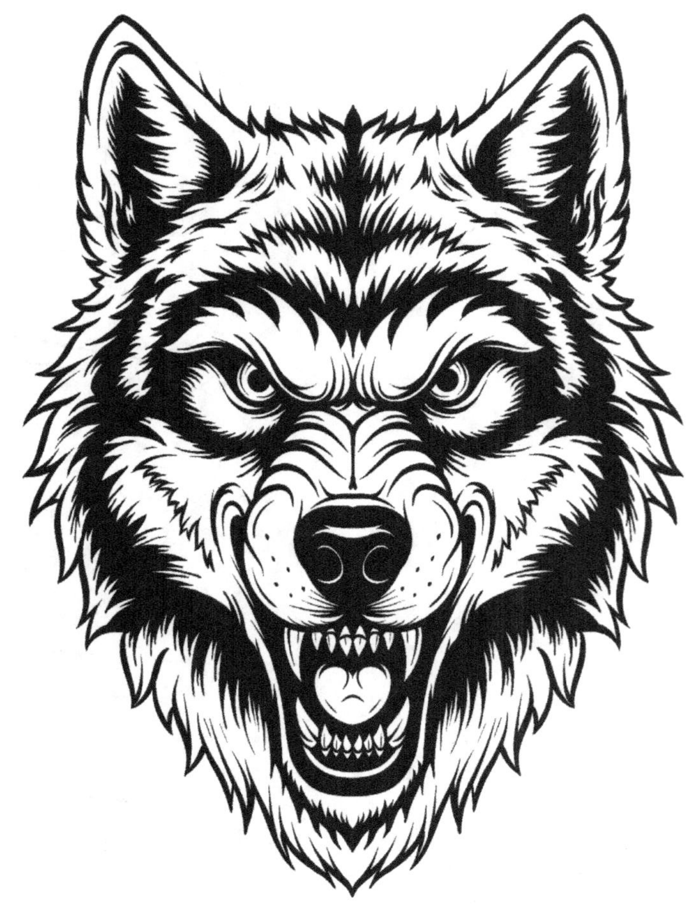

Pro tip:

Start with a head circle, then hang the muzzle circle centred on the midline at about one third of the head circle's diameter, touching the bottom edge.

01   **02**   **03**

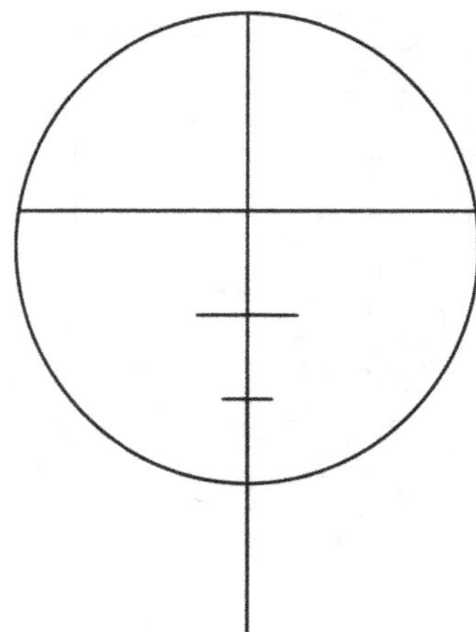

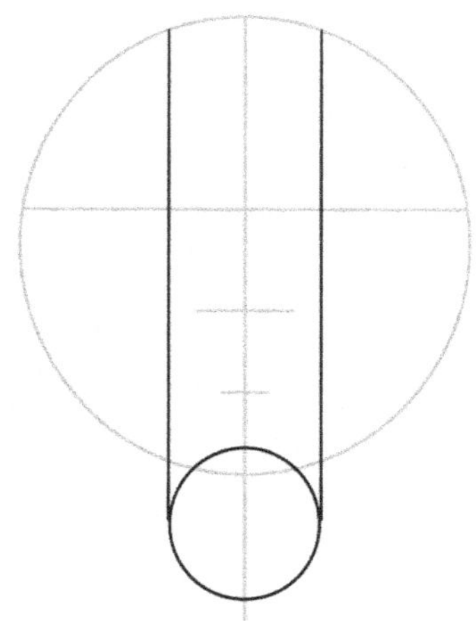

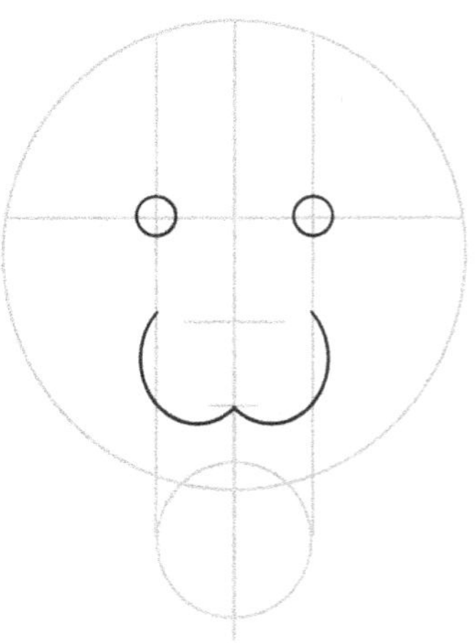

04

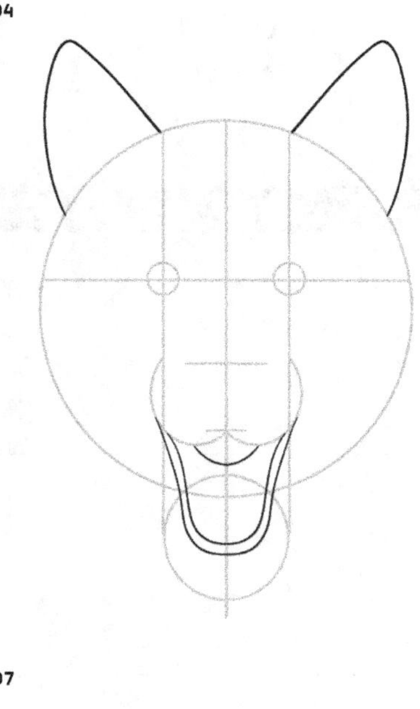

05

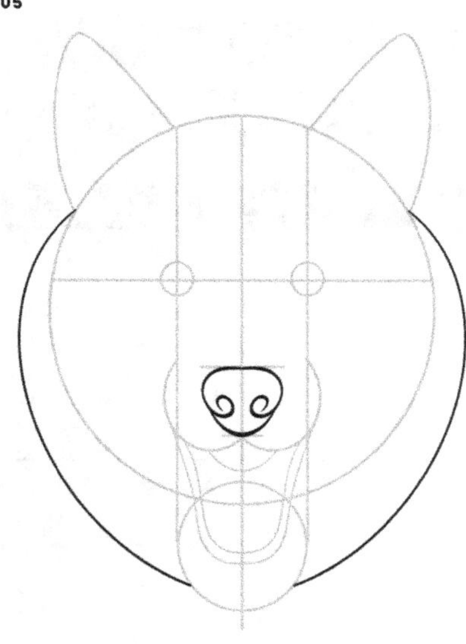

06

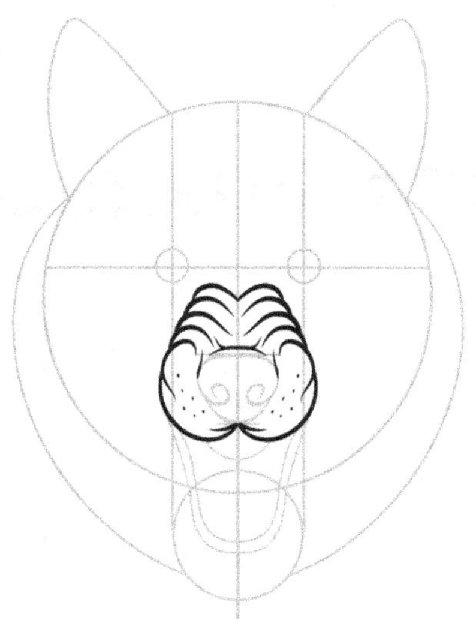

07

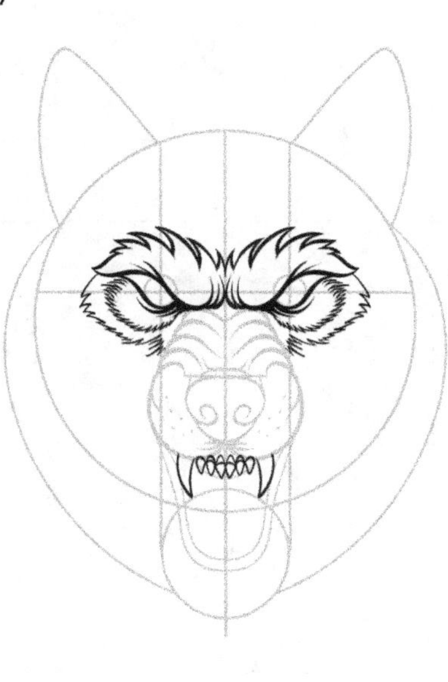

08

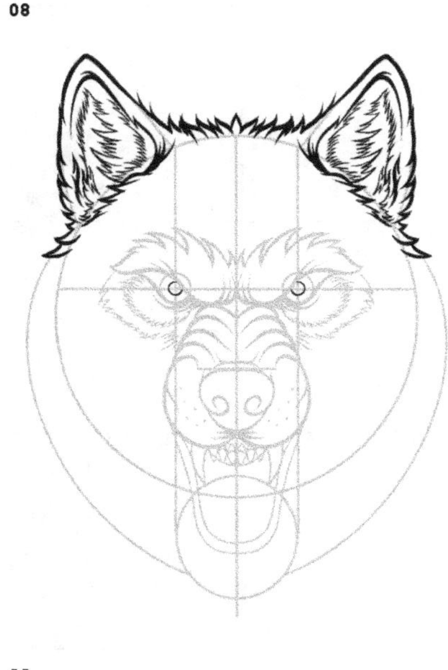

09

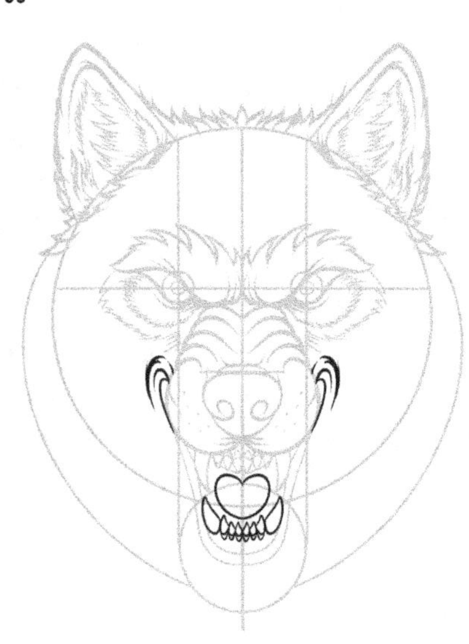

10

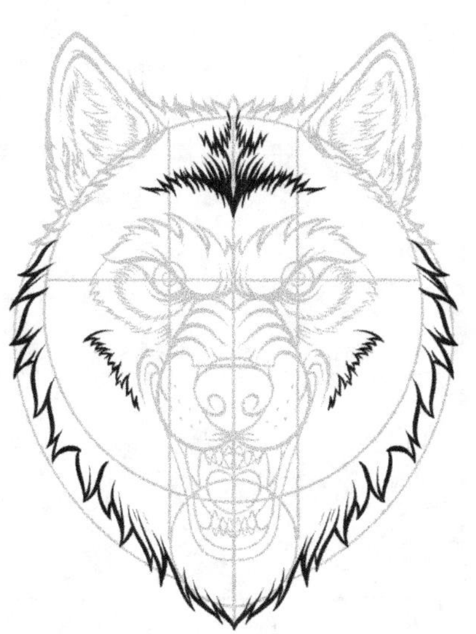

11

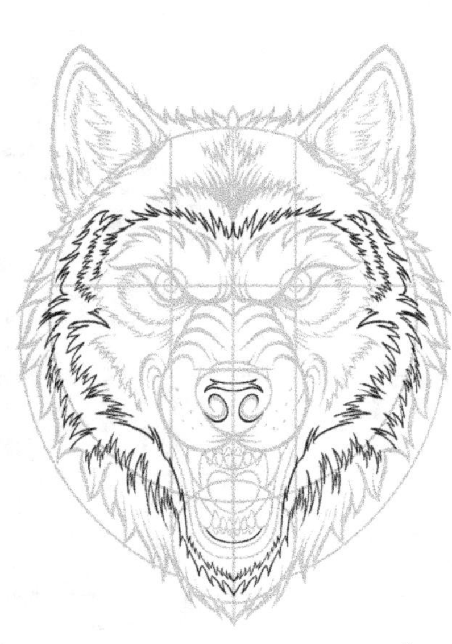

12

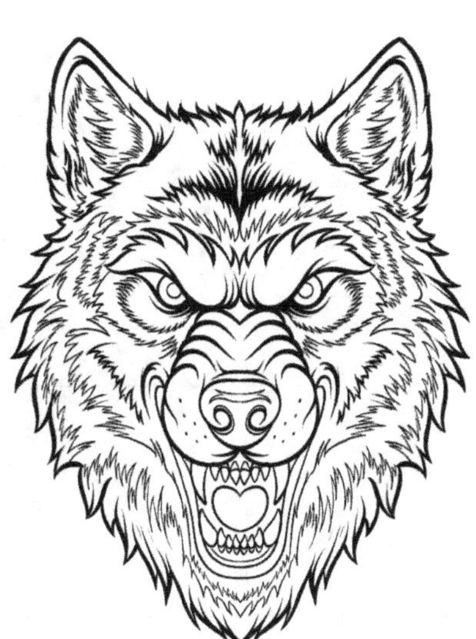

HOW TO DRAW COOL THINGS

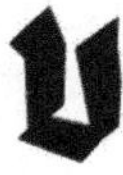
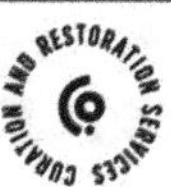
CURATION AND RESTORATION SERVICES

HOW TO DRAW
PRACTICE BOOK

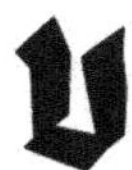
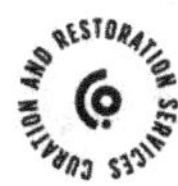

LEARN MORE
VAULTEDITIONS.COM

HOW TO DRAW
PRACTICE BOOK

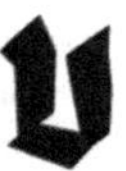
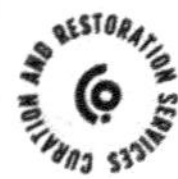

LEARN MORE

VAULTEDITIONS.COM

HOW TO DRAW
PRACTICE BOOK

PRACTICE
MAKES
PERFECT
T R D
M R K

PRACTICE
MAKES
PERFECT
TRD
MRK

HOW TO DRAW
PRACTICE BOOK

PRACTICE
MAKES
PERFECT
TRD
MRK

HOW TO DRAW
PRACTICE BOOK

Vault Editions Ltd

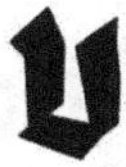

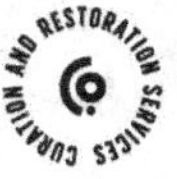

LEARN MORE

VAULTEDITIONS.COM

PRACTICE MAKES PERFECT
T R D
M R K

HOW TO DRAW
PRACTICE BOOK

PRACTICE MAKES PERFECT
T R D
M R K

CONCLUSION

In this book, you've drawn designs rooted in punk, street culture, fashion graphics, skate art, and pop imagery, from bold icons and characters to strong-silhouette animals, plus favourites like skulls, roses, eyeballs, and surreal mash-ups.

Along the way, you've practised the core skills that make this style work: building forms from simple shapes, keeping proportions consistent, refining linework, and controlling value through mark-making and rendering. More importantly, you've trained your eye for design, how to simplify an idea into a clear read, push contrast for impact, and choose details that strengthen the overall shape rather than clutter it.

Every drawing in this book is a starting point, not a fixed design. As you keep making new artworks, remix what you've learned. Swap features, combine subjects, change moods, push proportions, and make variations that feel like you. Turn a clean icon into something rough and punk, or take a dark design and make it playful. Keep drawing, experimenting, and finishing pieces. Style is built through repetition, but owned through reinvention.

LEARN MORE

At Vault Editions, our mission is to provide the highest-quality reference materials for artists and designers, offering meticulously curated resources that inspire and empower creativity. If you've found value in this book, we invite you to explore more of our expertly crafted titles at vaulteditions.com, where you'll discover a world of visual inspiration and practical tools designed to elevate your creative work.

REVIEW THIS BOOK

As a family-owned and operated independent publisher, reviews are essential to the success of our business. Please leave an honest review of this book wherever you purchased it.

JOIN OUR COMMUNITY

Are you the creative and curious type? If so, you will love our community on Instagram. Every day, we share bizarre and beautiful artwork ranging from 17th and 18th-century natural history and scientific illustrations to mythical beasts, ornamental designs, anatomical drawings and more; join our community of 300K+ people today by searching @vault_editions on Instagram.

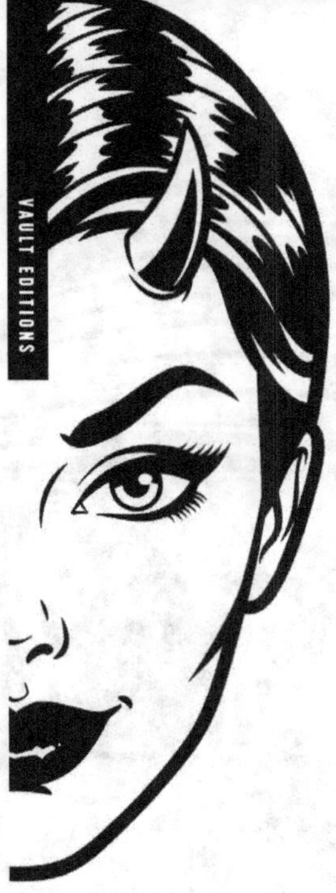

DOWNLOAD YOUR FILES

To enhance your creative journey, *How-to Cool Things* comes with a digital PDF version of the book and a specially designed set of Procreate brushes. These resources are tailored to help you refine your skills and streamline your workflow, whether working traditionally or digitally.

The digital PDF provides easy access to the book's contents on any device, so you can reference the designs anytime, anywhere. It's perfect for artists on the go, allowing you to study and practice whenever inspiration strikes.

The custom Procreate brushes are designed to support the drawing process by helping you improve your draftsmanship and build stronger technical skills. They offer precision and flexibility as you sketch, refine, and finalise your artwork, making it easier to develop clean, confident lines and consistent forms.

Download yours now and get creating!

STEP ONE

Enter the following web address on a desktop or laptop computer in your web browser.

vaulteditions.com/pages/hct

STEP TWO

Enter the following password to access the download page:

hct49825sxda

STEP THREE

Follow the prompts to access your high-resolution files.

CONTACT

For technical support, please email:
info@vaulteditions.com

Copyright © 2026
Vault Editions Ltd

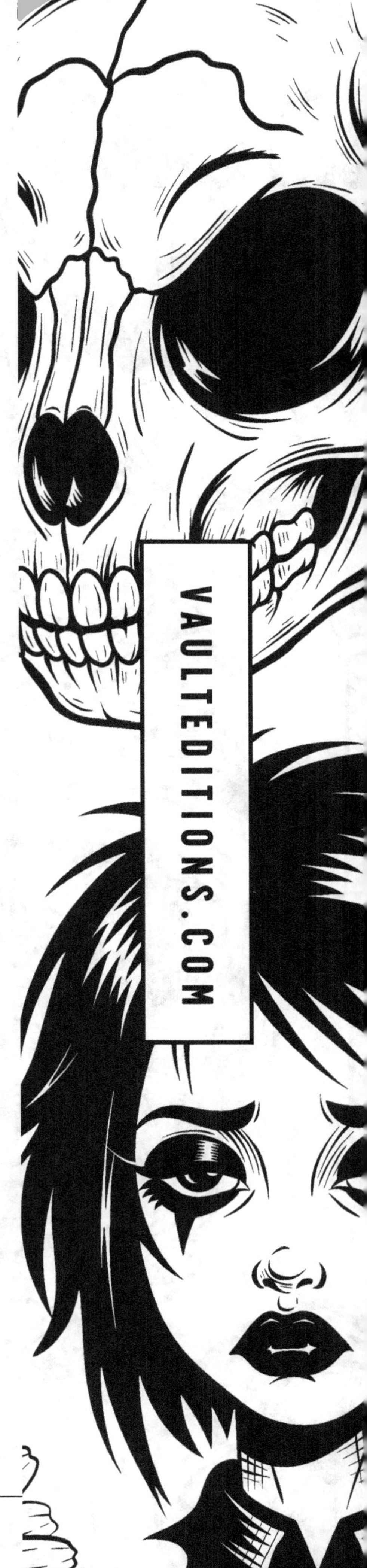

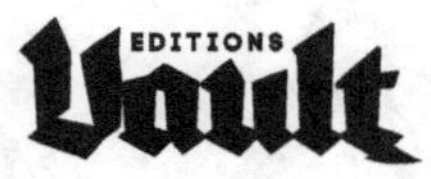

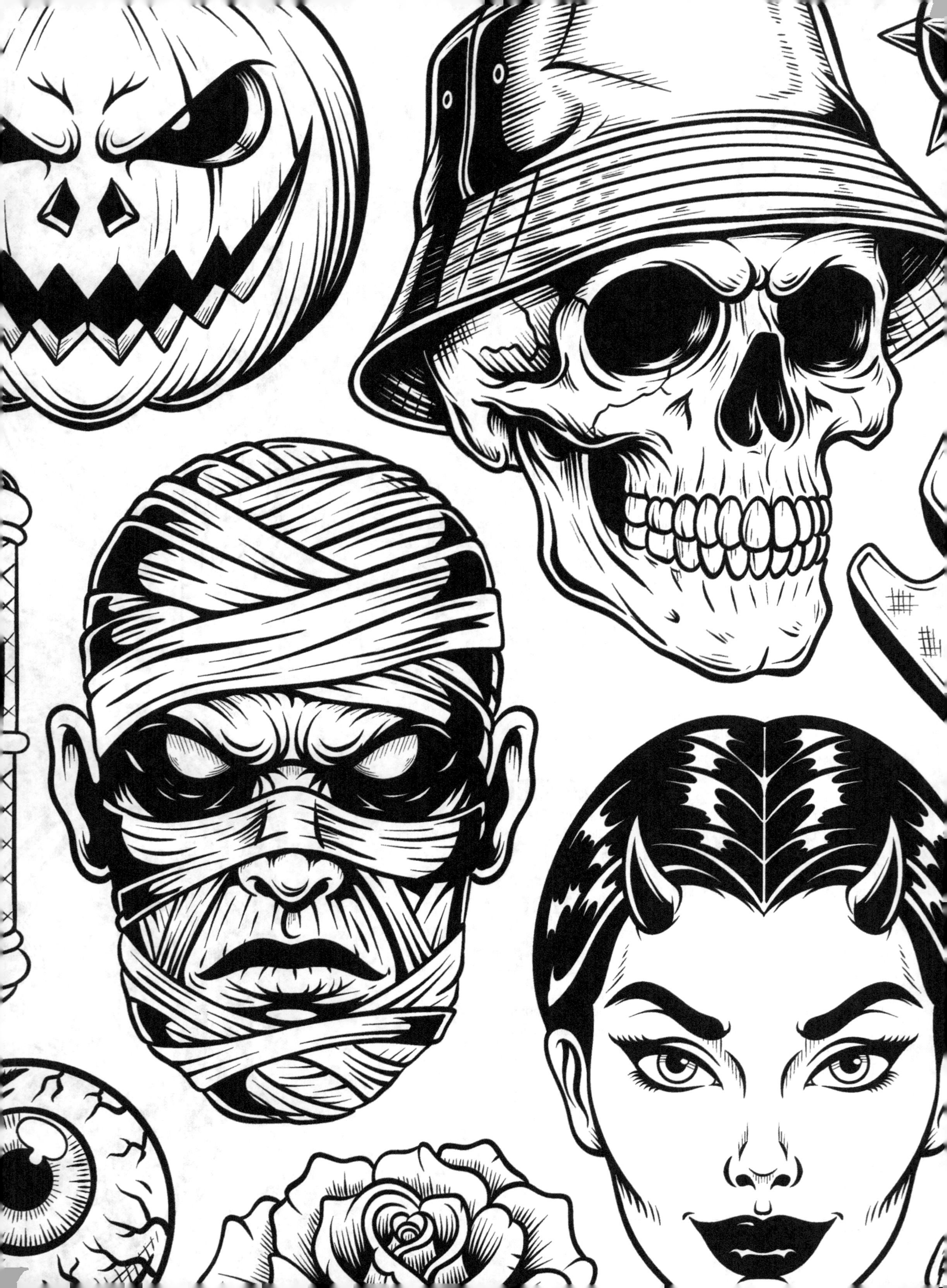